UNBURDENING MOTHERHOOD

A GUIDE TO
BREAKING CYCLES, HEALING TRAUMA,
AND BECOMING A SELF-LED MOM

DR. ANGELE CLOSE

Health Communications, Inc.
Mt. Pleasant, SC

www.hcibooks.com

Library of Congress Cataloging-in-Publication Data
is available through the Library of Congress

© 2026 Angele Close

ISBN-13: 978-0-7573-2557-1 (Paperback)
ISBN-10: 0-7573-2557-2 (Paperback)
ISBN-13: 978-0-7573-2558-8 (ePub)
ISBN-10: 0-7573-2558-0 (ePub)

Publisher: Health Communications, Inc.
1240 Winnowing Way, Suite 102
Mt. Pleasant, SC 29466

Cover, interior design, and formatting by Larissa Hise Henoch

Praise for

UNBURDENING MOTHERHOOD

"IFS therapy has transformed my mothering, and here in your hands is the definitive guide toward shedding our false skins and finding a safe home inside ourselves. As a mom with a very hard parenting road, I feel seen, I feel celebrated, I feel hopeful that motherhood doesn't have to slowly destroy me. IFS gives us to tools to feel it all, and Dr. Close gives us the wisdom to find our own freedom. This is a gentle guide to true liberation for mothers of all kinds."

—**Amanda Diekman,** author of *Low Demand Parenting: Dropping Demands, Restoring Calm, and Finding Connection with Your Uniquely Wired Child*

"*Unburdening Motherhood* is a gift to all mothers who are navigating the challenges of matrescence and wish to step into motherhood without the burdens of their pasts. With humor and great warmth, Dr Close reminds mothers that they have everything they need within them to raise their children with confidence, compassion and love."

—**Chris Parrott,** British Psychological Society chartered counseling psychologist and board-certified coach BPS Chartered Counseling Psychologist, Board Certified Coach

"Reading Angele's book feels like walking through the dark forest of motherhood with a wise, funny friend who's been there. She gets the guilt, the mess, and the beauty, and offers IFS as a gentle map home to becoming the Self-led moms we were meant to be. She reminds us that motherhood can be a powerful path to healing our deepest wounds."

—**Tammy Sollenberger, LCMHC,** author of *The One Inside: Thirty Days to Your Authentic Self*

"*Unburdening Motherhood* is the compassionate permission slip I didn't know I needed. Dr. Close offers both a mirror and a map—one that gently reflects the truth of our pain while guiding us toward healing and self-trust. As a mom of older kids, I find comfort in knowing that no window has closed on my capacity to love or repair. The book's blend of structure and grace—clinical insight delivered in plain, caring language—makes it uniquely accessible. I'm grateful for this hopeful reminder that even in the hardest moments and seasons, there is still a way back to peace."

—**Sarah Cassidy,** author of *Swaddled: Sage Stories to Wrap Mothers in Love*

"Becoming a mother both cracked opened my heart and gave me a portal to my own painful, childhood memories. I wish I'd had Dr Angele Close's gentle and wise book when embarking on my own healing work. She names and normalizes the inner struggles we face as mothers and offers a road map to enter a new, more-nurturing relationship with ourselves and with our children."

—**Sacha Mardou,** author of *Past Tense: Facing Family Secrets and Finding Myself in Therapy*

"In *Unburdening Motherhood*, Angele Close offers mothers something rare—permission to be fully human. Through courageous self-revelation and the lens of Internal Family Systems, she shows how the messy, painful moments of parenting—anger, shame, exhaustion, self-doubt—can become gateways to healing and self-compassion. Her voice is down-to-earth, warm, and real—like a trusted friend who walks beside you and tells you the truth. This is not another book that tells mothers to be perfect; it's an invitation to remember that every moment of imperfection can open the heart."

—**Anne Cushman,** author of *The Mama Sutra: A Story of Love, Loss, and the Path of Motherhood*

"Becoming a mom is one of life's most beautiful experiences—but no one prepares you for the emotional, physical, and mental toll modern motherhood can take. Unburdening Motherhood is the book every mom needs to better understand herself and break free from the trauma, triggers, and burnout that come with intensive parenting. Dr. Angele Close offers an easy-to-follow, compassionate pathway to healing and wholeness."

—**Darlynn Childress,** life and parent coach and host of the
Become A Calm Mama podcast

"*Unburdening Motherhood* offers mothers the gift that they desperately need: permission to be human. Dr. Close compassionately guides readers through the Internal Family Systems approach, helping them recognize that the critical voices and overwhelming feelings that arise in parenting are not character flaws but protective parts that can be understood and healed. This is a practical road map for mothers ready to break free from shame, honor their own needs, and parent from a place of greater wholeness."

—**Jenna Riemersma, LPC,** certified IFS Therapist and IFS clinical
consultant, bestselling author of *Altogether You* and *IFS Integration*

"*Unburdening Motherhood* is exactly what we need in order to identify and shed limiting beliefs regarding what it means to be a mother in our current society. Close unveils how our internal world has taken on roles that no longer serve mothers in their process of being loving and present for their children. She shares many ideas and exercises that will help mothers be the mothers they want to be. Read this book on your journey to break old cycles and plant a new garden of motherhood."

—**Seth Kopald, PhD,** certified Internal Family Systems (IFS)
practitioner and presenter, author of *Self-Led: Living a
Connected Life with Yourself and With Others*

"No matter how long I've been doing this work—personally or professionally—it is always so validating to know I am not alone. Close is brave and courageous, sharing so vulnerably and with such authenticity, clearly walking the talk. She gives readers not just validation for their experiences, but context and a clear map forward. IFS, one of my favorite clinical approaches, is distilled here in a way that is accessible, relatable, and immediately useful. This book is a gift for anyone navigating the complexities of self, relationships, and growth in motherhood."

—**Chelsea Robinson,** motherhood therapist and matrescence educator

"*Unburdening Motherhood* invites mothers into a tender journey of compassion, courage, self-acceptance, and, ultimately, joy. Through the illuminating lens of Internal Family Systems, Dr. Close serves as both guide and companion, helping readers untangle the inherited expectations and unseen pressures that shape a mother's inner world. For every mother longing to feel whole, seen, and understood, this book is an essential, comforting friend."

—**Frances D. Booth, LICSW,** IFS clinical consultant and lead trainer

"Dr. Angele Close normalizes the real, messy, emotional realities of motherhood while offering a clear path to healing and self-trust. As both a clinical psychologist and a mother, I found *Unburdening Motherhood* to be a compassionate and grounded guide that helps mothers to parent from their truest selves."

—**Dr Hilary Claire,** clinical psychologist, author, and host of *Wild and Well* podcast

CONTENTS

FORWARD

FOR MORE THAN A DECADE, I have listened to the voices and stories of mothers around the world—and I can tell you that motherhood often brings women to their edges.

Despite our expectations that we'll immediately love it, or we'll do better than our own parents did, or whatever 'story' we tell ourselves, every single one of us is eventually faced with our own flaws, guilt, and shame. And without the right understanding or support, that can be incredibly isolating—and scary.

But I deeply believe that becoming a mother is an invitation to look deeply within yourself and heal. It's a chance to change generational patterns and forgive yourself.

When I first learnt about matrescence and the deep transformative journey it can be, it changed my life. However, it took me years to gather the tools and insights I needed to actually *do the inner work.*

You, beautiful mama, do not have to do that.

In your hands, you have a book written with such a depth of understanding and personal reflection on both the experience of motherhood and the deep healing work it requires.

All those feelings of guilt, shame, and self-doubt will be redefined. That worry that you're not doing this 'right' will be relieved. Most importantly, you will begin to truly understand yourself in a whole new way and have the tools to be able to support yourself in every area of your life from now on.

You don't need to spend years searching as I did, and as so many before me have done.

Here is the path forward.

In *Unburdening Motherhood*, Dr. Angele Close walks you through all you need to know. She masterfully shares the insights of matrescence that bring to light intergenerational patterns and unresolved wounds that resurface in parenting and then shows you how IFS offers a gentle yet transformative approach to healing these cycles. Together, IFS and matrescence empower mothers to create a legacy of compassion and connection for future generations.

This book is a gift to mothers seeking to thrive in their parenting journey.

With love and admiration for the journey ahead,
Amy Taylor-Kabbaz, founder of Mama Rising
and Global Matrescence Foundation

INTRODUCTION

NO ONE WARNED ME that I wouldn't always love being a mom. Dare I write for anyone to read that sometimes I have a part of me that hates being a parent. Now, settle down before you pass judgment (or maybe you feel relieved to know you're not the only one). Not all of me feels that way, and certainly not my true Self.

I read all the *What to Expect When* books . . . but no book, person, and certainly no village prepared me for all the ways that my emotions would react to this new child-rearing life. When things really got challenging—when my kids were no longer so adorable and little that I could justify they "didn't know better"—a voice would rear up and scream in my head, *This is bullshit! I didn't sign up for this shit!* Admittedly, I even called up a *Fuck this shit!* in the toughest moments. Thinking such thoughts doesn't align with what a "good mother" thinks, so I'd end up feeling even worse, adding alone and ashamed on top of the resentment and rage I felt.

The fear that people will judge you and think you either don't truly love your kids or you're not a good mom if you think or feel that way keeps moms from opening up, from being vulnerable, from being real. There's also the sense that to share the inner struggles or the ambivalence will sound like complaining. No one wants to be gaslit and shamed, misunderstood and alone in their pain. So moms silence themselves and sit alone in isolation, self-blame, and in the worst moments, shame.

I'm here to tell you, sweet mama, it's not you. It's not your fault. All those thoughts and inner voices, feelings and moods you've had along the path of motherhood (maybe even before pregnancy) are okay. They don't discount the love you feel for your children, and they don't mean you're not a good mom. They all belong. It'll seem radical to consider, but even the thoughts you don't dare say out loud make a ton of sense because they're there for a good reason, even if you don't yet know what that reason is.

Motherhood for me started like entering a joyous, lantern-lit pathway into a beautiful, inviting forest that I felt called to. I had only imagined the love, connection, and laughter that awaited me. It never occurred to me that I wouldn't—or shouldn't—become a mom. And yet, unexpectedly along this lovely forest path were thick roots jutting out from the ground that caused me to stumble. There were multiple crossroads, each with their own contradicting signage that promised the right way forward. I found myself frozen with surging doubt and fear that I'd pick the wrong one, then I'd shame spiral, thinking that I wasn't doing the best for my kids. Then I found myself getting angry multiple times a day—every day. I hate being angry. I don't like conflict, and I never wanted to be that "angry mom," so I felt horrible. All that is to say, motherhood has at times been a very dark and scary place that left me feeling ill-equipped, unprepared, alone, and afraid that my failures await me in the future blaming faces of my children, who I'm setting up for years of difficult and expensive therapy.

Maybe, like me, you wanted to do better than what you experienced in your childhood but found that this motherhood gig is way frickin' harder than you expected. Along the path of motherhood you noticed memories arise—old wounds from the past getting triggered more and more frequently—and despite your resources, smarts, and inner resilience, you can't seem to break out of unhealthy patterns you find yourself caught in (over- or undereating, drinking or shopping too much, zoning out on TV or social media, etc.). You feel like you're killing yourself to meet all the expectations of what we're told a good mom does, is, and should be, but it's exhausting, and you feel like you're falling short.

Your kids don't listen, they have *way* more feelings than you knew was possible, and you find yourself saying things your mother or father said, which you swore to yourself you'd never say. You have moments of feeling anger, resentment, guilt, and shame. You feel alone in this and misunderstood. The thought might have even crossed your mind if you should've walked down this path, thinking maybe you're just not good enough. You don't know what to do, who to turn to, or what to do next, but you desperately want to feel better and stop white-knuckling this parenting gig, just hoping things will somehow get easier. A part of you is saddened by the fact that on tough days you fantasize about them going off to college, but you also know that you will miss them deeply.

I'm here to tell you there is another way. Motherhood can be easier, more joy-filled, fulfilling, and fun. It can also be the gateway to our own deep healing. There is a reason we feel torn at times, seem to sabotage ourselves, and can both love being a mom and love our kids to the moon and back and still have disappointments in motherhood. There can be and often are two truths: I love my kids, and I love being a mom, truly, and a part of me tells me she did not sign up for this, *WTF, can I get off this roller-coaster ride please—or at the very least take a nice long nap?!*

Our inner turmoil and what feels like a tug-of-war of feelings and thoughts are the result of having different parts within us, and we're made up more like a system than just one singular person at all times. For example, on the one hand you have a part that wants to dive into motherhood and devote all your energy to your kids. You have another part that resents your kids and their incessant needs at times and feels grief that she's missing important aspects of her old life. And still a third part judges you for this, making a part carry feelings of shame that are often silenced and suppressed. Or you know you shouldn't care so much about what other people think of you, and yet you can't seem to unhook from worrying about others' opinions of you, your parenting, and if they think you're a good mom.

The mind-body of humans is inherently and unconsciously self-protective. Rather than one united person, our inner world is more like a committee of parts, with different parts having different roles to guide us in our daily lives. This is why we can experience what seem like opposing thoughts—multiple simultaneous emotions, beliefs, and sensations—much of which are being processed unconsciously.

A lot of what your inner thoughts are telling you is simply regurgitation of the direct and indirect messages they've picked up on trying to navigate the world since you were born. Now as an adult and a mother, a lot of the messages your brain is registering are around how a mother should be, what she should do, and what she should look like. These messages are passed down from one generation to the next.

In today's Western culture, our "village" comes with messages of judgment, a sense of impossible expectations and burdens that a mother do all the things (like raise happy, healthy, well-behaved kids while being a kick-ass career woman at the same time) without any real understanding of what she is going through or providing her with the support she needs. This dark forest of motherhood includes the expansive digital world filled with thousands of images on social media that present perfectly groomed, beautiful, smiling mamas and their happy, smiling children in beautiful clothes with aesthetic and beautifully curated tiles and reels that make you feel like it must be you who can't get your motherhood shit together.

If you aspire for something different—for a real representation of true motherhood, messy and mixed, filled with awe, love, grit, and vulnerability, then keep reading. This book is for the moms who want to do motherhood differently: moms who want to change things for their kids and not repeat the patterns they experienced growing up. Moms want authenticity, realness, and freedom to parent on their own terms.

We are a generation of parents who want kids to know they matter, to be allowed to express their feelings, and to not have to earn the love and connection they—and we—all long for. But actually doing this—creating this family system when you might not have had this experience in your childhood—is not easy. When you don't have a model for what that looks like and how to actually do it, it can feel nearly impossible. It's even harder when motherhood is a minefield for the resurgence of your unmet needs, insecure and vulnerable parts, and desires for something better.

You hear your angry mom voice as you snap or shout at your kid in a way that sounds rote and familiar. You'll know in your gut this was not a good parenting moment, not how you wanted it to be, and you might feel really angry at yourself for losing your cool. You might numb the shame and frustration with some lighthearted toxin or minimize or suppress it all, feeling unsure how to change this dreaded cycle. You promise yourself to do better, and you do, until the next trigger when your kid is saucy, and maybe this time there were observers. Lather. Rinse. Repeat.

How do you get off this ride? How do you break the cycles of your childhood patterns and stop getting triggered altogether? How do you manage parenting in the way you envisioned where you consciously connect with your kiddos in a supportive, loving, and trusting relationship? Where is the harmony? How do you get there?

THE PATH TO UNBURDENING MOTHERHOOD

In *Unburdening Motherhood*, I share the map I used to go from daily triggers of anger and shame spirals to a more settled, balanced, and even joy-filled experience of motherhood. Instead of continuing to stumble through the dark forest of motherhood feeling alone, confused, and inadequate, I discovered a pathway to understanding myself, trusting myself, and healing in ways I never imagined.

First, I learned that all the changes, feelings, and the inner split I was feeling were all normal and explained in the term *matrescence*. Matrescence refers to the multifaceted changes and identity transformation a woman goes through along the journey of motherhood. Having a word to explain my feelings of self-doubt, self-criticism, and mother wound resurfacing was a game changer in dissolving much of the shame and self-blame I was carrying.

Then, learning about and applying the *Internal Family Systems (IFS)* model of healing and psychotherapy helped me navigate my challenges in matrescence. Through leaning on the principles and practices in IFS, I experienced true and deep changes in my experience of motherhood.

IFS is a nonpathologizing therapeutic model that offers a specific method of healing trauma and fostering personal transformation. Generally practiced by therapists and clinicians who train in the model, IFS is now branching out into other areas, with coaches, lawyers, spiritual teachers, and leaders leaning on this model as a pathway of hope to improve many of our world's social and cultural problems. There are clinical trainings and a certification process, but IFS can also be learned through self-study, such as courses, webinars, podcasts, and books.

IFS is an approach to understanding our psychology or our inner world—our emotions, thoughts, and beliefs—as well as the patterns that lead to our actions and experiences. By turning our attention inward—focusing on the rising emotions, bodily sensations, images, and thoughts—we can understand ourselves and our experiences with much more clarity, insight, and self-compassion. IFS provides a map so that we can learn to relate to our inner system in ways that bring deep healing, wholeness, and integration of being.

INTERNAL FAMILY SYSTEMS (IFS) AND MOTHERHOOD

Originally a family systems therapist, Dr. Richard Schwartz (widely known to friends as Dick) developed IFS by listening to his many clients describe their different thoughts, kind of like voices in their heads. He realized that in the way that families carry certain dynamics, his individual clients each also seemed to have an inner system that was creating inner tension and turmoil in their lives. Recognizing that these emotions, views, and beliefs were almost like their own separate personality with a specific role within the person's system, Schwartz called them *parts*. By connecting with the individual parts of the client directly and coming to understand and witness these parts and the pains they carried, he saw how these parts could let go of and unburden the injuries and pain from the past and release the beliefs and emotions in a deep and lasting way. Releasing or helping the burdens release from a person's system also allowed for new and healthier energies and natural gifts to emerge within the person.

Dr. Schwartz identified different types of parts, called *protectors*, as well as the more vulnerable parts of us, called *exiles*, which are typically buried deep in our system to avoid feeling and experiencing emotional pain from our difficult life experiences. Finally, we all have what Schwartz called *Self*, which refers to the energy of love, compassion, and all-knowing wisdom that is not a part but is a profound source for us to heal and awaken to the truth of our goodness and deservingness of love and compassion. Self is not damaged by life circumstances, and it is the core essence from which we begin to transform our daily experiences with our parts and their strong feelings and reactions. Self is our anchor, and the practices in *Unburdening Motherhood* will help you connect with your Self-energy, guiding you to become a Self-led mom.

The profound transitions of matrescence mean that a mother's inner system of parts will be completely shifted and disrupted by her new role as a mom. A solution is provided through the lens of IFS to begin to turn your attention inward, to notice your feelings, sensations, and thoughts and to get to know your parts—so that instead of feeling like a roller coaster inside, you can make sense of and have a say in what you're experiencing in motherhood. Understanding yourself as having an inner system of parts that seek to protect you from pain and prevent further pain or harm from happening is a game changer in self-understanding. Learning how to build a trusting relationship with your parts has the potential to completely transform your experience of matrescence and will help you parent with more calm, groundedness, and self-trust.

Consider a new pathway through the forest that offers you a way of understanding your reactions, the many different inner thoughts and feelings, and the beliefs that have been keeping you stuck. Understanding yourself as a Self with a committee of well-intentioned inner soldiers is the key to getting closer than you've ever imagined to truly knowing yourself—to making sense of the inner struggle, turmoil, and pain, and flowing through motherhood with ease, grace, and self-compassion.

If you open to the ideas offered here and follow the experiential practices in this book, you'll learn a healing method to help you release the myths and burdens you've unknowingly absorbed and you'll transform your pain into newfound clarity and purpose. You'll break cycles and shed residues from wounds that don't serve you or your family as you establish motherhood on your own terms and show up as the mom you always thought you'd be. With the healing map I share in this book, motherhood will be a gateway to a deeper awakening and self-actualization. I would not suggest to you there is such a hope if it were not from my own personal experience.

MY STORY

The baby-through-kindergarten years were smooth and un-eventful for my motherhood. Physically exhausted with three kids in four years while attending graduate school in clinical psychology, for sure, I was tired! But my task-oriented survivor mode seemed to manage fairly well, and I remember thinking (and based on ac-knowledgments from others), *Hey! I can do this motherhood thing!*

Their cute faces and funny ways of saying words kept some of my reactive parts at bay because kids are . . . small. They don't know. They can't help it. I seemed to have oodles of patience. For many years I was also able to ignore and push back the spikes of resent-ment, grief, and intermittent flashes of my traumatic childhood that peeked through into my thoughts every so often. I powered through, thinking *I can do this! I can do this* . . . with the help of happy-hour wine while I make dinner (because, in all honesty, I hate making food every single day for other people, and I'm so incredibly bored and my brain is mush from playing with babies all day, and I miss my passions and my work and talking to other adults . . . but I can't admit this to myself because that's my job now and I'll feel trapped and powerless, and wait, does that make me a bad mom? So, I'll make it more fun and tolerable by treating myself to a crisp glass of Sau-vignon blanc that temporarily quiets these thoughts and feelings).

When my kids grew beyond ages eight and nine, I started to think that at that age they should know better, and my tolerance and patience began to wane. I'd wonder why they are saying such things to me: *In a million years I wouldn't say that to my mom!* When my strong-willed kids started pushing boundaries (i.e., not listening to my instructions), protesting or negotiating every directive, and fully expressing all their feelings—which is something I encouraged as a therapist and wanted for my children—shit got real.

These kids had *way* more feelings than I ever remembered having (no duh, cause their environment is much more permissive of a range of expressed emotions!). My inner committee began to revolt in unavoidable ways in this new territory with an array of my kids' extensive and frequent needs and demands, meaning that an angry part intensified, an exasperated part poked out in little sighs, and my inner critic grew louder, pointing out how I must just suck as a mom.

When one of my children began having really big feelings—frustration, rage, defiance, and resistance to simple demands and requests—there was no book that helped prepare me for their reactions to things and my reactions to their reactions. My naive pre-mom self thought parents had way more control than they do. My child didn't respond to a stern directive or threat of punishment the way I thought they would. Consequences didn't seem to influence them. I accumulated daily evidence that my kids' behaviors would trigger all sorts of stormy reactions and ultimately unprocessed wounds within me that I didn't understand.

As a trained and certified mindfulness meditation teacher and therapist, I thought I would be better at this—that I'd be able to find peace, calm, and Buddha energy to meet my kids wherever they were. Instead, my meditation practice began to make me keenly aware of the many voices in my head and the huge inner identity tug-of-war that left me feeling confused and frustrated with myself. I felt weak, inadequate, and more insecure and unsure than I'd felt since middle school.

I felt stretched and split between my newly credentialed career as a clinical psychologist and a mom to three beautiful children whom

I had wanted and adored. I was dropping balls trying to juggle it all and felt like I was doing a half-ass job at everything. I was being triggered regularly and living in survival mode—you know, the kind that makes you freeze like a deer in headlights when your kid is having big feelings and needs a sturdy leader to trust and lean on . . . not a deer!

My confidence was at an all-time low, and I felt lost from myself. *Who was this woman who's sucking at everything that matters? I don't recognize her. She's not the strong, independent, confident woman who was the top of her class in grad school. Where did she go?*

I needed to fix myself as fast as I could because I knew I wasn't showing up the way my kids needed. I knew that having a miserable, shame-filled mom wasn't going to be good for my kids—and it certainly wasn't good for me. I didn't want to pass on what I came to understand was some of my shitty baggage (aka intergenerational trauma) onto my innocent children.

Thankfully, Internal Family Systems came into my life when I needed it most. I was fortunate to work with and learn from Dick Schwartz while studying the model on my own and attending institute trainings, as well as my own therapy and consultation. Through my own experiences of healing with IFS and bringing it to my work with clients, I realized how profoundly IFS can help moms through matrescence.

Healing through IFS helped me quickly let go of many of the old wounds that were blocking me from enjoying motherhood and from showing up for my kids as the mom they needed. I was amazed at how swiftly I could release and unburden from internalized myths and faulty beliefs about what it means to be a "good mother" and feel more lightness, joy, empowerment, and inner liberation using IFS. The impacts from the early attachment traumas that I endured underwent a transformation as I found myself feeling more confident, strong, and trusting in my capacities to be the mom my kids needed . . . to grow into the woman I always aspired to be.

My profoundly deep and transformational healing inspired me to help as many mothers as I can. I wouldn't have written this book if I didn't know for myself that change is possible. That your children will be your greatest teachers is not considered in pregnancy and baby-preparation books. I want to shout from the rooftops so that all mothers know they're in matrescence and in it lies the potential for deep self-understanding, healing, and soul-aligned evolution. You can heal. You deserve it. You're worth carving out a little bit of time to turn inward and get to know your parts.

We can break cycles of trauma and heal ourselves, our families, and ultimately there's hope for communities and the world if we were to accept the invitation. To be a cycle-breaker, the work starts inside. In this book you'll learn an effective and powerful method for transforming how you relate to yourself that will help you dismantle and release the toxic myths you've internalized around motherhood while breaking the cycles of trauma that you've been carrying so that you can show up for your kids with the presence, compassion, and confidence they desire from you.

This book gives you a basic understanding of the model of Internal Family Systems, an evidence-based psychotherapeutic healing method, and how it can help you understand and change what's blocking you from the personal healing and expansion that await you through matrescence.

HOW TO READ THIS BOOK

The most important message I want you to hear before venturing into this book is an invitation for you to embrace an attitude of openness, curiosity, and self-compassion. I avoided reading parenting books for years because I was afraid of the self-blame, shame, and judgment cycle I anticipated would be triggered. I expected that as I read about what experts say parents "should do," I would inevitably crumble down a shame spiral when I saw and remembered how I've made what I thought were deep, penetrating mistakes.

I don't want that for you, sweet mama. I can help you avoid that spiral by first stating that there is no perfect parent—no expert who does it all right. One of the greatest gifts of IFS is to understand that all our parts have good reasons for doing what they do. It is the most compassionate and nonpathologizing model I have come across to understand and make sense of even some of the most unsettling or harmful behaviors humans do.

There is a saying in IFS circles: "No excuses, but good reasons"—meaning that if you're a mom reading this book, you are open to learning. You want to do better for your kids, for your family. You know in your gut there's gotta be a way to enjoy this motherhood gig more. And you're right. You are not alone, and all of your parts are welcome. The fact that you are reading this book is proof that you are an awesome mom! Engaging in the practices in this book will change your life. The shifts that come with understanding yourself and learning to relate to your parts with curiosity and compassion will have profound ripple effects, like improving your connection with your kids and all your other relationships. Your family life will change, and as you heal you are ending patterns from past generations.

I also understand that every mama is at her own place in her journey. It takes courage and openness to pause—meaning, to turn our attention inward and get curious about our thoughts, emotions, and beliefs—and get interested in our pain. It takes bravery and readiness to enter a dark forest not knowing where it will lead us.

Give yourself permission to pace yourself. There's no rush. Be brave, Mama. Be kind to yourself. Remember that you are not alone. This is not a one-shot quick fix. We are all works in progress. Notice what resonates and what makes sense with your experience. Let the rest flow by. The promise in this book is that even if you take one new insight away—you learn to be a little more curious or compassionate with yourself as a mom—then amazing shifts will happen in your life. If you open to the ideas in this book and experiment for yourself, you will be amazed at how more energy, power, hope, and self-trust are available to you.

Each chapter explores matrescence and how the IFS method can help moms understand themselves with more clarity and compassion. You'll learn why our kids trigger us and why our old wounds rearise in motherhood. Then we'll move into the myths of the good mother, hearing from moms around the world who experience parts that carry these myths.

Then I'll share with you my theory of the motherhood legacy burden, which outlines how mom parts cluster together and loop through cycles, manifesting from the internalized myths of the perfect mother that's been handed down through generations. You'll read about different moms and how their parts react in some common ways because of patriarchal social and cultural scripts and pressures on how moms should be.

We'll expand from here to include some common mom protector parts, each with its own respective chapter and examples from brave mamas who share their stories of healing to help all moms learn and grow from their witnessing. We'll then look at the parts moms have that carry emotional pain and wounding that are exiled throughout life but get triggered in parenting. To illustrate, I share an excerpt from a session I had with Dick Schwartz that was profoundly healing and transformative.

Then I offer you a chapter on being a Self-led mom, presenting different ways you might access Self-energy, helping you parent from that place to align with your intention of becoming a conscious and attuned parent. The next two chapters will help you consider the importance of finding your own village for support and then show you the promise of what becoming an unburdened mother offers for us, our families, communities, and the world.

I acknowledge that everything written here reflects my perspective and position as a white, cisgender, heterosexual, able-bodied, neurotypical, and economically privileged woman. While I have made intentional efforts to recognize the limitations of my lens, I know there are places where I may have fallen short. I offer the teachings in *Unburdening Motherhood* with humility, a deep openness to continued learning, and a commitment to engage in dialogue and grow—especially as I work to uncover and unlearn unconscious biases and internalized cultural legacy burdens.

Exercises at the end of every chapter can help you reflect on and process your learning. When we awake to the realization that our experience of motherhood has been socially and culturally constructed—influenced by our past, our ancestors' pasts, and a very broken and ill society—we are renewed with a sense of power and hope. This new awareness helps us see that we have power to change—to consciously curate our own version of motherhood.

Mothers are rising to break the toxic cycles that limit our light and mute our love for ourselves. Mothers right now are ending intergenerational cycles of trauma and embodying a more whole and empowered model of mothering for our daughters. Sisters around the globe are braving the inside work and learning to release burdens from generations of devaluing vulnerability and the feminine to foster a new way of healing and hope for our children. You are not alone, even though some days it may feel that way. I commend your bravery for facing the dense forest alongside me. You've got this, Mama. Welcome to a true paradigm shift: the Self-led mothers' revolution.

The first step is to understand how our kids are our greatest teachers—why and how our kids, motherhood, and parenting serve as our most potent triggers of intense emotion and unprocessed past pain. Knowledge is power, after all, so let's start making sense of this foreboding forest called motherhood.

CHAPTER I

MOTHERHOOD AND UNHEALED TRAUMA

On some level unconsciously,
we think our kids are going to heal us,
and the truth is our kids trigger us.
—DR. BECKY KENNEDY

THERE ARE MANY REASONS why we all know parenting is the hardest job. I can quickly list five or more reasons off the top of my head. But the one that tops my list, without a doubt, is that motherhood can be a minefield where unprocessed pain or traumas from our past can be triggered.

After hearing the stories from many mothers and developing my own case conceptualization, I see how our children act as little mirrors of our own childhoods. If we were lacking in nurturance, attention, interest, or acknowledgment in our childhood, we can't help but notice the incongruence as we offer our own children our attention and interest, our energy, and care.

For example, as a teacher and married mother of a five-year-old daughter, Tatiana noticed these unmet needs in terms of what she called her "jealous part" when planning and preparing for her daughter's first birthday party. She described her thoughts to me: *"How come I—I never got to have this that way? . . . She gets all the attention. . . . She has . . . everything. I should have had that."*

As we hold them dearly and value them, wanting the best for them and doing all we can to ensure they thrive, we come up against the errors of our parents, who missed the mark. Our unmet needs will be revealed to us as we build our motherhood muscles and parent our kids.

A part of me is still embarrassed to admit it, but despite my years of clinical training and personal therapy, I was completely naive to the fact that my old traumas would resurface alongside mothering. I had gone through a good chunk of therapy alongside graduate school to become a therapist. I thought I got it. I was a trained, skilled psychotherapist with extra training in emotional processing. I had my PhD after thousands of hours of clinical experience and knowledge accumulation. I thought I had healed my childhood wounds and that I'd be the Best. Mom. Ever.

Little signs or clues that my past was not still in the past began to pop up along the way. Watching my four-year-old daughter during her bath time every night, I began to have random thoughts about my own childhood. Seeing the innocence, dependence, and vulnerability in my children, I found myself wondering how anyone could hurt such a beautiful, vulnerable creature like a child.

If you're wondering why my thoughts would go there, you might be right in guessing that my childhood included sexual abuse. For me, it happened at the ages of three and seven. I thought I'd healed from these abuses and processed them in EMDR therapy years before my first pregnancy. Here I was faced with my beautiful, precious daughter at the age that I was abused, and I couldn't seem to avoid these thoughts popping up in my mind.

For a long time, I was able to shove those thoughts right back down. Not consciously but somehow automatically, I managed to place them somewhere in the recesses of my mind without too much effort. It made sense to me that showing up for my kids in ways I missed might trigger some tenderness. Because I could conceptually make sense of it, I could fairly easily discount these thoughts and feelings in the early few years of motherhood. Focusing on the litany of daily mothering tasks kept me distracted and too busy to investigate what might be happening here with this resurgence of thoughts about my past.

Then sadness started to creep in with the thoughts. I'd get a bit moody, melancholic—you might say "more emotional." My husband thought I was unhappy, and I'd assure him, "I *AM* happy, Goddammit!" I wanted to be happy. I should be, after all. I had three beautiful and healthy children one after the other, the way we wanted. I was in the career I'd worked so hard to achieve. But he was right. There was a simmering weather storm beneath that I couldn't quite name or understand. I was busy enough as a mom, so I kept my eyes forward trying to just get everything done and not allow too much time for self-reflection. But eventually, the signs and clues that I had more healing work to do became impossible to ignore.

When my kids grew a little older, when they started to really protest and test boundaries, things got extra bumpy. Even though I felt like I had no model or map to know what to do since my kids were not "just behaving" the way I did as a kid, I found myself avoiding reading parenting books. Eventually, I pushed through my resistance, recognizing that I was terrified of reading all the ways that I was doing it wrong: I was scared to feel the shame that was lurking inside that I was failing as a mom. Even worse, I was afraid that I'd learn that it was too late to fix what I'd already broken.

When my firstborn was nine, my daughter eight, and my youngest son six, we moved from Canada to the United States. Six months later was the COVID pandemic lockdown. In a new community with no support, I found myself bumbling through trying to stay strong and confident for my kids during the uncertainty of that time when inside I was riddled with insecurity, fear and worry, shame and inadequacy, and grief.

Yet the realization that I needed to take action and change something came months later when I found myself zoning out when playing a supposedly family-fun game of baseball. My deeply feeling, competitive then-nine-year old grew angry and emotionally dysregulated. I just sort of froze. I could vaguely hear my husband call out to me. "Hello? Where are you? You're like a deer in headlights." Walking back home from the park, I realized I had some inner work to do.

My years of clinical study and my skills in case formulation helped me interpret that, somehow, I was having a freeze response in the face of my son's anger episode. I thought that maybe the reason was witnessing the constant, intense arguing between my parents that happened throughout my childhood that was leading me to somehow automatically shift into this deer-in-headlights state. My father was never physically violent, but he was the loudest person I knew, and he would have shouting matches with my mother, who was chronically unhappy with him and perpetually exuding misery and resentment. Or maybe it was a freeze response from experiencing sexual abuse. Or maybe both. To know for sure was splitting hairs—I knew for sure that I was reacting to my son's emotional outbursts in automatic ways that seemed to come over me. I was not feeling conscious and in control, and that was a problem.

Humans are hardwired for survival. I learned long ago in my clinical training about our physiological stress response that our bodies have a parasympathetic system, which is when our nervous system is in a state of calm and rest—called *homeostasis*—and a sympathetic system, which is when we're triggered into fight-flee-freeze-or-fawn mode. I realized in that moment that my past trauma and my automatic ways of reacting and coping in certain parenting moments was getting in my way of being able to show up as the mom I wanted to be.

All my clinical training and knowledge did nothing in these real-life moments with my kids. It was like everything went in one ear and out the other, and I was functioning completely in reactive and automatic ways. Despite my years of mindfulness meditation and training to teach others how to live with more presence and consciousness, here I was living with what felt like inner chaos. I was perpetually shifting between trying to do all the motherhood tasks, as though I was treading water, trying not to drown, and feeling so angry most of the time that eventually I would yell, stomp, slam doors, and burst into uncontrollable tears. I believed I should have known better and done better, which only added to the already overflowing feelings of inner shame I was carrying.

LITTLE-T OR BIG-T TRAUMA

When I say our old wounds and past trauma get re-triggered in motherhood, it's important to clarify what I mean by "old wounds" and "trauma." Big-T trauma is what's outlined in the clinician's handbook in which diagnoses of mental disorders are labeled (*The Diagnostics and Statistical Manual of Mental Disorders, 5th ed.*). You've likely heard of post-traumatic stress disorder (PTSD), the diagnosis given to people who develop a number of symptoms (such as disturbing thoughts, feelings, dreams or mental or physical distress, hypervigilance, and avoidance of things relating to the traumatic event) that persist more than one month after experiencing a traumatic event. Big-T traumas, according to the DSM-5, are sexual assault, warfare, vehicle collisions, child abuse, domestic violence, or other threats to one's well-being or that of someone they care for.

Not formally included as a diagnosis in the *DSM-5*, but complex post-traumatic stress disorder (CPTSD), first defined by Judith Herman in her 1992 book *Trauma and Recovery*, has been more readily acknowledged in the field and is commonly used by clinicians. Based on her clinical experience working with women and many children and adolescents, Herman proposed that children and women in enduring relational and environmental situations where there is chronic dysfunction, lack of safety, abuse, or witnessing or experiencing violence can lead to symptoms and struggles across many areas of life that weren't accounted for in the PTSD diagnosis.

Wounds is the term many therapists use to refer to critically significant or chronic injuries to a person's sense of self and safety, usually in childhood, that impact their psychological and emotional development and beliefs about themselves and the world, which then color their experiences in relationships (attachment), coping behaviors (e.g., addictions), and overall happiness in life.

Thanks to decades of developmental psychological research over the past century, most of us in the United States understand that physical abuse or mental and emotional abuse of children has significant negative impacts and outcomes for the children. What's less understood is that many people experience wounds and what is referred to in the field of psychotherapy as "little-t traumas" that stem from unmet needs or living in dysfunctional environments (e.g., being raised by emotionally immature caregivers), as well as from some historically common parenting practices.

For example, shaming was historically a parent's tool to try to motivate their children or have them behave in what's thought to be socially acceptable ways. Parental criticism—such as pointing out the child's errors after a sports game, academic report card, or public performance—has been typical across generations. Gaslighting, which refers to intentionally invalidating, dismissing, or denying a child's emotions and perception of reality, can also have long-term influences on the child's development. Not to say that occasionally these parenting tactics will traumatize or forever harm a child, but when they are chronic, harsh, and void of positive connection or affirmation, they can be impactful and wounding.

Attachment wounds can happen when parents don't support, connect with, or provide for the needs of the child. This is inevitable if the parent him- or herself is not healed and is burdened with unprocessed traumas and pain from their own childhood. This is how wounds are passed down from one generation to the next. As Dr. Jonice Webb has explained, childhood emotional neglect, which is common for many people, is less obvious than abuse or maltreatment. You can't remember because there's no memory of a trauma, but emotional neglect by a parent still has an impact.[1] What you didn't get—such as emotional support and acknowledgment, validation of your feelings, and help with how to process them—is a small-t trauma. The challenge lies in the fact that we can't give our children what we ourselves didn't get.

> ## *A loving note, dear mama—*
>
> I invite you to pause here. You might have a reaction that makes you think of your own childhood and what you might have experienced that would be considered an attachment wound. Or, like I sometimes do, you might remember the times you weren't attuned to your children. Take a deep breath in, inhaling loving and compassionate energy toward yourself and exhale out any thoughts of self-judgment. Remind yourself you can brave the dense forest of reflecting on motherhood because you are learning and healing and aiming to break cycles. This means you must invite forgiving and compassionate energy to your past behaviors. You were doing the very best you could with what you knew. Mistakes are not failures when they lead us to learning and growth. Give yourself grace to learn a new way.

Innovations and voices in the parent coaching space, like Daniel Siegel (*The Whole Brain Child*) and Dr. Becky Kennedy (*Good Inside*), are shedding light on the ways that past behavioral interventions with kids—like focusing on punishment and negative consequences and rewards in trying to get the hoped-for behavior—are not the best, and may even have negative repercussions for our children and our connection with them.

These experts are advising parents to stay connected with their children, helping them learn the skills they need to be resilient and well-functioning adults—the kind who are confident in their ability to navigate and tolerate the full range of their emotions while integrating the capacities they need to be happy, healthy, and successful in life. We're in the age of parenting through valuing our children's sovereignty, emotional needs, and rights to make mistakes and learn without shaming or judgment. Ways of parenting through fear, authoritarianism, and corporal punishment are slowly dissolving as the young generation of parents want to correct the mistakes of their parents. That's a good thing. That's how we grow and evolve.

This is no small task, however, especially when we are from a generation of parents who were raised with general absence or neglect, or for those whose parents didn't know better than to rely on threats, punishment, or abuse—parents who invalidated, dismissed, and punished our emotions/emotional expressions and our experience in the world because that's how they were raised and they were carrying unhealed trauma without the skills and abilities to show up for parenthood with attunement, emotion regulation, and steady connection. You can't teach what you never got.

Many of us didn't get a highly attuned and attentive parent who was able to sit with, validate, and witness the full range of our emotional expression. Getting curious about our kids, or how Dr. Kennedy suggests we view our children's behaviors with "the most generous interpretation," was not many people's experiences. Parents of the 1970s and 1980s didn't have this knowledge and understanding, and like every generation before us, we do the best we can with what we know. The wounds that go unhealed in one generation will be passed on to the next. Wounds might manifest in similar ways (e.g., addiction) or they might look different (e.g., overachieving in lieu of addiction). The reality is that many small-t traumas arise from unhealed parents, as well as from the impacts of gaslighting, criticizing, shaming, and authoritarian modes of parenting.

Having a parent or both parents who suffered either big-T or little-t trauma can lead to the passing along of unintended emotional injuries and pain. Having parents who struggled with some type of addiction, for example, has undeniable impacts in different and varied ways. Having lost a parent through death or abandonment, and not having been able to process or grieve, can leave lasting imprints that will resurface during motherhood.

Kids are bad interpreters, and they are too young to process big feelings or unsafe experiences on their own. With brains still growing, they don't have the capacity to formulate and understand that the bad or challenging things that might be happening in their household are not personal. Instead of being able to see errors, problems, or difficulties as "something bad happened to me," their internal systems shift into various forms of self-protection, like dissociation, denial, distorting reality, self-loathing, or self-blame to cope with feelings that are too big and to help them survive.

Injuries get filtered and imprinted in kids' psyches as "I'm bad," or "This bad thing that happened to me is because of me and my badness." In this way, most of us are walking around with wounds inside from difficult experiences in our early lives that we misconstrued and misinterpreted. Many of us have buried parts of ourselves from early life experiences that were too painful to process and release. Deep inside, on some level, we still believe that we are somehow bad and unworthy, too *this* or too *that*. These parts can be triggered in the face of our own children behaving like typical, normal children.

A loving note, dear mama—

Notice with a loving energy what's coming up for you. You may be thinking about your own childhood, or you may be thinking through the lens of a parent. Either way, this learning and growing can be hard. In the words of Glennon Doyle, "We can do hard things." You're not alone. No one is perfect. Healing and repair are always possible. Hang in there! You're here trying to heal and change for yourself and your kiddos. Self-criticism, self-blame, or self-condemnation is asked to sit in the waiting room in your mind. Give yourself some grace, Mama. Deep breath . . . You got this!

EXAMPLES OF SMALL-T TRAUMA:

- When Joanne was young, she was not a big eater, and she recalled feeling anxious when her mother would become angry with her for not eating. Now, with her eighteen-month-old, she has noticed she feels angry and anxious when her daughter resists eating. She said the degree of emotion felt seems "disproportionate," and she doesn't know what to do with this strong emotion.
- Liz described her father as an angry and sometimes rageful man. Now, with a four-year-old and two-year-old, she notices she won't allow herself to feel any anger because of this. But she's human, so sometimes her anger bubbles up. This creates inner turmoil, self-blame, and shame—not to mention the fear that she will become—or is—like her father.
- Milena was taken from her mother right from birth and put on her own in a separate room, not being held by anyone,

including her mother, until twelve hours later (as was custom in the hospital at that time). She connects this important absence in her development to sometimes feeling a deep sense of aloneness and hurt that overwhelms her when she reads the news and learns of stories of children being harmed.

- Rachel felt like she was reliving her own struggles as a deeply feeling kid when "shhhhing" her daughter and realizing that she had been a deeply feeling kid who didn't get the parenting she needed. She realized she had learned to believe she was "too much" and that something was wrong with her through her mother's not knowing how to best respond to her big feelings.

- Stephanie felt triggered when her son was in a phase of wanting her partner more (which is developmentally normal). She noticed feeling salty and withdrawing from her son, which she later blamed herself for and then tried to compensate by self-sacrificing to fix what wasn't broken. Going inside and getting to know her parts, she realized she had a wounded part that felt "unwanted," which was now showing up in her reactions to her child.

There are many examples of small-t trauma—too many to list here. When a child's needs for safety and security; agency and independence; and exploration, play, and fun—and validation of their emotions and experience—are not met, there can be misinterpretations and wounds that follow the child into adulthood.

When gone unhealed and unprocessed, big-T trauma experiences will also manifest in ways throughout motherhood. Statistics from the Centers for Disease Control and Prevention (CDC) and

RAINN (the Rape, Abuse & Incest National Network) tell us that one in four girls will experience sexual abuse or assault before they turn eighteen years old. Based on reporting data (which may under-represent true numbers), 82 percent of sexual assault victims under age eighteen are female. These shocking and sad statistics suggest that many mothers will likely have symptoms of trauma that can manifest in motherhood.

For instance, violations against one's body mean that parts within her system will learn to cope in ways to buffer emotional pain from trauma. Women cope with this in different ways, and one common way is to live disconnected from one's body. This isn't hard to do in our very emotionally avoidant culture, where we tend to rationalize away our feelings and try to live in our heads rather than feeling our emotions, which live in the body.

The experience of pregnancy, giving birth, and breastfeeding can move a mother into confused territory, with emotions and coping strategies that have yet to know how to respond to this kind of use of her body. Consider the example I shared in the introduction: I had developed the capacity to sort of tune out—like a deer caught in headlights. This self-numbing capacity evolved from my experiences of sexual abuse. It also helped me cope with the constant yelling and fighting between my parents that was traumatic to be forced to live with. I could just tune out most of my life.

I've noticed that some of the feelings of powerlessness, help-lessness, and lack of control that arise from physical and sexual abuse can be retriggered in the dynamics of motherhood. The self-sacrificing of one's body, time, energy, and complete attention asked of moms today can feel similar to those feelings derived from trauma and victimization. Feeling trapped, powerless, or angry, or even feeling taken for granted or used, can trigger us inside, but most moms don't put the two together when they're activated in parenting.

When becoming a mother and along the course of raising and parenting our own little beings, these wounds will inevitably be triggered. What this looks like is similar and different for everyone. Old wounds resurfacing can appear like intense or disproportionate emotional reactions, like anger, rage, anguish, depression, or despair. For some people, it shows up in excessive worrying or fear, anxiety, and hypervigilance in situations that don't warrant such a response. Feelings of shame, inadequacy, and insecurity are common imprints from abuse or neglect and from overall bad parenting (criticism, shaming, contempt, or rejection).

It might be a chronic sense of emptiness or hopelessness that leaves a residual shadow in a mother's life. Deeply entrenched beliefs often come with emotional wounds, as do critical or negative thoughts and despairing or victimlike mindsets that block a mom's ability to feel joy, lightness, play, or creativity. The impact might look like a mom showing up with excessive seriousness, irritability, resentment, or misery.

For some moms, these wounds can evolve into developing more serious mental health issues, like clinical depression or anxiety. What's underlying the disorder, however, is often not fully understood. While there's some evidence to support a genetic component to depression and other mental health disorders, these conditions are better understood as imbalances manifested from and within a broken world.

Traditional and medical theories about mothers' mental health, as in diagnoses of "perinatal mood and/or anxiety disorder," do not account for the powerful process of transformation mothers are going through when becoming mothers. They don't consider the ways that we can accommodate multiple roles to try to function, cope, stave off pain, and survive. What the mom experiences is inner turmoil, most often because the outer world doesn't understand nor support the multiple truths and polarized parts within her. As a result, she doesn't understand and instinctively blames and judges herself for it—making it all the worse.

Moms love their kids, so the stakes are high. We don't want them to suffer, and we want to show up as the best version of ourselves. What makes trauma resurfacing in motherhood even more challenging is we often don't realize this is what's happening to us. When we can't make sense of our inner turmoil, our discontent, and our seemingly unconscious reactivity, we feel even more confused, ashamed, and alone.

Becoming a mother brings us face-to-face with how we were mothered; how we might have been misunderstood or disconnected from our fathers; how our needs for connection, acceptance, love, and affirmation were met; and how ancestral wounds have been passed down to us. Things that happened to us that we thought were behind us have a strange way of cropping back up in motherhood. No one prepares moms-to-be to expect that one's own childhood wounds and trauma might await them, rearising along their journey of motherhood. This is because matrescence has unfortunately yet to be fully understood and embraced in our social and cultural understanding of motherhood and maternal mental health.

WHAT IS MATRESCENCE?

Motherhood is a journey unlike any other. It is a transformational process of identity that is infused with meaning. It stirs us up, changing every aspect of our life. It opens us to places where we need to heal and in this way offers us potential for spiritual awakening.

Becoming a mother is so much more than the physical changes following childbirth. Moms who adopt or use a surrogate also undergo an invisible process of transformation by stepping into mothering another soul in this human life. We can't truly understand and acknowledge our experiences as mothers without understanding matrescence.

Though still unknown to most people, the term *matrescence* was coined in the 1960s by Dana Raphael, an American anthropologist and breastfeeding advocate. She saw the need to rethink beyond the birthing process the way we view how a woman becomes a mother, considering the implications and effective support systems.

Carrying the torch of Raphael's work years later, Dr. Aurelie Athan expanded our understanding of matrescence through her work at Columbia University and laid the groundwork for women to begin to view motherhood as a rite of passage in the same way that adolescence is an understood and recognizable process and shift in identity that comes with emotional, psychological, physical, and hormonal changes. Matrescence is like adolescence.

Author, coach, and podcast host Amy Taylor-Kabbaz explains that "matrescence is the complete transformation and identity shift of a woman as she moves through motherhood—psychological, social, emotional, physical, economic, cultural, and spiritual."[2]

Taylor-Kabbaz states that matrescence is "the split between who you used to be and who you are now. It's the tug-of-war between your old self and your desire to be there for every moment of your child's life. And we don't name that transition—when we ignore it and tell women they just need to multitask and get on with it, we deny her the truth. And we deny her the opportunity to define what motherhood means to her, in her own way."

No one tells you that you'll feel feelings you never expected. Perhaps you'll have joy and bliss, but you'll also have despair, fear, dread, sadness, and grief. No matter how many prenatal books you read or how beautifully decorated the nursery is, you can't mentally and emotionally prepare for your personal transformation into becoming a mother. The changes are subtle and significant. They are nuanced and invisible. They will impact every aspect of your life, and too few mothers know that this process has a name.

It's different for every mom, just as unique as our own fingerprints. For me, it was the lack of words to name the feelings I had, feeling torn between my career (I had just had my third child when I graduated with my doctorate) and motherhood. I'll always remember what my husband often cautioned me about those first few years. Seeing me split my attention from the kids and the pull I felt to focus on my work and my career passions, he'd warn me, "They're only little once!"

As if I don't know that—thanks so much! I'd think, not knowing about matrescence and not having the words to name what I now know is a common and significant inner shift that many moms experience. I didn't know there was what Taylor-Kabbaz calls "the inner split" between the woman before you became a mom and the woman you are after becoming a mom. Matrescence helped me name that I was grieving deeply in my core, feeling like I had to jump off a path that I was excited about, interested in, and fulfilled by. I lost the freedom to run (literally, because childbirth wrecked my body), the choice of my daily routine and time (you mean they must breastfeed that many times a day—and it takes how long?), and the space to paint, write, think, and grow as a psychotherapist, and as the spiritual seeker I'd been for thirty-four years. I was thrown into a new world where it felt like I was supposed to naturally, comfortably, and willingly give all of that up. I also had no clue that motherhood would break me open to past experiences I thought I was over and had healed.

I had desperately wanted to become pregnant. I had no doubts about wanting to be a mom. I was just completely unprepared for the inner feelings that followed. I thought I was being ungrateful. I had three healthy babies in the order we had wanted them—who was I to complain? Confused and saddened by my discontentedness, I would assure my husband, "I *am* happy, damn it!" The truth is I was. I was just going through a layered, intense, and powerful transformation that I had no words for, no understanding of, and no support to help me move through it with ease and grace. When I learned about matrescence, I felt showered in validation and understanding. Maybe I wasn't so bad after all. Maybe I wasn't—as I'd feared—a bad mom just because I had these mixed feelings.

An eighty-seven-year-old grandmother, talking about motherhood, said that when her first child was born, she didn't feel that immediate "knowing" of what to do, how a mother should just "know." I told her, "I think that's the greatest myth to any mother and that actually we are learning and growing too." I told her that there is a word now for what we go through: *matrescence*. She paused and said, "Thank you. For all these years I've blamed myself. Thank you."

According to Dr. Athan, matrescence is "a developmental passage where a woman transitions through preconception, pregnancy and birth, surrogacy, or adoption, to the postnatal period and beyond. The exact length of matrescence is individual, recurs with each child, and may arguably last a lifetime! The scope of the changes encompasses multiple domains—biological, psychological, social, political, and spiritual—and can be likened to the developmental push of adolescence."

For adolescents, we have a common understanding about the unique needs—the hormonal shifts, awkwardness, and mixed emotions—that arise from a changing body over which we have no control. We have books written on it, coaching programs, and cultural grace toward teens.

For mothers, who are going through their own developmental passage, there's some awareness that their bodies will change, and their emotions will be all over the place until their hormones settle back down—eventually. But she's expected to be happy regardless of, or even with, all the changes that arise from becoming a mother. As one mom shared on a coaching call, when she expressed some of the challenges in motherhood, her partner responded with "You chose this." In other words, don't complain. Matrescence makes room for the nuanced emotions, the thoughts that seem contradictory or even scary—for the challenges and valid things to complain about. Knowing about matrescence helps a mom not feel crazy or alone in what can sometimes feel like an inner tug-of-war.

We understand that adolescence is rife not only with milestones in identity development but how we relate to it, and we can have a major influence on how we feel and grow into adults. While teens are officially, legally, and culturally considered adults once they've walked through the developmental milestone of completing adolescence, mothers are not honored in this way. The shift into motherhood is not seen for how multifaceted and transformational it is.

Matrescence represents how once we birth or adopt a child and take on the role of mother, we are no longer the same person. We're being created moment by moment through the process of matrescence, never to be the same again. The lack of acknowledgment of this potent process within our culture makes what could be an honorable, deep, and spiritual transformation feel instead like a confusing, scary, and isolating journey for most women. Instead of connection, validation, and recognition in community, silencing and discounting women's experiences in motherhood perpetuates competition among women and sets the stage for internalized feelings of shame and inadequacy.

Whether we want it or not, becoming a mother involves our own experiences of being raised, and we are influenced by our ancestral and familial lineage in the maternal experiences that were passed down. In a *New York Times* article, Dr. Alexandre Sacks writes, "For better or for worse your maternal identity is founded in your mother's style, and hers in her mother's." When our parents carry unhealed wounds and emotional burdens from their unprocessed pain, they pass either a similar wound or a different wound onto us. In this way, we understand that motherhood and its unhealed traumas are passed along from one generation to the next.

There's proof of this in epigenetic studies showing evidence that we pass our stress and trauma off to our offspring.[3] Recent writings about what Bethany Webster called "the mother wound" are shedding light on the painful impacts of wounded mothers raising their children without doing their healing.

Whether painful or positive, or a mix of both, matrescence brings us face-to-face with our childhoods and with the ancestral patterns that we might want to change. If we're brave, if we're open to it, and if we're ready to change our relationship with ourselves, we are gifted an opportunity to heal and to reparent ourselves at the same time we're trying to raise healthy, happy little humans. This is the gift offered through matrescence: a chance to heal, evolve, and emerge as the wisest, most compassionate, and most authentic version of ourselves.

This was the result for me in learning and using the principles and practices of IFS. Once I had the language of knowing that all of my mixed feelings and the inner tug-of-war I felt between my kids and my career were understood as normal in matrescence, I began to soften the inner critic that was turning against myself in self-blame. Understanding that my old wounds and unhealthy patterns were rising up to the surface, as they do in matrescence, I was kinder to myself and I accessed an inner drive to do the work it would take so that my children wouldn't inherit and absorb what I wasn't willing to face and heal.

What did this look like exactly? Through guided meditations or sometimes without guidance, I started turning my attention inside my body with curiosity and patience. I invited in the parts that were activated and started listening to what they wanted me to know. With interest and openness, I grew to know each part that would be activated during parenting, in my relationships, and sometimes seemingly randomly, like when watching a show. Over time, my parts came to trust me, as I worked through and released old wounds and faulty beliefs. They became less charged as they saw how I would care for them, listen to them, and help them unburden outdated feelings of not being safe, good enough, or loveable. With each caring visit to my inner world I would feel more clarity and self-confidence, finding less reactivity in all of my relationships. With each part that I connected to with compassion, I felt more space open up in my heart, and my inner judge or angry mom part began to soften and relax. I didn't need to be so armored anymore as my heart opened to myself, making room for more joy, creativity, love, and faith.

This is possible for you too. I will be your guide in *Unburdening Motherhood* as I share with you the pathway that helped me transform an experience of pain, confusion, and having parts that hated motherhood to feeling like the most confident, free, empowered, and true version of my Self. Wherever you are in your matrescence journey, the practices offered here will meet you and light a path forward to knowing yourself and being able to care for and heal yourself right away.

We'll start by exploring the many myths of what it means to be a good mother, and you can see what, if any, you've unknowingly absorbed. We all have, to some degree, as the subtle messages of what it means to be a successful woman and a good mother are infused in the tapestry of our culture and society. The good news is, with awareness, we can choose a different belief system. We can create a motherhood that aligns with our own hearts and values. So while recognizing the wounds and hardships we've endured is hard and takes courage, there is also hope. The truth is that we all have power to create the life we want. So, dear mama, let's get started!

Woman, standing on a hillside, peering, peering into blue
space...

 ...what will woman be?

  ...not yet fully seen

   ...not yet fully revealed

    ...but coming

     ...coming

      ...what will woman be?

    JUDITH DUERK, Circle of Stones

EXERCISE: REFLECTION ON MATRESCENCE

I invite you to pause. Take a deep breath. Find a comfy place for a few moments. I know you're a busy mama, so there's no requirement to get out a journal or to take more than five to ten minutes. You might write this down if you're a journal person (I was before becoming a mom), but you can also just pause, close your eyes after reading each question, and bring your attention inward with a curiosity as you reflect on the questions below.

1. If you didn't know about matrescence before reading this chapter, what thoughts and feelings came up for you with this new concept as a way to interpret and understand your journey of motherhood up until now?

2. Now that you understand matrescence, do you see, feel, or interpret your experiences differently? How?

3. How has your identity shifted since becoming a mother?

4. Have there been any surprises in motherhood—things you didn't expect or anticipate? Maybe things you wish you knew?

5. What emotions have you noticed during motherhood? Grief, anger, sadness, love, joy, fear, anxiety, confusion, disappointment? There are no wrong answers. All feelings are welcome—they all make sense in matrescence.

6. What ways have old wounds, small-t traumas, or big-T traumas impacted your experience of pregnancy, birth, motherhood, and parenting?

Now, dear mama, give yourself a loving embrace in your mind, or literally wrap your arms around yourself and squeeze. Or you might place your hand on your heart and say, "I'm here. I'm listening" or "I care." Take a few slow, deep breaths, and notice how that feels in your body. Now I invite you to do something soothing and caring for yourself. You deserve it!

CHAPTER 2

THE MYTHS OF "A GOOD MOTHER"

*Did you hate that part of you before someone
told you you should?*

—L. E. BOWMAN

FOR SOME MOMS, motherhood has been all they thought it would be. They are prepared, they correctly anticipate everything, and they fully embrace and love almost every minute of being a mom. For others, motherhood feels like they are hit in the face with a cast-iron pan. Over and over.

For a long time, I was in the latter group. Motherhood kicked my ass. Like many of the moms I've worked with, there was an unanticipated surprise or even shock of what motherhood was actually like compared with what I expected and how good I thought I'd be at this gig called Mom.

For me it was constant defiance and negotiation with my kids that led me to feeling daily anger and frustration. The never-ending demands of their daily routines, meal prep and cleanup, organizing and coordinating social and extracurricular activities that I found myself responsible for, and the ups and downs of helping three kids manage their emotional expressions and frustrations left me completely exhausted by the end of every day. And never feeling satisfied or proud, I should add.

Instead, my inner dialogue was typically pointing out the places I could have done better or should be doing more. More reading, more playing, more making them tidy up (instead of doing it myself because it's faster). After a lengthy bath time and story time and finally getting three kids in their beds, I'd collapse on the couch excited to finally tune out my mind and body, only to start up the engine again the next day with a plan to try harder and do better.

In the thick of parenting and realizing this isn't what I expected, I realized that subconsciously I expected motherhood to be like it was for my mom, not realizing that raising my kids quite differently—tending to them, doing things for them, and prioritizing their emotions and needs—meant a very different experience for everyone. My mom's experience of motherhood was different because I was a quiet, conflict-avoidant, people-pleasing "good girl" who never argued or protested. As a child who, as a result of both small- and big-T traumas by age five, deeply didn't believe her needs mattered, I was an easy kid to raise. I unwittingly assumed I'd have easy kids to raise despite raising them completely differently and also in a digital environment that previous generations never had.

In tough moments of frustration and feeling fed up, I'd tell myself, *You have strong-willed kids, Angele, who are no one's doormat. That's a good thing! You want your kids to know they matter—that their emotions and needs are important. It's a good sign that they feel safe with you to express all their emotions and not hide parts of themselves to fit in or get love.* This viewpoint would ease my anger and worry somewhat, with part of me truly believing it and another part of me wondering if I'm just kidding myself to reduce my worry and shame for messing them up and doing a shit job.

A quick scan of TikTok and Instagram and the many mom accounts tells me that I'm not alone in feeling this way. Moms are using humor to express and share their moments of overwhelm, making folly of the insane and unrealistic expectations that plague them. Many cycle-breaking moms are sharing their tears around what it's like trying to raise good humans and enjoy motherhood while having old wounds and past traumas simultaneously resurface throughout motherhood. Having no good model for an emotionally healthy parent, some moms are feeling lost, stressed, and alone as they try to navigate the rocky trail of motherhood.

The *What to Expect When* series did nothing to prepare me for the roller-coaster ride that awaited in motherhood. Maybe that's been your experience too? Maybe you've felt blindsided by raising kids in the 2020s where the world seems to have become unrecognizable from the context in which you grew up. Maybe, like me, you were committed to parenting differently than your parents—better—but found yourself lost on how to actually execute in a new way without any models, map, or compass to find your way through to what you thought would be a happy, harmonious, loving, and functioning family life.

Maybe you've talked about your experiences with friends, but you've held back a bit, fearing the potential judgment from others that you can't be a good mom if you sometimes feel dissatisfaction, confusion, or ambivalence. The thought that you must be doing it wrong might have stopped you from having real conversations with your closest people—your best friends, family, and partner.

Or maybe you've never felt more anxious. Your friends and family are tired of trying to reason with your fears, frustrated that their logic doesn't seem to calm your chronic insecurities. Keeping these thoughts and feelings locked inside might seem like the best alternative, only leaving you to feel more lost from yourself, unsure about how to move forward, and wondering why being a mom isn't more fun and joy-filled, the way you thought it would be—the way some of those moms on Instagram seem to be loving all of it.

Or like so many moms, you're just plain exhausted and functioning in survival mode, rushing from one task to the next while thinking and planning and navigating the mental load of motherhood, without any space or energy left to reflect on what it's like for you to be a mom. *What? "Motherhood"? That's a thing?*

THE MOTHER LOAD

It's no wonder moms are struggling, considering all they're trying to balance. On top of the tasks and day-to-day demands that moms are still mostly responsible for—pickups, drop-offs, housecleaning, groceries and cooking, social coordinating, hosting, holidays, and for many moms, caring for elder parents—mothers' work also includes what's now popularly referred to as "the invisible mental load" of parenting. The invisible efforts of daily mental tasks, like remembering appointments, anticipating children's needs, keeping track of activities and social times, school involvement, organizing, and essential life project management—all of this takes up mental space and emotional energy. This significant mental labor has been shown to negatively impact mothers' attentional resources, cognitive functioning, and psychological well-being.[1] This unseen yet taxing work of parenting is folded into traditional and current models of motherhood, and it can lead to overwhelm, resentment, and burnout.

Mothers also appear to have taken the brunt of many of the consequences of the COVID pandemic. Most parents who took on the labor, educational, and childcare shortages because of the COVID pandemic lockdowns were moms.[2] Research into the impacts of the pandemic showed that moms suffered the most in leaving jobs and careers to uproot everything and accommodate the new remote needs of their kids, referred to as the "motherhood penalty."[3] Taking years of progress and earned time away, moms were set back, not only in work, but they were the ones to help their kids cope with and recover from their mental health because of pandemic life.

Increased rates of anxiety and other mental health issues for kids were noted across the United States since the COVID pandemic, with over 20 percent of children ages three to seventeen formally diagnosed with anxiety or depression, according to the CDC. These are concerning numbers. And who is finding therapists, social workers, and psychiatrists to help while reading the parenting books, listening to the parenting podcasts and webinars, and integrating their recommended interventions and treatment protocols in the home—oh, and monitoring their screen time? Yep, moms.

It's clear moms are juggling *a lot*. A recent U.S. surgeon general conducted an advisory review of the mental health and well-being of parents. The review of recent studies showed that nearly 70 percent of parents say parenting is now more difficult than it was twenty years ago, with children's use of technology and social media as the top two cited reasons.[4] The advisory points to the "intensifying culture of comparison" that's perpetuated by social media influencers and online trends that promote unrealistic expectations around child development, parenting strategies, and goals and status symbols, which kids and parents alike absorb and think they must achieve. The surgeon general's report states, "Chasing these unreasonable expectations has left many families feeling exhausted, burned out, and perpetually behind." Of the parents interviewed, 41 percent reported feeling so stressed most days they cannot function, with 48 percent reporting that most days their stress is completely overwhelming compared to other adults (20 and 26 percent, respectively).

The surgeon general offers many recommendations on mass cultural, institutional, policy, and systems change to improve the plight of modern-day parents and the state of their mental health, which impacts the health and well-being of children. One of these expectations is to "talk openly about the stress and struggles that come with parenting," recognizing that doing so can ease feelings of shame and guilt while helping to "build the momentum needed to ultimately shift practices and collective expectations to be more consistent with health and well-being." We're advised to take care of ourselves and reduce our stress with many commonly understood self-care strategies like sleep, exercise, a balanced diet, meditation, and doing activities that bring us joy.

And while the advisory briefly differentiates the impacts of parenting according to gender—noting that women have a higher prevalence of mental health conditions than men—the report acknowledges that paternal mental health conditions and impacts on children are less studied. Apart from pointing to the statistics on perinatal health for mothers and that 22.7 percent of pregnancy-related deaths are related to mental health conditions, including suicides and overdose or poisoning related to substance use disorders,[5] nowhere is the influence of patriarchal cultural ideologies and practices—the underlying causes of why women's mental health is more negatively impacted by parenting—mentioned in the mental health experience of mothers.

Why is mothers' mental health worse than men's when it comes to parenting? Are the pressure and responsibility for raising children equal for fathers and mothers? Not yet. Not only does society rely on mothers for this massive, perpetual undertaking of raising the next generations, but there are social and cultural rules and expectations on *how* moms should be doing it. It's hard not to compare or measure ourselves against what other moms appear to be like on social media, or the baseball game, or the school's open house night. Whether we're aware of it or not, motherhood carries societal expectations that have been woven into the cultural tapestry across generations. Messages around what is expected of mothers persist through the myths of motherhood.

What do I mean by myth? As defined by *Webster's Dictionary*, a myth is (a) "a popular belief or tradition that has grown up around something or something," such as "embodying the ideals and institutions of a society"; (b) "an unfounded or false notion"; or (c) "a person or thing having only an imaginary or unverifiable existence," such as the myth of the unicorn. The myths of motherhood go by different names, but they all reflect the same impossible ideals and standards. The most well-known to date are Super Mom and the perfect mother, or the good mother myth.

THE MYTH OF THE GOOD MOTHER

In 1953, British pediatrician and psychoanalyst Donald Winn-
icott coined the term *good enough mother* after working with and
observing babies and their mothers. He concluded that despite the
commonly held belief in a "perfect mother," children benefit from
mothers failing them in certain reasonable and manageable ways.
Based on his observations, he concluded that by mothers gradually
reducing their responsiveness as their infants grow, their children
adapt and develop their own skills such as through delayed gratifi-
cation (not getting what they want instantly), respecting boundaries
(Mom saying no), and building independence (trying it first on their
own). He concluded that by not meeting a child's every need and
whim in mild and reasonable ways, the child would become better
equipped to adapt, build skills, and develop resilience. Despite this
permission to be imperfect, moms still get caught in the pervasive,
deep, and thick tar within the collective consciousness that carries
incredibly high and unrealistic standards for mothers.

Today's good mother (aka Super Mom) is an intensive mother.
She might have it all, including an important job or career on top of
being a mom. If she doesn't work in formal paid employment, she
busies herself by volunteering at her children's schools and maybe
caring for elders and neighbors. She buys organic and makes fresh
wholesome meals on top of keeping a clean and container store–
organized house. Her children are engaged in multiple enrichment
activities and extracurriculars for which she also volunteers. She's
not angry or tired, she's got a healthy glow, and she thrives in her
motherly duties. She's on top of it all and completely responsible for
raising healthy, happy, well-behaved, successful children on track to
go to the best colleges and grow to be upstanding American citizens.

Oh, and did I mention that she's also supposed to be hot? Society's beauty standards for women have barely changed over the years, meaning that on top of the never-ending tasks and to-do lists around managing households and parenting children, moms are also supposed to keep fit and look their best. The term *MILF* ("mother I'd like to fuck") is an example of how on top of being Super Mom, we're also supposed to be sexy. Body dissatisfaction is so rampant among women that the term "normative discontent" was coined to reflect its commonality.[6] One study found that 68 percent of mothers reported dissatisfaction with their postpartum bodies[7] and feel pressure to lose weight. Body-image struggles in the postpartum period have been linked to mental health concerns, with higher rates of postpartum depression.[8] Of course, these standards don't end for new moms but continue to impact women into their perimenopausal years, where magical serums, creams, treatments, and diets are marketed to women to prevent the inevitable changes in their aging and naturally shape-shifting bodies.

It's important to recognize that the Super Mom ideal in the United States is deeply intertwined with broader systems of power and domination, where white supremacy, racism, capitalism, ableism, and heterosexism persist, both overtly and subtly. As a result, images in pop culture, mainstream media, and marketing aim to reflect the dominant subjective identity, idealizing white, middle- to upper-class, heterosexual, cisgendered, and able-bodied women as the benchmark for a "perfect mother," obviously leaving out BIPOC, adopting, lesbian, trans, and other women who don't fit the promoted mold. So, for many moms, meeting the standards of societal and cultural expectations is quite literally impossible.

This ideal is represented on the cover of magazines (yes, they still make some of those), in popular television shows and movies, and across social media in the seemingly perfect and easy-lived style of "momfluencers." Each is the archetype of motherly perfection—the model that all moms have absorbed knowingly or unconsciously as the gold standard of what a good mom looks and acts like, how she feels, and what she does.

There is intense pressure on moms to do things a certain way or the right way. Mother-blaming biases have been passed down to us from early psychological and scientific theories where mothers and mothering were taken as the cause of all ailments, behavioral and emotional concerns, and disability observed in children. In the 1950s and 1960s, we had the example of Dr. Bruno Bettleheim (who, as it turned out, had a doctorate in art history and not child psychiatry) blaming "refrigerator mothers" for causing autism in children. There was also the concept of the "schizophrenogenic mother" in the mid-twentieth century, when mothers were told they were responsible for causing schizophrenia in their children. And in case you weren't aware, later psychoanalytic theories of the 1960s and 1970s brought the idea that overprotective mothers were most responsible for causing borderline personality disorder in their offspring.

Mothers were considered inadequate to parent without leaning on so-called experts in child development and early psychology theories that prescribed "correct" mothering practices, spanning from how to hold and feed an infant to when and how often children should be hugged, kissed, scolded, or spanked. "Psychologists claimed correct maternal behavior would lead to hard-working, self-disciplined, law-abiding adults; any variance would create weak-minded, badly behaved, aberrant adults with a propensity for crime and radicalism."[9]

From one generation to the next, we live in what motherhood sociologist Dr. Sophie Brock describes as a fishbowl, where we are immersed in culturally and historically subjective expectations of motherhood, often unaware of the social and cultural scripts shaping how we think we should be as mothers.

This type of taken-for-granted-ness has come through in my work with mothers. When asked about their sense of the myths of the good mother and our current script toward intensive mothering, some moms realized that they never questioned this or saw that this is not necessarily the truth but a model of current times. But they could definitely see that it's the model against which they hold themselves. For example, when I first suggested to Rachel, a fellow psychologist and mom to two daughters, ages three and six, that the current cultural standard for mothers is characterized as "intensive" and is tied to myths of the good mother, she shared her process with me:

> I had a part that was like, Well, of course, it's intensive.
> Why wouldn't it be? Why would that be a myth? And then I
> separated a little bit, and realized, Oh, I think that's because
> of the culture and the generation that I'm in.... I don't even
> question it, like, having it framed as a question or a myth to
> consider.... Yeah, that was a bit of a process to sort of unblend
> or sort of step back from my assumption that parenting
> should be intensive to sort of ... imagine that of course there
> could be other ways to parent.

A smart, successful, and accomplished therapist, Rachel is not unique in internalizing the notion of being an intensive mother. Taking it for granted as truth, we swim in what is toxic water without pausing to reflect on its toxins, to question their presence, or to confront their inevitability.

Unfortunately, because of patriarchy, many of the ideas, beliefs, and scripts that persist for women and mothers are demanding, dismissive, and devaluing of mothers' experiences, contributions, and heavy burdens. They have become taken-for-granted assumptions of what a mother is like, subtly creating prescriptions of what mothers *should* be like. Women absorb these myths and other scripts that are passed down through generations. They influence and impact their experiences of becoming mothers in sometimes very disruptive and harmful ways.

A loving note, dear mama—

This may be a good place to pause, take a deep breath in, and slowly exhale out. It's common for feelings of anger, frustration, helplessness, or even cynicism to arise when naming the inequalities and insufficient support mothers are faced with (and have been for millennia). These feelings are valid and understandable. And it's not where we want to stay. We will use the energy of our anger and sense of injustice to fuel our awakening—to inspire social and cultural change for ourselves and our sisters. For now, I invite you to validate your own feelings that have come up in reading thus far and to remember that there is a pathway for hope and change. When we learn to lead from Self, we have the potential to make immeasurable powerful changes in our lives for ourselves and our children. One more deep breath. . . . Let's keep going.

While many myths around motherhood have permeated culture and society across generations, I highlight five here. I think these represent some of the most salient, influential, and harmful beliefs and scripts that all moms are subjected to and held against—whether they realize it or not. These myths make up the standards, the blueprint, and the unquestioned shoulds in the unconscious collective minds of mothers, starting with a myth that influences women at the outset of pregnancy.

Myth #1: *A good mom gets pregnant easily and "naturally" and has a smooth birthing experience, after which she bonds instantly and naturally with her child.*

This myth sets up women to feel inadequate from the start should there be any infertility issues in trying to conceive. Feeling less than, or not whole, unable to "give" their partner a baby triggers feelings of shame and self-judgment for many women. This narrative of natural pregnancy and birthing perfection completely misses the not-uncommon experience of mothers who have miscarriages, adopt, or go through surrogacy and makes women who have any delay in becoming pregnant or resort to innovative medically assisted means feel stressed and insufficient.

Take Stephanie, for instance, a therapist and member of the LGBTQ community who shared that, right from the start, her son's birth was difficult and traumatic. She described it this way:

> I think before I got pregnant, I would have said, I know, that's a myth, and I'm not gonna buy it! And then I had my son and from the get-go, he was a planned C-section because I'd had surgery in the past. And then I realized that right from the jump, I automatically felt like I had done something wrong.

Many moms I've spoken to share a similar self-blame and struggle around breastfeeding. Whether not producing enough milk, or the milk is coming out too quickly, or the baby isn't latching easily or at all, moms internalize these challenges and—in part because of this myth of motherhood—interpret the challenge to mean they're already failing at motherhood.

The reliance on medical experts and so-called research findings leads moms to mistrust themselves and their experience with their infants. If a baby isn't developing according to their charts (which are based on statistics, meaning 67 percent will be considered average, leaving 33 percent outside the middle) and breast milk is promoted as "the best" for the baby, Mom is left feeling inadequate and bad. We're told what is the best and what it should look like so that when Mom's experiences don't track according to the experts, self-blame is the outcome for the mom.

When I think about breastfeeding, I remember the frustration I felt learning it, the grief and sadness for those who cannot, and the irritation and guilt for moms who would rather not have a baby latched to their breast so often—thank you very much—and I think about my mother. While I am a Gen Xer and, at the time I became a mother, breastfeeding was promoted and strongly encouraged, the standards were very different for my mother. She bitterly recalled how her doctor told her breastfeeding was "disgusting"; mothers at that time were not supported to breastfeed based on the then-current medical opinions. This is an example of the fishbowl in which mothers operate. Issues around pregnancy, birth, and feeding are ripe territory for mothers to feel judged, judge themselves, and erroneously blame themselves, thanks to myths of motherhood that mothers and the public hold.

In Stephanie's words,

> I had internalized a lot of expectations of myself to be able to
> breastfeed, for it to be easy. For it to be "natural," so to speak,
> and for it to be pleasant for me, for it to be enjoyable, and for it
> to be a really bonding experience. So, when I couldn't do that
> without choking him, I felt like I'd failed.

Experiences of postpartum depression are often linked to this
myth, with many women reacting to their own ambivalent thoughts
and feelings with an added layer of shame and self-blame. This can
spiral quickly into depression and anxiety postpartum. Where there's
no space or acknowledgment of matrescence for women, they unknowingly absorb the myth that triggers self-judgment, fear, shame,
and grief, when the reality is that bonding isn't necessarily quick
or instant. Bonding commonly takes time, but new moms feel bad
and perceive something is personally wrong with them. This self-
judgment fuels negative thoughts and feelings about themselves
during motherhood as they interpret their emotions as proof that
they're failing or not good enough.

Myth #2: *A good mom always loves motherhood.*

The motherhood mandate, which carries the view that all females
are meant to be mothers, sets moms up to believe that since we're
born to become mothers, it must be our calling and so we should
love all of it. And the idea that if we wanted to get pregnant and
therefore *chose* this path, we should be happy about being a mom at
all times.

Ambivalent or even dreary or negative emotions are part of being
human and are certainly part of our journeys through motherhood.
So when moms experience this contrast to the cultural script of

loving all aspects of motherhood, they can feel sad, ashamed, anxious, or confused; they fear telling others about their inner thoughts and feelings, thinking they'll be seen as a "bad mother." They feel guilty when they don't love it all. They judge themselves and wonder if they're doing it wrong. They think it's personal, like they're failing at being a good mom.

If you're a mom and have ever been admonished or encouraged (often by elders in public) to "enjoy the moments. They go by so fast!" you are experiencing the manifestation of this myth. I remember chasing after my three kids, who decided that wrestling in the grocery store was a good idea. Exasperated, exhausted, and frustrated, I worried about what the many observers would think of me and my parenting skills that were on display in the produce section, worsened by the fact that my kids were clearly not listening to me. This older couple who saw all these emotions on my anguished face offered me this "sage" advice, likely from their vantage point of missing their children who are now grown and out of their house. I knew I felt bad, but because I didn't yet know about matrescence and have awareness of the myths of the good mother, I didn't realize what I was feeling—I just felt like I was a bad mom. *Why am I not enjoying all the moments? I must be doing this wrong*, I concluded.

As if I didn't realize that my kids would grow quickly and that somehow this couple's unsolicited comment would transform what, in that moment, was truly frustrating and hard. Their advice made me feel like I shouldn't be feeling the actual feelings I had but should open my eyes and see how this is all just fleeting—enjoy it, Mama, enjoy it *all*! This and similar comments from people gaslight what moms are really feeling and perpetuate the myth that moms should be happy, grateful, and uncomplaining, essentially enjoying all aspects of motherhood—"'cause they grow up so fast!"

Rachel described this myth as her "oh-shit" moment:

> We wanted so much to get pregnant. It happened within a few
> months, and it was so intentional. I was determined—we are
> getting pregnant—and then, the moment I was pregnant, I
> was like, *What have I done? I don't want this.* It was like
> I played God, and it worked, and now there was no turning
> back....And I don't know that that's talked about enough.
> There's so much talk around infertility and pregnancy loss, I
> don't know if we're talking about the pregnancy ambivalence.
> ...Are we allowed to talk about the parts that are scary, or
> the parts that would turn back time, or maybe do it a little
> differently, like ... if I had known it would be fairly easy, I
> would have waited maybe another year or two or three.

Myth #3: *A good mom sacrifices her needs for her children and family.*

This myth comes from a long-established archetype of the
mother as martyr and saint. The traditional gendered role of mother
in the postindustrial North American world is rooted in piety, do-
mesticity, selflessness, and charity. Mother Teresa's unwavering and
relentless sacrifice for others is the gold standard for the good and
selfless mother. Anything other than self-sacrifice elicits judgment
and beliefs of being selfish as it contrasts with this ideal of mothers
as all-giving.

The myth of mothers' self-sacrificing as a benchmark is stifling.
Modeling self-sacrifice at the costs to our own health and well-being
has been the dominant model for countless generations of women.
This model of total self-denial leads to many moms becoming ter-
ribly and totally depleted. Neglecting our physical, emotional, and
mental needs can lead us down a path to anger, resentment, or rage,

or feeling trapped and helpless or panic-stricken. When unaddressed and chronic, self-neglect will eventually lead to more significant disorders, like clinical depression, burnout, and even suicide for some moms.

Sacrificing our own needs, dreams, and things that light us up is not only not good for us but it doesn't benefit our children. Having no boundaries that honor us as our own person to our kiddos gives the message that we're not deserving of our own integrity; we're merely to serve others and aren't powerful, gifted, creative, and worthy in our own right. This shows our sons that women are there to serve them, and it shows our daughters that they are destined to serve and care for others, perpetuating the motherhood mandate.

In *Untamed*, Glennon Doyle speaks to the silencing of mothers' freedoms of authenticity and the pain of martyrdom:

> I burned the memo presenting responsible motherhood
> as martyrdom. I decided that the call of motherhood is to
> become a model, not a martyr. I unbecame a mother slowly
> dying in her children's name and became a responsible
> mother: one who shows her children how to be fully alive.

The archetype of the selfless martyr doesn't create permission for women to thrive. It shackles moms who have been promised that we also can be successful career women. The traditional roles in the home didn't change much at all, but added on were the ambitions of second-wave feminists that encouraged us to follow our dreams and goals and take our place in what had been male-dominated spaces and workplaces. What was needed, and what didn't happen, was navigating and letting go of something, creating new boundaries and support systems that would allow for adding on careers on top of mothering tasks, duties, and responsibilities. The myth of the self-sacrificing mother didn't shift at all; it morphed into the Super Mom complex, and moms are killing themselves trying to do it all and blaming themselves when they can't.

A loving note, dear mama—

Notice whether anything resonated for you in these first few myths. If it did, you might feel angry, sad, frustrated, or any other emotion. That would make sense. I invite you now to give yourself a deep, loving breath of love—Say, *I care about these feelings*—or you might say to yourself, *It makes sense that I feel this way.* Getting angry at the impacts of patriarchy makes perfect sense. Don't worry, you won't get stuck there. But it is a part of your awakening. Keep going when you're ready, sweet mama.

Myth #4: *A good mom can do it all on her own.*

This myth permeates culture in subtle ways. Slights or judgments against moms who hire nannies, night nurses, or other childcare reveal the underlying myth that a good mom doesn't need help, and she's less than if she accesses it. The lack of childcare support, after-school programs, and community assistance with early child-hood development is also a manifestation of this myth. Many jobs are 8:00 AM to 5:00 PM, and yet daytime childcare and kindergarten programs often end at 3:30 PM. Double-income families are forced to figure it out, and often it's Mom who takes the hit in either lower work performance or the motherhood penalty.

I felt this when my kids were young. I was often the last to show up at work and the first one running out the door to pick up my kids.

I made a special arrangement with my manager that I could forfeit the hour they give us for lunch to skip or take half so that I could leave early. This circumstance created so much stress for me, and it trickled into less confidence at work.

Feeling there's no other option, this myth can lead moms to silence themselves. Moms will struggle to damaging depths of depletion before eventually opening up to their physician or partner to share the struggles they are experiencing. This is shown beautifully in the movie *Tully*. Charlize Theron plays a mother who just gave birth to her third child and is run totally ragged. Not to spoil the plot for you, but this story perfectly reflects how moms are breaking themselves apart to meet the impossible demands of motherhood, which can lead to crisis, despair, and even danger.

Sadly, too often it takes a crisis or total breakdown for some moms to access the support and help they desperately need and deserve. Moms will suffer in silence believing that they should be able to manage and do it on their own; otherwise, they're failing at motherhood—a belief that carries with it more painful emotion than any mom deserves.

Myth #5: *A good mom raises good kids.*

The myth that "a good mom raises good kids" comes from generations of mother-blaming. From post–American Revolution to postindustrialization, women's roles have taken on the raising of "good American citizens." The social construction of mother as the child raiser and character curator brings with it the erroneous notion that Mother alone is ultimately responsible for—and should carry guilt and shame for—any difficulties her children experience. The idea that how children act is a direct reflection of their mother's skill and success as a child rearer creates rich grounds for negative internalized beliefs and the development of parts for moms that can be difficult, painful, and even damaging to their mental health and their relationships with their children.

This belief discounts the fact that children are their own people. They make their own choices (they try to and eventually are supposed to), and they are influenced by all sorts of other people (like friends, peers, extended family), things (like social media and video games), and places (like their school and community). Children are developmentally supposed to make mistakes and mess up, and they each have their own personality and temperament. Any parent with more than one child knows that you can say the same thing or use the same strategy with two kids, and there's no guarantee they'll react the same way.

To be honest, I didn't realize how little control and influence parents have until I became a parent. I used to be the one to judge kids' behaviors in public places, and my first thought (I'm ashamed to admit) was often, *What did that mother do wrong with that kid?* I see this myth play out on local mom Facebook groups where pictures or descriptions of children's behaviors are highlighted, followed by the praise when a kid was seen being kind or helpful ("Good job, Mom") or—more commonly—criticism and blame toward the kid who did something wrong ("Who's the mom of the kid who nearly bowled me over in town with their electric scooter?"). Every time I read comments like these, the part of me that buys into this myth gets reinforced, making me feel like it's all my fault when my kids aren't happy or when they "act out".

THE PAINFUL IMPACTS OF SUPER MOM

This list of myths is far from exhaustive. There are also myths about breastfeeding, returning to work or careers (some camps stating it's wrong while others say it's right), and hiring childcare help. There are myths that mothering is natural (the motherhood mandate) and that moms will instinctively know how to mother, leaving moms to feel guilty or inadequate when they don't. At the same time, mothers are set up to turn to the many so-called experts and trust others to tell them the one right thing to do for their child.

The impacts of the myths of motherhood run deep. They influence and toxify our experiences of motherhood and our relationships with our children. This blueprint of motherhood shapes us without our realizing it, bubbling beneath the surface as chronic inner tension or stress, and it activates our inner system to live in a self-protection mode in ways that limit our experience of life's fullness.

Self-criticism (and shame) was the most commonly reported consequence of absorbing the myths of the good mother among the mothers I've worked with and interviewed. Feeling guilty, resentful, exhausted, lost, and trapped were also expressed. In their own words,

> *"I felt guilty for just wanting to pee in solace and didn't love motherhood in those moments."*

> *"I feel guilty if I feel frustrated with my toddler's behavior or my newborn's crying. I manage the situations fine with effort, but if I feel intense negative emotions or feel overwhelmed, I tend to criticize myself harshly for experiencing those feelings. I suppose I believe that great moms never feel frustrated. I know it's not rational but deep inside I feel I should be perfect."*

> *"When I break down and ask for help, it causes me to feel like a failure. That if I was a good mom I could've handled all this."*

"It has made it feel impossible to exist alongside my kids. I always feel like there is no room for me."

"It feels like dads add another identity to theirs when a child comes into play. But for mothers, there is a trade-off."

For many moms, especially moms who haven't yet heard of matrescence, they're not sure what they're feeling. Their emotions are suppressed only to resurface with intermittent spikes of energetic charge they can't quite understand. These myths impact our emotions and behavior in ways that make us conform and adapt to avoid judgment or social rejection, but they are not usually aligned with what *we* want, and they're definitely not based on what's best for our children.

The lack of support for mothers combined with high to impossible expectations is a predictable setup that leaves mothers suffering and too often blaming themselves for their own mental, emotional, and physical pain.

Seeing this pattern of despair and poor health while working with mothers for years led Dr. Oscar Serrellach to identify a phenomenon that he named "postnatal depletion,"[10] which refers to the physical, emotional, and psychological impairment of moms' health that new moms experience because of the current constraints and lack of support. Postnatal depletion is not limited to but can include fatigue and exhaustion, digestive problems, low libido, and brain fog. While Dr. Serrellach says this depletion is most common in the first seven years of a baby's life for the mother, in my experience, depletion varies in its forms and manifestations, and I believe mothers experience it throughout their children's lives in different ways. For instance, moms have often expressed to me feeling selfish or guilty for taking time away from their kids at all different ages, suggesting that the myth of self-sacrifice persists and leads moms to continue to deny their own needs for agency, nurturing, and care.

The pressure on moms is massive, and the social, cultural, economic, and institutional systems do not support mothers in meeting the demands. One survey of 913 mothers commissioned by *Time Magazine* found that half of all new mothers had experienced regret, shame, guilt, or anger, mostly due to unexpected complications and lack of support. More than 70 percent of moms felt pressured to do things a certain way, most from, the reporter added, "society in general" as the primary source of the pressure, followed by doctors—and interestingly, I think—other mothers.[11]

There's a disconnect between what mothers are told is available to us and what's provided in our communities to support us. Amy Taylor-Kabbaz explains, "Although we are told 'she can have it all,' the only way she actually can is to sacrifice her health, her time, or her relationships to prove she can keep up."

Society is good at telling moms how they should be, what they should do, what they should look like, and how they should act. But what moms aren't provided in a postindustrial world are the supports, structures, and spaces to examine their experiences of becoming mothers—a space and place to express, name, and acknowledge the multiple changes and transformations they will inevitably go through on their journey of becoming a mom.

Where are the spaces and interest in inviting new moms to reflect and explore their transformative experience of motherhood? Who is asking a mom how she feels? What's changed or is changing? What does she miss? What does she love most? What is scaring her now? Where does she feel her power? What does she need? What's it like

for her now in the world? In her work? In her family and relationships? What has she lost? Is there space for her to express, share, and
grieve? How is she relating to herself—to the thoughts, emotions,
and beliefs that have arisen since she's become a mother? I know
my mother and mother-in-law never asked me these questions. The
moms who joined a postpartum group and were lucky enough to
find a mothers' group or circle were the exception. Many moms I've
worked with and spoken to lacked this space and invitation to understand and explore their experience of matrescence.

Without these social and community systems and spaces to
support mothers, and an understanding of matrescence and what
mothers need, they are continually subjected to meet impossible
standards they'll never attain, keeping them feeling small, sad, angry,
confused, self-blaming, and alone. All moms have on some level unknowingly absorbed many of these myths, expectations, and beliefs
around women and motherhood. Deep individual and collective
awakening, healing, and transformation are needed so that moms
can parent on their own terms and in a way that is aligned with their
highest health, well-being, and soul's purpose—for themselves and
as a healthy model for their children.

HOW TO RELEASE THE MOTHER LOAD

As a cycle-breaker, which I'm guessing you are if you're reading
this book, you've likely connected with some, or maybe even all, of
the myths listed above. You might be one of the 2 million Dr. Becky
Kennedy Instagram fans feeling torn in your experiences, frustrated by trying to not parent your kids the same ways you were
parented, but it's not working. This mothering gig is not at all what
you expected—it's way harder than you thought. You might even be

suffering with old wounds resurfacing that you don't know how to handle.

At this point in your reading, you might be wondering what the plan is here. Now what? How do I dissolve these negative and mistaken beliefs from my psyche to heal and live and parent with more consciousness and joy? How do I deal with the disruptive and sometimes painful emotions resurfacing from my past? How do I walk this journey of motherhood with not only joy but from my true Self? Why can't I just embody the sturdy leader model that Dr. Becky talks about on her podcast?

When we have a language to label and understand our experiences, as in knowing about matrescence, along with an effective and evidence-based method for our own healing, like IFS, we have a plan. We know what to do. We have a pathway out of this painful cycle of holding ourselves to invalidating and dismissive myths and impossible standards that create undeserved pain in our experience of motherhood. These internalized myths and mistaken beliefs that block our capacity to enjoy motherhood and pollute our relationships with our children can be deconditioned and unburdened from our psyches so that we can make room for what is healthy, compassionate, and true.

The wounds and burdens you carry as a result of these myths—believing you are not a good mother, you are failing and less than, you suck at parenting, and your kids will be messed up all because of you—are *not* true. The fact that you are reading this book is already proof that you care about your kids' well-being. You are doing your best, and I'm sure you are doing way better than you ever give yourself credit for! You are taking responsibility for your influence, and you are brave enough and courageous enough to devote your time, energy, reflection, and heart to break the unhealthy cycles and burdens that you carry from your culture and familial line to make a change: *incredible!*

Understanding matrescence is the first layer of unburdening that naturally occurs through having a term or concept to acknowledge and articulate the many painful experiences of mothers who've absorbed social and cultural myths that influence their daily lives, their relationships with their children, and their experiences of motherhood. Having language to point to the faulty beliefs and burdens on mothers and the space and permission for moms to express how matrescence has been for them create a magical and therapeutic space to begin the transformation of freeing moms from the shame and self-blame that they don't need to carry.

As Dr. Aurelie Athan states, "Words create worlds," and without the term *matrescence*, there's an invisibility to the lived experiences of mothers. There's no space to express, acknowledge, and heal what needs healing, to change what needs changing. Matrescence is the launchpad women need to come together, as women have powerfully done historically across time, to empower and validate one another in the process of activating their inner strength and capacities to create the worlds our children need. It starts with understanding our inherited constraints within a rigged system through the internalization of myths and the motherhood legacy burdens we carry.

Next, we begin the work of unburdening ourselves from the faulty conditioning and myths of a good mother that we've unknowingly absorbed. We turn inward and begin to relate to our parts with interest, curiosity, and compassion. One by one, we can get to know the parts of us that are believing these myths and are working so hard to follow suit and to be perceived as a good mother by our communities—sometimes at high costs to our physical, emotional, and mental well-being. The most painful of costs, of course, is feeling disconnected from our true Self and living in self-protective modes that dull our vitality and toxify our connection with our kids. We can change these parts to align with new beliefs, with new standards that are self-prescribed. Moms can access the heartfulness and joy that we deserve.

THE MAP OF IFS IN PRACTICE

Using the map of IFS over and over, I've been able to meet each part of myself that was believing she wasn't a good enough mom. This belief was triggered often when I would drop the ball in my motherly duties, like forgetting to sign up my son for a camp he wanted but then realizing it was full, learning that my son had multiple cavities and pummeling myself in shame and self-blame because it was all my fault, and missing my son's team-building charity event because I got lost and couldn't find the right address. Before learning IFS I would usually end up bawling in my closet with unbearable shame and self-disgust until my husband would help calm me down or coach me through to a more regulated state by trying to counter my inner critic. My own internal system would also sometimes kick in by numbing out or distracting me because sometimes the pain of the shame spiral was too much.

Using IFS practices, I started to go inside (i.e., turn my attention inside my body) with a curious attention to start to know my different reactions or parts. I came to know the sad part that carried shame and the part in my system that was often being very self-critical or judgmental, basically my inner bully, or what Taylor-Kabbaz refers to as the "Mean Inner Mama."

How you can work with your inner critics and transform the deep burdens moms carry using IFS is explained in more detail in

Chapters 5 and 6. For now I want you to consider that while many types of therapies or self-help books encourage you to change your beliefs—such as through daily affirmations or suggesting that writing down and reading a new belief will simply work to replace mistaken beliefs for healthier ones—understanding that we have parts and getting to know them directly through experience is different. It's more effective at leading to real and long-lasting change.

We get to know the part that's believing she has to be perfect and not drop balls to be a good mom. We let that part know it's not alone, and we are interested to understand it. We ask, Where did it learn that? What's it afraid would happen if it didn't hold you to that idea or standard? How does it feel doing its role as a sort of drill sergeant (or whatever other image of this part might come to mind)? One of my parts that was driving me to be a Super Mom and triggering disappointment and shame inside when I'd inevitably fail showed up in my mind looking like a 1950s housewife. She was pointing her finger at me, stern and rigid. When I asked her these questions, she shared with me that she wants us to be good. She expects excellence, and she explained how she pushes me toward it. When I asked her what she's afraid would happen if she wasn't pushing me and wasn't driving me toward perfection, her fears were revealed. "If you're not a good mom, then you're a loser," she said. *"No one will want you."* With this insight I suddenly had a sense throughout my body that she'd been there for a long time. She was the one trying to help me be a good girl in order to be accepted and loved (in an early environment where these needs were often not met), and now she was trying to make sure I would continue to get the love I've always wanted—through doing things right or perfectly.

I let her know that I could see she's been there a long time in my life, always trying to help me be accepted and loved. Seeing and sensing her positive intention for me, I felt a warmth and gratitude in my heart toward her. Tears of gratitude welled up seeing how all these years this part had tried to help me get the love and positive attention I craved. I saw with such clarity that of course this made sense in my childhood, and I could see that now she was still trying to do this job; though it wasn't working, her intention was good. I expressed my gratitude to her, which she appreciated receiving.

I let her know that I'm a grown-up now (our parts often still think we are vulnerable children because they've been doing their jobs since our childhood). With this new update of my age and my strengths and abilities, I let her know that I am capable of choosing now. I let her know that I have love (from my husband, friends, and children), and she relaxed and softened, realizing the love that we have in our life. We never want our parts to feel like we don't want them, so I gently invited her to choose a different role in my system. How does she want to help me, now that she knows we don't need to follow all the social rules—especially the wrong ones? She was happy to know she didn't have to keep working so hard to be perfect. She told me she wants to serve as my consigliere of sorts, to be consulted on decisions to make sure they align with our values, with our desire to cherish and raise our children the way *we* want, not how society tells us we should. I agreed to listen to her, and I expressed my deep gratitude for her openness to change and reconsider what rules or norms we follow.

I experienced a deep opening of space in my body as all tension and tightness left, and I felt love and hope tingling throughout my body. I felt more fully myself—at peace, clearer, and more confident. This is healing. You can also learn to go inside and be with your parts with curiosity, interest, and an intention of self-understanding as you create new beliefs and new roles for your inner system that leave you feeling more aligned, centered, and harmonious. The work starts by getting to know a part. Experiment for yourself with the closing exercise.

EXERCISE: IDENTIFYING INTERNALIZED MYTHS AND GETTING TO KNOW A PART

This guided meditation is designed to help you discover a part of you that may have absorbed one of the myths of being a good mother. You may wish to read this and keep your eyes open as you follow along in the instructions, or you may prefer to access the audio recording of me guiding this meditation (www.unburdeningmotherhood.com/guided-meditations). You may also choose to follow along and simply write or journal about what comes up for you. There's no right or wrong way to do this exercise. I encourage you to experiment and see what feels right for you.

Find a space that is private and quiet (if possible) where you can feel undistracted for a few moments. I invite you to start by closing your eyes or gazing downward, taking in a few deep breaths, and letting your exhale be slower and longer than your inhale. Once you've had a few deep breaths to help settle into the present moment, turn your attention inside. Now, offer a gentle invitation for a part to be known, perhaps focusing on a reaction you had when reading this chapter. Was there a myth that resonated most with you, where you noticed a strong emotional or physical reaction? Invite this part in with kind attention.

Parts can show up in various ways. They may arise as an image in your mind or as a voice or thought in your head. They may be a feeling or emotion or a sensation somewhere in your body. Some parts will be sort of sensed slightly outside your body, like to the side of your head or as if they're sitting on your shoulder. Don't try to force anything or think about it. I invite you to be open and curious.

Sometimes more than one part can arise, and that's fine. Let them know you want to know them all, but that it's best if you can be with one at a time. And then allow your attention to settle on one part. Invite in a part that resonated with the myths listed in this chapter and perhaps is a part that pushes you to be a certain kind of mom in some way.

Ask the part where it learned to believe what it believes about motherhood. Ask how it's trying to help you. What role does it play in your system?

Now ask what it's afraid might happen if it didn't do its job, or if it let go of this belief that it's carrying. Note what it tells you. Does this make sense to you in your life experience and from your childhood?

If it feels sincere, let it know you understand why it came to believe this and how it has been trying to help you, in its own way. Notice how you feel toward this part now. Do you feel bad for the part? Compassion, gratitude, and a softening toward this part are signs you are in Self-energy. Let the part know you appreciate what it has been trying to do for you.

If it feels right for you, you may wish to give it an update on what you know now and what is a more true belief for you. You might invite this part to send the mistaken belief(s) out into the air, a fire, the earth, or water—or any way its imagination would wish. Notice how your body feels. Pay attention to any sensations in your body.

Ask the part what gifts it carries or what role it would like to play in your life now. It may not know right away, and that's fine, but just see if there's anything it wants. Ask it, "What do you need or want from me?" See if the part is ready to negotiate a new role. If it's not sure, that's fine. Just let it know you will come back, and you are always there for it/her/him.

End the practice by taking a moment to notice what your body feels like. If any or all of these steps didn't seem to work or flow as printed, that's totally fine. Wherever you are in your system, that is also fine. Just beginning to turn inward and get curious about your parts, letting them know you're there and you care, is a huge step toward transforming your relationship with your parts and ultimately your inner experiencing. Send yourself a loving breath of pride or acknowledgment for taking this time and doing this inner work. Notice how that feels in your body.

Way to go, Mama! Remember, we're just getting started. Next, let's get even more clear on how IFS can help you on your motherhood journey. I want to be specific about how motherhood affects our parts—because when we see it clearly, we can finally let go of the old stories and expectations that keep us stuck in cycles we didn't choose.

CHAPTER 3

MOTHERHOOD THROUGH THE LENS OF INTERNAL FAMILY SYSTEMS

Through them, we learn.
But for them, we grow.
—AMY TAYLOR-KABBAZ

LEARNING INTERNAL FAMILY SYSTEMS (IFS) while in matrescence saved my life. I realize that sounds dramatic, and maybe I am exaggerating for effect. But honestly, IFS helped me understand that when I had a thought that screamed, *I can't fuckin' take this anymore!* I could also calm down and know that this wasn't completely true—*only a part of me was feeling this way*. It gave me a map to know how to work with this part of me so that I didn't have to hate motherhood and keep feeling ashamed about it.

I hope you were able to try the end-of-chapter exercise, or perhaps you've started to just notice your own parts by getting curious and seeing for yourself. Not everyone likes the language of "parts," and if you prefer, you can call them "energies" or "reactions." The wording is less important than the experience. If you have a cynical or doubting part that feels resistant or thinks this is hogwash, that part is welcome too. Let me try to explain it simply.

We are all born with parts that are kind of like their own little subpersonalities. Like little inner beings, our parts carry gifts, skills, and energies that allow us to function and adapt in life, to achieve our goals, to create and express ourselves, and to experience joy and the aliveness of being human.[1]

For example, I've always loved making art. You could say that painting and mosaic are my hobbies. It's not all of me that always wants to create art, but since I was a child, I have been drawn to painting, and when I'm in the activity, I feel alive, in flow, in sync with a sense of at-homeness. I also have a part that is very task oriented. This part of me helped me go from poor grades in college (because at the time I was unmotivated and coping with unprocessed trauma in unhealthy ways) to top marks so that I could get accepted into a competitive graduate program to become a therapist. This part was skilled at learning, executing academic assignments, and meeting our goals. This part wasn't, however, always in balance, as sometimes I became obsessed or taken over by it in an extreme way. I'd see my friends less, I wouldn't rest as much as my body needed, and I went over my assignments repeatedly to try to make them perfect. It worked to get me into graduate school, but it felt out of balance and I went without more experiences of fun, lightness, and relaxation.

When traumatic, wounding, or difficult experiences too challenging to process arise—as is the case in many people's childhoods —instead of being able to flow with what life brings, parts take up roles in the system to not get hurt. They tend to carry intense feelings, rigid thoughts, and skewed beliefs that can translate to outward behavior. Unless we know about the theory of multiplicity in the human psyche, these reactions, emotions, and behaviors are typically out of our conscious awareness.

I realize that this can seem perhaps radical or outlandish. But when I first learned about multiplicity, it was like the answer to what I'd been grappling with both personally, in my own mind and emotions, and professionally, in feeling burnt out with clients after many years as a therapist. I had often naturally used "parts" language with clients because it was organic and natural. But I didn't have the full language or map that Dick Schwartz created for IFS. Multiplicity explains why we can feel two different feelings, urges, or even intentions at the same time. We can have opposing parts within, and often this is what keeps us stuck and struggling.

For example, understanding we have an inner system of parts explained why I wanted to be fit and was trying to lose weight *and* would find myself taken over by a part that just wanted to indulge in chocolate and French fries. It helped me make sense of my ambivalent feelings about motherhood—it explained why I both loved my kids and wanted to be a mother more than anything, and I also had a part that felt resentful of motherhood because it was an ambitious part that had worked hard to achieve a career that it didn't want to put on hold. Multiplicity helped me understand that the voices in my head weren't thoughts I should keep trying to ignore (which wasn't working), but I could get curious about these parts I had inside. IFS gave me a map and a pathway that I could follow to change my inner despair and my internal struggles.

This model also helped me feel less ashamed of myself for not being able to change my thoughts. When we understand the idea of multiplicity, we can be less identified with some of our thoughts, feelings, and actions. This turns out to be very healing and deeply relieving when some of those thoughts, feelings, and behaviors are not so helpful (or let's be honest, we might judge them as wrong or bad). This understanding of ourselves helps us see that we are not our thoughts. We are the ones observing the thoughts. This was the beginning for me to soften my chronic self-blame and shame.

In the 1990s, the publicized story of Truddi Chase, her book *When Rabbit Howls*, and the subsequent documentary and interview she did with Oprah Winfrey put the possibility of multiplicity onstage. Truddi was a survivor of profound trauma and abuse and was said to have ninety-two known personalities. But back then, the diagnosis of multiple personality disorder (now dissociative identity disorder, DID) was considered the exception and only for those who, like Truddi, had endured significant abuse and trauma.

But the same psychological functioning of multiplicity that helps survivors of trauma cope by differentiating their parts into completely separate personalities is similarly true for all of us. In fact, Truddi explained to Oprah that her parts "keep [her] sane." Though there are differences from people who have a DID diagnosis, we all have parts within us that we are born with, which aim to help us function and cope with our human circumstances—our trials, tribulations, threats to self, and safety and security in life.

I think it's useful to think of our parts like the Alanis Morissette music video for her song "Ironic." If you haven't seen it, basically she is dressed as different people—or parts of self—sitting in different seats in the car driving somewhere. Like a road trip of our life, we might see our parts this way, each part taking the wheel at different times, as they see the circumstances warranting their particular role.

TYPES OF PARTS AND THEIR ROLES

As he developed IFS learning from his clients, Dick Schwartz identified different types of parts that serve different roles in one's system. The most active parts of us that help us function in the world are understood as our *protector* parts, which include *managers* and *firefighters*. Our protector parts help us adapt to our environments and move through the world in ways that aim to achieve goals, meet our needs, and avoid emotional pain and discomfort. They also have the important role of keeping our exiled parts suppressed. Our exiles are the more vulnerable parts of us that carry the emotional pain or wounds usually from early childhood, such as embarrassment, rejection, emptiness, terror, or fear.

When helping clients heal in the IFS model, we first meet—often many—protectors before we are able to unburden what the exiled parts are carrying. In fact, as discussed more fully later, we need the permission of our protectors before connecting with and trying to heal and unburden our exiles. Our Self (or Self-energy) is an essential element to our system but is not itself a part. Let's break it down so that this makes sense.

MANAGER PARTS

Manager parts are focused on preventing the emotional pain that exiles carry from being triggered and brought to the surface, as well as avoiding any new experiences of rejection, abandonment, or social disappointment from happening. They work hard managing to keep pain and all things awkward and uncomfortable at bay. Manager parts are often task driven, future focused, and goal oriented. Workaholics, people-pleasers, and perfectionists are common manager parts, as are busy bees and parts we might call *controllers*.

Manager parts are often reinforced and affirmed in society, as cultural ideas around being successful that are associated with financial wealth, reputable or high-status employment, or exceptional achievements (e.g., in athletics) tend to align with high achievement, which often requires time-intensive persistence, commitment, and sometimes a degree of obsessiveness or perfectionism. The negative impact of overworking manager parts can show up as stress-induced ulcers, headaches, or other physical ailments, and loneliness, disconnection, anxiety, and feelings of imposter syndrome.

You achieve that goal you always thought would make you happy only to find emptiness. When the goal is to attain success and the underlying drive is to feel good enough, loved, or accepted, any external achievement will pale in comparison, unable to meet this human need for validation and connection. What happens then is that once the goal or title is achieved, the happiness is fleeting, as you realize it doesn't fill you up the way you thought it would or the way society promised you it would feel. So the manager part will come up with a new goal and try again and again.

FIREFIGHTER PARTS

As we know in life, eventually something or someone will trigger us. It's impossible to permanently keep our exiled emotions down and buried forever. When we feel disproportionate emotional reactions to seemingly small issues, this is a sign that an exile part has been activated. Sometimes things we don't realize—often things that remind an exile of a past trauma—will trigger them. It'll feel like we are just overcome with intense emotions out of the blue. When this happens, *firefighter* parts become involved. Their role is to take over when even a little emotional pain comes up, and they react by trying to stop that pain in its tracks. They do this in many ways, such as addiction (alcohol, substances, sex, gambling), shopping or spending, food, or numbing and dissociation. Anything to dull or stop the pain or vulnerability from getting bigger is the firefighter's role.

In this way, for example, workaholism can serve as both a manager part, which pushes and functions to avoid uncomfortable or difficult feelings from surfacing, and as a firefighter part. Consider when vulnerable feelings are triggered, such as feeling incompetent as a parent, and then the firefighter takes over by distracting from the parenting issue and going into their office to do work.

All protector parts are trying in their own way to help you. Ultimately they're trying to keep you from feeling pain that you experienced earlier in life when it wasn't possible or safe to process it at the time. If you grew up in an environment where all of your childhood needs were met (safety, fun, agency, emotional expression, physical well-being), and you had a trusted and safe adult with whom you could process any difficulty or challenge you experienced growing up, then you are lucky—and I suspect you are rare. The human condition is such that therapists today recognize that no person is untouched by big-T or little-t trauma. Whether from family-of-origin wounds and intergenerational traumas, or the battleground that school and peer groups can feel like, or the broken and discriminatory systems that permeate our social and cultural realms in the form of racism, classism, ableism, heteronormativity, and sizeism, it's nearly impossible for anyone to grow up unscathed and unburdened.

Our systems adapt to these early experiences and throughout our lives such that we are hardwired to stay as safe as possible; try to get our needs for belonging, love, and connection met; and avoid discomfort and emotional pain and heartbreak. Our manager parts get pushed into roles to try to prevent more harm, while our firefighter parts rally when hurt, pain, or discomfort inevitably arises, stopping the pain at all costs. The problem is that despite their intention to help us by preventing vulnerability in the case of managers, or firefighters putting out the fire of emotion, our parts' extreme roles can result in additional pain and even trouble in our lives, sometimes creating the very thing they're trying to avoid.

For example, Karen, mom to a six-year-old son and a two-year-old daughter, came from Eastern European immigrant parents who were very strict and critical. She had protector parts to help her cope through her childhood that also became self-critical, untrusting of other people (fearing their judgment), and anxious, which came across on the outside as Karen being somewhat rigid, cold, and reserved with others. Feeling lonely in motherhood in a new community, she attempted to find connection with other moms by attending a mother's circle. After one session, she put herself out there by being more open and vulnerable. However, her protector parts backlashed and her critic gave her a vulnerability hangover that she found too uncomfortable to try again, so she left the circle. In this way, despite wanting a deeper connection and to be seen and validated in relationships with others, her protectors—designed to try to keep her safe and not get hurt—came in and sabotaged her opportunity to have her needs met, ultimately leaving her still feeling disconnection from others and alone.

Similarly, Natalie, mom to twin boys in middle school, felt very alone. Deep down she believed she wasn't lovable or good enough. She had a firefighter part that used alcohol to help calm her worried part, and she enjoyed the liquid courage it gave her to go out and socialize more, eventually making several mom friends in her neighborhood. However, because these relationships were mainly in the context of drinking wine together and letting off steam, she continued to feel empty inside, believing that if these women really knew her, they would reject her. In this way, her firefighter part was trying to fix her feelings of loneliness and low self-worth, only to reinforce the feeling that she was an imposter, and no one would truly love her if they knew the real and sober Natalie.

Until we can understand and heal the parts of us that are wounded, burdened, and believing we are unlovable and less than, our protectors will continue to behave in ways according to their roles that prioritize avoiding more hurt and pain. It's not possible to live as our most openhearted, whole, and authentic Self as long as we are living in fear and self-protection, focused solely on avoiding pain and discomfort.

EXILED PARTS

From the very start of our lives, we have experiences that create emotions that are too painful or potent to understand and process. Emotional or physical neglect, invalidation, shaming, and rejection or abuse, such as physical abuse and aggression, can be too painful to bear. The emotions from these experiences get buried deep in the unconscious mind and body because it's not safe to feel or remain vulnerable. We stealthily and unconsciously learn and adapt to our environments in order to survive. Our protectors help us by pushing down and suppressing what's too big or painful to make sense of, which is often our young and tender parts. The buried parts are removed to the depths of our psyche and are known in IFS as *exiles*.

Along with painful emotions and beliefs, the natural energy of the part—such as the exuberance, excitement, or bold wonder of a child—might be shunned or rejected by a parent whose own trauma or extreme parts are threatened by a display they experience as over-stimulating or triggering for them, like when a parent reprimands a child for being too excited, loud, or messy. I'm not talking about occasional frustrations or the odd "Shhhh," but I heard one example from a mom who shared her exiled part with me that carried the pain of being constantly "Shhhhed" because her five-year-old "ADHD excitement" was often too much for her mother. Her exiled part felt rejection and internalized a belief that she is too much and bad. In this and similar circumstances, the child's parts learn from the pain or censure that it's not safe to live in its full expression without some type of punishment within that family dynamic or environment. The part shuts off from its natural energy, often by shutting down or hiding its energy deep inside, being exiled.

Another example would be a family's unwritten rule, such as "We don't get angry," which might manifest in consequences like "Go to your room," or verbal reprimanding or punishing expressions of anger or frustration. The child then learns to push down and suppress the part that was expressing anger to avoid more punishment or disconnection from Mom and Dad. Being shamed for misbehaving or embarrassing our parents, being punished or rejected for things that are usually typical and developmentally appropriate for kids has always been common in U.S. culture.

Exiles are often our more vulnerable young parts of ourselves—the parts that were highly sensitive to the lack of care, abuse, or trauma we endured early in life. For example, many of the exiles whom I've healed and unburdened were young, some still in diapers and some when I was around three or five years old. I had one exile part who carried the pain from experiencing molestation around age three. From connecting to this young and vulnerable part, witnessing her, and finally processing the emotions (fear and disgust) and beliefs she came to hold (*I'm not worthy of being protected*), I was able to help her release these emotions and the energy from the trauma and be freed from this pain that was locked in time in my mind and body. Healing this exile, I felt a powerful shift in my body and heart. As I released her feelings of shame and beliefs of my unworthiness, I felt a deepened love and compassion for myself.

Exiles can carry all kinds of emotions and beliefs, such as terror, fear, disempowerment, rejection, humiliation, or abandonment. Exiles can also carry experiences from preverbal times. For instance, many people have healed their exiles from being an infant in an ICU or having undergone scary and traumatic medical procedures.

Our exiled parts are trapped as if in a time capsule, like little inner children. Protectors keep them down because they don't understand that you're a grown adult now with the resources and capacities to consciously manage your life. They wait deep within for a time when they can be seen, witnessed, and healed.

A loving note, dear mama—

You might want to pause here and take a slow, soothing breath. Sometimes, reading about painful emotions can stir up our feelings, perhaps triggering an exile who is waiting for attention. In case this feels like a lot, I invite you to stop for a moment. Most of us aren't super excited about going through hard feelings. But the good news is that when we understand how we have this amazing ability to adapt, survive, and shove down our emotional pain when we need to, it means there's hope to heal. As an adult, you now have the resources, strengths, and skills to process what you couldn't back then. There is hope, and there is light. You got this!

SELF: THE CORE HEALING ESSENCE WITHIN US ALL

Fundamental to IFS is the understanding that, in addition to our parts, we all have Self—the core essence within each of us that is never damaged, no matter what we've lived through. The Self—also called *Self-energy*—is always within us, but for most of us, we become blended with our protector parts as we live our lives. Being blended with a part means that one of our protectors has taken the wheel. In these moments, Self is blocked by our fortuitous protector parts, who hold their posts to keep the exiled parts from surfacing.

But when our protector parts learn to trust that you (i.e., in Self) are there, when you can for a moment access Self-energy and connect to your parts from this space, they can begin to let go of their reigns of self-protection. When they trust you enough to share what they've been carrying and you can witness them from this Self-energy, you can release the pain and transform it finally, no longer needing to carry and hold it in the safety box of your unconscious.

Self is our healing agent. This trust in you—in Self—is done as you regularly meet your parts with curiosity and care (turning your attention inside in meditation, writing dialogues, and other exercises shared in this book). Chapter 8 is devoted to exploring more in depth what Self is and how to access it in motherhood.

Now, with a basic understanding of IFS, let's consider how motherhood is a fertile ground for old wounds and traumatic patterns to surface—meaning that, unintentionally, our kiddos will behave in ways that trigger our system of exiles and protectors.

KIDS ARE OUR *TOR-MENTORS*

The term *tor-mentor* is used in IFS to refer to people, places, or situations that trigger the emergence of our exiles or activate strong protector parts, showing us where we have some healing to do. Anyone can be a tor-mentor to us. It might be a boss, family member, or maybe another person in a moms' group who reminds your exile of a mean girl from middle school. In IFS we also use the term *trailhead* to refer to awareness when a part of us is activated. In this way I would argue that kids can be our tor-mentors, and motherhood is a journey ripe with many trailheads!

Our kids are powerful tor-mentors because there's already strong emotion involved (we love them a ton), there's a lot at stake. We tend to place our own happiness and sense of okay-ness in relation to the happiness and success of our children (ever heard the expression "You're only as happy as your least happy child"?). We don't want to be our kids' mother wound, and more than anyone else in the world, we want their happiness. When there's a lot at stake, there's a likelihood of parts being triggered. In this way, our children can be our mentors if we can see this as an opportunity. In other words, when an exile rises to the surface, we have an opportunity to heal it.

Our kids are also tor-mentors because, like all of us, they each have their own inner system of parts. They have needs (some have a lot of needs), and sometimes our parts' intentions—for example, being seen in glowing terms in our community—can clash with our children's wants, desires, and ability to express themselves. Our kids' jobs are to explore the world and learn. They're trying new things and testing the limits and boundaries. That's what they are supposed to do. And yet the ways they express their wants and needs, their protests and challenges and attempts at agency, can be confronting to us parents who want them to be behave in certain ways. Our parts are bound to have reactions that are automatic and often emotionally charged.

For example, our manager parts might feel anger or even rage when this little being doesn't listen and is now in the way of us doing what we think we need to do in life (e.g., getting to places on time or following the plan for the day). Our manager parts that try to control others' perceptions of us and try to help us avoid social judgment, embarrassment, or rejection will have something to say when our kid starts screaming, protesting, or maybe even playing loudly in a public space. Our firefighter parts might see a lot of opportunities to quickly soothe or stop feelings tied to boredom in the monotony of mundane or repetitive tasks, the loss or a lack of satisfaction, a sense of perceived failure, or a stress or pressure that feels like too much.

The ways that our protectors try to manage the demands and experiences of motherhood are endless.

Through matrescence, mothers are faced with finding their own maternal style while grappling with their own childhood (what was great and what wasn't great at all). A combination of the weight of the responsibility that comes with the care and raising of another human being paired with the deepest and most profound love for the little being—on top of intensive demands and stress that is the reality for modern-day parents means that our inner systems will reconfigure in ways that render our protectors as the default. Without having healed our wounds or released burdens from our own childhoods and earlier experiences, the stress and demands of parenting and identity transformation inherent in matrescence result in exiles being easily triggered and us living most of our moments from our protector parts.

More times than I can count, I've felt like I have no inner map for how to parent. I'm afraid of messing up and what other people will think of me. *Do I look like a bad mom to other parents, teachers, principals, and—well—everyone?* No one has been able to push my buttons as much as my kids. Sure, my spouse takes a close second, but the day-to-day demands of care and responsibilities, paired with the deep pressure to guide and parent well-behaved, praiseworthy human beings, are ripe grounds for old wounds to resurface and inner protector parts to take the wheel.

Living mainly from protector parts can look like constantly anticipating the future (hello, worry and anxiety) or getting stuck in the past (depression, regret, and ruminating over what you did wrong). Living from protectors can feel like constant tension, tightness in our bodies, and strong emotional reactivity. When I'm trying to control my kids as I'm feeling frustrated, or when I feel the urge to deny their feelings and needs, I know I am reacting from a protector part. When I'm trying to control them, it's often coming from an anxious part that believes that if they're not happy and successful, it'll be my fault—and of course, I want the best for my kids and don't want them to struggle or suffer. When I mentally beat myself up for the mistakes I've made in the past—because no one gets this parenting thing perfect—I know a part has taken control.

Whereas Self is in the present moment and exudes calm, centeredness, openheartedness, and clarity, our protectors are the armed guards of our hearts, and their focus is to minimize threats and avoid harm. But what they evolved to prepare for and protect in our childhood is not the same as the challenges we face in motherhood and parenting. It's like wires getting crossed, which can feel confusing for moms who are exhausted and unsure of what they're feeling or how to feel better.

Often our protector parts are young. They're easily overwhelmed and not as capable of handling our lives and relationships the way our heart wants. Think about it: Have you ever felt like you reacted to something like a child? Or that in the face of a parenting challenge —such as confronting another parent about a conflict with your children—you felt terrified, anxious, and ill-equipped, or maybe you became loud, controlling, or aggressive? In tons of typical parenting situations, we can be taken over—or what in IFS we call *blended*— with our parts.

A loving note, dear mama—

This is a gentle reminder to remember that you are learning. If past experiences are popping into your mind, see if you can note them with kindness, with grace, and without judgment. When we gain new insights, often what can follow is grief or regret that we wished we knew them sooner. This is life; you've not done anything wrong. Take a deep and loving breath, sweetheart, and trust in divine timing. You're on the right track. Forgive yourself for what you didn't know.

We love our kids. We want the best for them. And like it or not, we don't have all the control. Our parts will continue to hold their posts until we can relieve them from the job they've been doing, likely for many years. Until we get to know them, helping them understand we aren't helpless children anymore, and we have resources and capacities to parent and live with more consciousness, they'll keep working hard to do what they've always done to protect us from pain and from exiles arising—unless they know that it's okay to stop or change, until they can learn to trust Self to lead. When we're little, there wasn't anyone to lean on, so they took up their posts. They will shift and change when they can trust someone else to take the job.

What this means is that we will be parenting from our protector parts. We will have, as I can attest, more not-so-great parenting moments than we'd like to admit. When you think about it, many of our protector parts and our exiles are young—like little children, since they evolved during times in our life when we were ill-equipped or it wasn't safe enough to process our difficulties or traumas. Until we get to know our parts and help them release their burdens and heal, we'll be living from them as we're blended with them and essentially parenting our kids like a kid would. Famous life coach Mel Robbins acknowledges this phenomenon in her popular book *The Let Them Theory*, where she paraphrased her therapist, who said that basically most adults walking around are eight-year-old children. She's not far off.

I don't know about you, but I felt awful realizing that I was not showing up as the mom my kids truly needed. My strong emotional reactions—my parts—were getting in the way of me being the patient, calm, wise, and safe adult I wanted to be and always thought I would be. Nothing motivated me more to get back into therapy and work on myself than when I realized that my wounds were in the way and I needed to heal them because my kids obviously needed me to heal.

The good news is it didn't take long to make a positive change. I started noticing benefits from the first IFS meditation I did. Each time I got to know a part, validate its feelings, and listen to what it needed, I felt more calm and integrated, more like my grown-up Self. The more practices I did to access Self-energy in my life, the better I felt. I noticed it in more steady and composed reactions, and in the ways I improved setting limits with my kids and not getting so angry or frazzled when they pushed them. The more I practiced, the more easily I could access Self-energy in the midst of tough parenting moments. I would be able to pivot and course-correct in the hard moments and walk away, feeling proud of myself for how I handled the issue. I also knew my kid felt better and safe, and we were closer and more connected. This is the hope that IFS offers all moms. The more we go inside and help our parts, the less we will be tor-mented by our kids or anyone, as we live more in Self and evolve into the women— and mothers—we want to be.

EXERCISE: GETTING CURIOUS ABOUT A TRAILHEAD

You can follow this meditation by reading along and pausing or you can access a guided audio of this meditation by going to www.unburdeningmotherhood.com/guided-meditations.

Begin this meditation by taking a few moments to settle into your body in the present moment. Find a comfortable posture and place to sit or lie down where you will not be interrupted.

If you feel comfortable, close your eyes or gaze downward. Take a few slow, deep breaths, seeing if you can extend the exhale, breathing out slowly. After a few deeper and slower breaths, allow your breathing to return to its natural rhythm.

Now I invite you to bring to mind a situation with one of your children, or somewhere else in your motherhood journey, where you get triggered. Refrain from choosing something too huge for this practice, but pick a situation where you get emotionally reactive or charged. Perhaps something came up when you read about how our kids can be our tormentors and you may wish to focus on that here in this practice.

Now, invite in the person or the situation as if it's happening on a stage in front of you. See the scene playing out with the players and people who seem to push your buttons. As you watch, notice the part of you that reacts the most in this moment. Turn your attention towards it with curiosity and interest to know it and understand.

Ask this part what it is afraid would happen if it didn't come up and protect you in this situation. What is important to this part about this situation? What's it afraid might happen if it didn't react in this way?

Now, with openness, listen to what this part shares with you, what it wants you to know. See if you feel any sense of appreciation for how hard this part has tried to protect you, how hard maybe it has been working to help you in the past to keep you safe, or to try to meet your needs. If it feels true, let it know you see how it is trying to help.

If you sense that beneath this protective energy there's a younger, more vulnerable part, notice that too for a moment. You may simply acknowledge its presence and offer a quiet promise that you'll return to it when the time feels right. If you notice any other parts, like judgmental or critical voices coming into the scene, with a kind attitude, ask if they could step back for now. Offer some assurance that you want to get to know them, but for now stay focused on the one part.

If it feels okay, ask your parts permission to go up on the stage on your own and respond to the person or situation as your Self. No pressure for them to agree, but if they're willing, try this as an experiment. Go up to the stage and rewind the play to the start and respond to the situation from this wise and clear place with your heart open and your parts observing from their seats. Notice what comes up for you.

If this feels out of reach or your parts don't allow this experiment, that's fine.

When you feel ready, thank your part for sharing with you all that its shared and for trying to keep you safe and protected. If you wish, you might ask them if they'd consider letting you respond to this situation in real life without their help—letting them know they can always watch from their seats. Just see if they might be willing to give it a try.

As you end, let all the parts that have come up in this practice know of your sincerity and your care. Let them know you are here for them and you will be back. Note their response.

Taking a few deeper breaths again, sense the oxygen flowing through your whole body, feel your feet grounded to the floor and earth, and open your eyes and shift your gaze again to the outside world.

CHAPTER 4

THE MOTHERHOOD LEGACY BURDEN

Becoming a mother is one of the few
experiences in life that really remakes a woman,
that dramatically unsettles her center of gravity,
and there is opportunity here: to connect,
collaborate, elucidate new visions,
and change the status quo.

—SARAH MENKEDICK

WE'VE LAID THE BASICS of the IFS model and discussed how our different protector parts, like managers and firefighters, try to guard our vulnerable exiles from being triggered in order to keep away emotional pain. And while we have burdens from our early life experiences, sometimes starting in the womb, we also carry the burdens of cultural and social myths that our parts internalize. In IFS, the beliefs, thoughts, and emotions that are informed and influenced by our culture and family line are called "cultural legacy burdens," passed down from generations of relatives and ancestors, known and unknown.

Recent studies in neuroscience and epigenetics are showing that we carry stress in our DNA and genetic makeup from stress and traumas before us for up to three generations.[1] Our psyche and our bodies carry the energies and wounds from generations before us through our ancestors. An example of cultural burdens is people's parts absorbing and internalizing the ideologies of white supremacy and racism, capitalism, materialism, and individualism that have persisted across time.

These cultural burdens intersect and influence the lives of individuals and collective groups, and they impact women's and mothers' lives in particular ways. For example, pervasive mother-blaming and the mother mandate are myths that influence women's lived experiences. Women who choose to not have children or, perhaps not by choice, don't have children still have many experiences of people—family, friends, and even total strangers—questioning and holding judgment around their childfree status. This pervasive attitude is an example of how the motherhood mandate manifests in society.

As Chapter 2 discussed, matrescence acknowledges the myths of motherhood that all mothers are subjected to whether we want to be or not, and it acknowledges the patriarchal messages passed down across generations to women and mothers that carry faulty beliefs about what a good mother is and should be, for example, the duty to attend to the health and well-being of children. Society holds the expectation that "a child must not be without its mother" and yet absenteeism among fathers is normalized. As Kelly McDaniel, author of *Mother Hunger*, puts it, fatherly love and attention are "a bonus."[2] The burden of the care and well-being of children remains in the hands and on the shoulders of mothers, as is the cultural scrutiny carried through the myths of the good mother.

Because of these intensive and straining cultural expectations and standards for moms that are infused with erroneous myths carried on from history, I propose that many mothers' parts carry what I call the *motherhood legacy burden*. This burden often shows up as beliefs and emotions that mothers take on (i.e., parts absorb), stemming from the societal motherhood mandate—the expectation that all women should become mothers and adhere to the cultural and social ideals of what it means to be a good mother.

The motherhood legacy burden refers to the cluster of parts that have absorbed and internalized the myths of a good mother and therefore carry faulty beliefs, feelings, and energies that create deep-seated polarizations and suffering within a mother's system. The ways that mothers are supposed to be—according to beliefs and standards carried across generations—live in the bodies and minds of women and are made manifest through how they feel about themselves as mothers and as people, and how they relate to their children, how they parent, and their experience of motherhood.

In a simplified form and certainly not prescriptive, I propose that there is a cycle or cluster of parts that many moms experience because of parts that have absorbed and internalized the social and cultural myths of the perfect mother. Experiencing this cycle through a constellation of parts within myself that I've come to meet and worked to help transform, I spoke with the many mothers I interviewed to receive their sense of this type of cycle or specific parts. The moms

I've worked with helped me elucidate the common themes and parts from their own experiences.

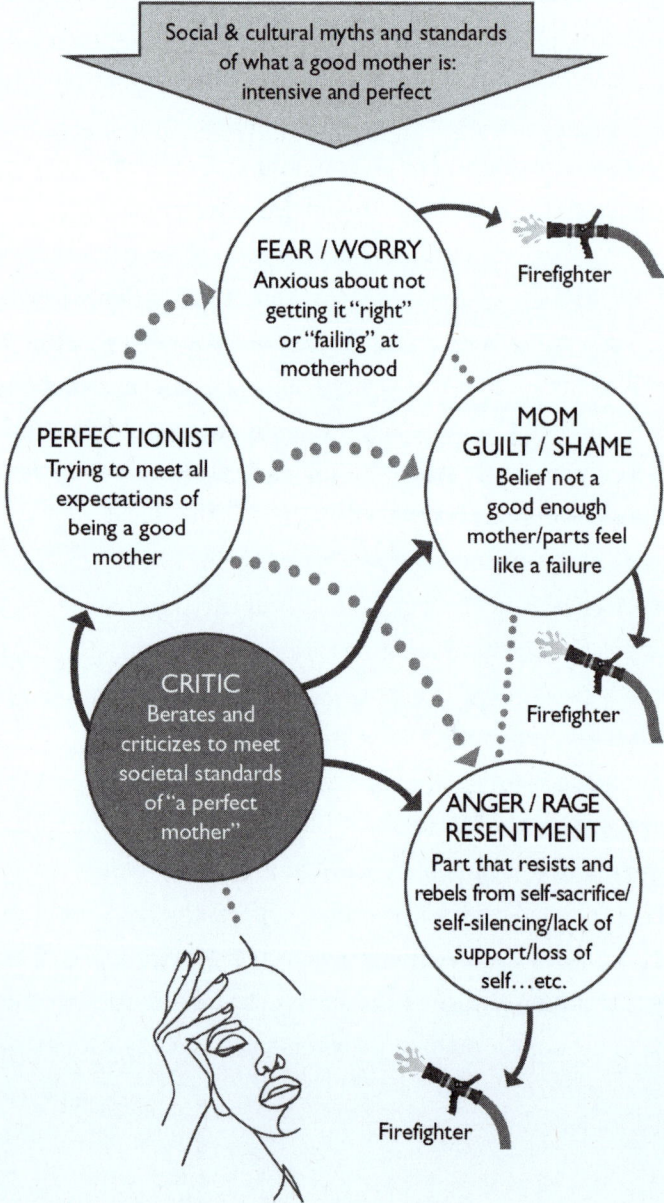

Social & cultural myths and standards of what a good mother is: intensive and perfect

FEAR / WORRY
Anxious about not getting it "right" or "failing" at motherhood

Firefighter

PERFECTIONIST
Trying to meet all expectations of being a good mother

MOM GUILT / SHAME
Belief not a good enough mother/parts feel like a failure

Firefighter

CRITIC
Berates and criticizes to meet societal standards of "a perfect mother"

ANGER / RAGE RESENTMENT
Part that resists and rebels from self-sacrifice/self-silencing/lack of support/loss of self...etc.

Firefighter

PARTS OF THE MOTHERHOOD LEGACY BURDEN

You may resonate with some of the parts, or a part listed here, but not necessarily. Our parts are unique to us, and there can be some universality to parts that arise tied to the motherhood legacy burden. Please know that I have selected the parts' names but yours might want different names. Also, you'll notice that I have chosen to title many of the parts in the cycle by their emotions. This is not to mean that parts are only emotions; our parts are like their own little being or personality with feelings, beliefs, and behaviors unique to them. But I chose to use emotions for titles because I think they constitute the most universal experiences that will allow more moms to resonate with them and to find their own part that shows up from the cycle of the motherhood legacy burden. Consider the parts in this cluster and see what resonates for you. Notice what might be the same and what may be different in your experience.

THE CRITIC

I'm starting with the critic because our critical parts are often very strong, influential, and a source of inner turmoil. They are also often the parts that have internalized societal and cultural norms and are somewhat the drivers of other manager parts, like a drill sergeant or conductor of an orchestra. Wherever there is a perfectionist part, a critic is pushing and driving the manager who is doing the work of trying to be perfect.

Mindfulness teacher Rebecca, mom to a four-year-old daughter and a two-year-old son, described awareness of her inner critic this way:

> The critic definitely shows up when or if I'm not behaving perfectly, like the way I think I should with my children. If I snap at them or something, the critic shows up to try to bring me back in line.

A part that tells us what we should have done or do, or that uses negative, self-deprecating, and judgmental language against us is a sign of a critic. Any inner voice, thoughts, or sense of inadequacy you feel tied to your role as a mother is likely coming from a critic. Motherhood studies sociologist Dr. Sophie Brock described the commonality of mothers being self-critical as "moms are should-ing all over" ourselves. That inner voice that tells you, "You're a bad mom" or "You suck," "You're useless," "You can't do anything right!" is all too common for moms.

Recall Stephanie, a mom to her son and expecting her second child at the time of this writing. She shares her experience of her inner critic:

> There's this overarching assumption that I would be an
> intensive parent. And then, when I fail at that—because,
> obviously, everyone fails at that because it's impossible—that's
> when the critic comes in. It's constantly nitpicking me, like,
> "Oh, I was distracted, and I wasn't paying enough attention
> to my kid," or "Oh, my work takes me away from my kids." It
> never lets me off the hook.

As you can see in the cluster diagram, there are three arrows from the critic to other parts in the illustration of the motherhood legacy burden because the critic can impact and influence all mom parts. It is particularly instrumental in driving the perfectionist or other manager parts that do "motherly" tasks or duties. The critic impacts parts who feel guilt and shame for moms, and it's active when the anger, resentment, or rage part is expressed outwardly, either toward the kids, the dog, the partner, or someone else. Because of the myth that "a good mom doesn't get angry or complain," the inner critic

will be quick to jab at a mom who crosses the line of societal standards and expectations of what a good mother is and does.

Critic parts can also be incredibly subtle—so much so that you
may not even realize that your self-doubt, feelings of inadequacy, or
perceived imperfections as a mom may be due to the inner berating
of a critical part. Many times in my life I realized my critical part had
been coming in through the back door: I didn't realize it was there,
subtly bringing me down and making me feel low and inadequate.
Often our inner critic has been in our life since childhood, so we
don't realize it's not true or that it's even there. We might have other
parts inside that believe it so we don't recognize the powerful influence the inner critic has on our system.

Like the name of his book *No Bad Parts*, creator of IFS Dick
Schwartz asserts that all of our parts, even the ones that seem to
turn against us or have ill will toward us, have our best interests in
their intentions. Both in my personal experience and in twenty years
working with clients this has always been true. Until you learn what
their positive intention is for you—what they're trying to protect
while going about it in ways that harm other parts and you—it can
be hard to believe. Once you begin to go inside and get curious about
this part, you will notice that you are not the critic. You are Self—you
are the one who can notice and listen to understand what the critic
is trying to accomplish in its role. The steps for working with your
critic are described in Chapter 5.

THE PERFECT MOTHER (PERFECTIONIST) PART

Ask any mom you know, and she'll be able to tell you what society
tells us a good mother is and does. Our manager parts take heed of

these messages—what it means to be a good girl, then a good wife, a good woman, and a good mother. Concerned with avoiding judgment, humiliation, embarrassment, or rejection, including also a berating from our own inner critic, most moms have one or more parts that have taken on the job to be a good mother by trying her best to meet the many standards and expectations of what that means today.

Single mom to her five-year-old son, Leigh described it this way:

> I definitely have the perfectionist that is geared toward being *perceived* as a good mom, or the perfect mom, rather than actually being a good mom. Because I'll notice—even when, say, packing my son's lunch or something—in my mind, I'm thinking, OK, nutritionally balanced and good, and packaged in a way that looks like, "Yes, I've done a good job." But when I'm honest with myself, this part is more concerned with how other people will see me—as a good mom—than really thinking about this is what my son needs to fuel his body properly.

Our perfectionist mom part is the one that is very attuned to the expectations in our world—to the tasks at hand as a mom and what others might think if she messes up. I remember one time when I was trying to make mom friends in my new community. I invited another mom I'd met at my daughter's dance class over to my house. My manager part had me stressed over tidying my house to an unrealistic display and making a healthy elaborate lunch that I would never normally take time to make.

I didn't realize fully what this was all about; I didn't know about IFS and my parts back then, but I had some awareness that I was going to great lengths to try to impress her. I knew on some level I wasn't myself. In hindsight, I see how I was very much blended with a manager part that wanted to impress this other mom or at least meet the standard of what I thought would make me appear to be someone she would want as a mom friend! What's ironic here is that once I saw her house, and she admitted to me that in her family it's her husband who is the "neat freak"—I realized my manager part was steering me all wrong. Our parts often miss the mark in trying to achieve what they want for us, which for me in this example was to make authentic and genuine friendships. (Big shocker: It didn't work out with this other mom.)

Do you have a perfectionist part? Perhaps it wants a different name, which is fine. Consider the myths of the good mother and the ways you might be trying to meet society's (or your parents' or friends' or community's) expectations. For example, recall from Chapter 2 the myth that mothers must be selfless and self-sacrificing. That translates to perhaps having a thought inside your head that you're being selfish if or when you take time to do something purely for your own interest.

I've heard many clients share with me that when they do take time away from their kids to be with friends or to do something for self-care, like go to the spa, go out with friends, or go shopping for themselves, the time isn't restorative anyway. They've shared that they still carry the mental load of concerns about how their partners are faring with the childcare duties, or worrying that once they get home, they'll have more tasks to do or some dreaded consequence for having taken this time. The father of a past client used to say this mantra to her throughout her childhood: "If you can lean, you can clean." So, as a working nurse with two young kids, she was run ragged, never letting herself rest or do anything restorative, because she would hear this voice in her head. Her parts had taken on this burden, and it was hard for her to care for herself in the way that she needed because of it.

If we look at the perfectionist part with curiosity, we can see that its attempts are well-intentioned. Within a culture where mothers are supposed to be all-sacrificing and selfless, it's adaptive and self-protective to be self-monitoring—to "stay within the lines," so to speak. Wanting others to see us as a good mom is a normal hope or wish. Pushing ourselves to get recognition, esteem, and even praise is a fundamental need for some parts. Our inner perfectionist isn't trying to create suffering for us or cause physical and emotional depletion. This part's positive intent is to avoid censure, punishment, and all the negative consequences that come with breaking the social and cultural rules of being a selfless good mother.

The judgments from others are painful. The threat might even include retribution. In some cultures, it could mean physical abuse and even death. The collective unconscious carries these myths across generations, and a spectrum of consequences can await mothers, depending on their social and cultural positions.

Our need to belong and avoid group rejection and harm is deep, primitive, and fundamental for our functioning. Our inner drive to avoid shaming from others, judgment, and punishment is beyond our conscious awareness. Our parts evolve to play a role that isn't inherent or even wanted. But without any other recourse or support, our inner psyche coordinates itself to help us survive in ways that bring about the least resistance and pain. For many mothers across time, this is accomplished by self-sacrifice and self-silencing—suppressing her dreams and desires, her feelings and longings—all for the good of her children and her family, and her own survival.

The perfectionist might show up for you like a drill sergeant, an unwavering boot-camp trainer, an A-type director, or hyperfunctioning doer. And, as the illustration shows, it's often connected to a critic. Where there is an aim to meet standards and expectations, a driver is often working hard to ensure that you meet your mark.

Trying to meet the benchmark for Super Mom or the good mother is like chasing a hologram. Moms today are facing a unique time in history where the benchmarks are especially unrealistic. Informed by the last three decades of research on child development and parenting studies, parents want a close connection to their kids. They value their children and want to raise them consciously, for them to have inner resilience, good values, and skills to become competent, kind, and contributing members of society. There are more parenting books than ever before—and then add in the podcasts. There's a longing for a paradigm shift from the younger generation to raise kids who aren't as shackled by outdated models of authoritarianism. We're also parenting a generation growing up in an established digital world, but the impacts of this monumental change are still unknown. The stakes feel incredibly high, and there are too many contradictory maps to follow.

Emma, a married mom with a five-year-old son and two-year-old daughter living in Southern California, put her experience of motherhood in the context of the current intensive-parenting age this way:

> I think the thing that feels confusing and challenging is, I feel
> like there's a cultural shift around parenting and motherhood
> right now. I feel like both realms are held and sort of polarized.
> I can't have a good, well-behaved kid while also meeting

> this new idea of being a cycle-breaker cause the way to do
> this is mostly by shame and control, and this other new way
> is different. Because you can't meet either, and then your
> perfectionist part is like, *Well, you're not meeting it here, and
> you're not meeting it here.* It's set up that I lose. In a sense,
> you can't meet both. You can't do it all, and managers are
> overwhelmed and overworked.

Our perfectionist manager parts are overworked and exhausted, which often leads to other parts carrying the burdens of feelings of guilt and shame for not measuring up, rage and anger in revolt of such impossible expectations that stifle our freedoms and identity, and parts that experience chronic worrying, fear, and anxiety.

THE FEAR OR WORRY PART

Because of the high stakes of wanting to do a good job as a mom—wanting our kids to be healthy, happy, and successful and feeling intense pressure that it's on us as moms to get it right—some mom parts experience a lot of worry, anxiety, and fear around motherhood and parenting. Not really someone who has struggled much with anxiety in my life, I have had many sleepless nights because of motherhood. I have lain awake into the night and then woken in the middle of the night with a potent worrying-manager part thinking, imagining, and rehearsing what I should do or say in stressful circumstances with my kids when they encountered various challenges at school or socially.

Moms have parts that worry for a million reasons. So many things are out of a mom's control, but she will suffer from or be blamed for them, which means managing parts that work hard to try to prevent potential bad things from happening. Moms who may have struggled with anxiety in their adolescence or early childhood are highly prone to carry anxiety into motherhood. I've heard from moms who experienced difficulty conceiving or suffered one or more miscarriages that they find a part that carries nervousness, fear, and anxiety for the safety and well-being of any pregnancy that follows or even later into motherhood.

For example, Kate, a married mom with twin daughters in kindergarten, described her fearful part this way:

> After having two miscarriages, I was so anxious during my whole pregnancy [with the girls]. It was like I couldn't breathe fully into my belly until they were born, out in the world, and I knew they made it. Then I could relax—sort of!

Sometimes the anxious part will quiet, but when the uncertainty of life pairs with the fear of not being able to prevent or control unwanted realities, parts will lock in and live with some level of chronic anxiety. Manager parts, like the perfectionist or similar manager protectors, will work hard to try to control or minimize the feelings of fear and uncertainty.

Parts where worry or fear is dominant can also seem to phase in and out at different times along the motherhood journey. When our children are little, we have more control over where they go, who they're with, and what they're doing. This can help some of our anxious parts settle because things seem, for the most part, under control. As our kids grow and require and deserve more independence, our parts that feel fear and struggle to trust can move powerfully to the forefront, blending with us and taking over.

Wanting to be a good mom can drive other parts in our system to feel anxious and worried. Unable to meet all the many demands and expectations, and also unable to prevent bad things from happening—which is part of this very fragile human life—means that one or more of a mom's parts will take on the role to try its very best to prevent harm from happening, often exhausting itself. The mom, like a hamster spinning in a wheel, goes nowhere.

While a part with a strong feeling of fear and worry might be very future oriented and pondering all the possible worst-case scenarios, a part that feels fear can also be fearing what might come after messing up: triggering the part that carries shame or guilt. For example, Rebecca shared that she has a fear part that comes up for her, and when we explored this, she connected it to her experience when her doctor told her that her newborn daughter was not gaining weight in the expected linear time frame. She recalled how triggering this was for her and how she fell into a shame spiral. She admitted to me that a part of her hasn't been able to let this go, so even as her children show no signs of any weight or health issues, she has a part that is vigilant around *Are the kids healthy?*, which for her is tied to the belief "It's my fault if they're not."

A loving note, dear mama–

This may be a place to pause and notice what might be coming up in you. Becoming aware of our Critic, seeing how we push ourselves to be perfect, and carry feelings of anxiety and worry for things we ultimately can't control can feel like a lot. I invite you to take a slow breath. It is possible to shift and change our inner landscape—to help these parts unburden from the mistaken beliefs that drive them and keep them stuck in a cycle that creates pain or suffering for you. You're on your way, mama. You're human. You're doing your best. There is so much more available for you. Keep going!

MOM GUILT AND SHAME PART

Whenever we have a voice inside telling us what we *should have done* or *shouldn't do*, you can bet that another part inside will feel like it was bad and is carrying feelings of inadequacy and shame. One of the most painful impacts of the perfect mother myth is burdening a part to feel guilt or shame when she perceives that she is dropping the ball and not measuring up. To blame oneself and feel like a failure at motherhood is incredibly hard and painful.

"Mom Guilt" is such a phenomenon that it's become a common colloquialism in Western culture. Guilt is an emotion that helps us recognize when we've acted in conflict with our values or moral compass. Inherently, when healthy, guilt can help us adjust our behavior, make amends, and learn from our very human mistakes. Human society thrives on this core emotion to help us survive and live in relationships and social communities.

But guilt is not always healthy and adaptive. When guilt arises because we feel we've crossed a line of a patriarchally informed myth or norm or someone else's ideals rather than our own, it is unhealthy. Plain and simple, guilt is not helpful if it's coming from a mistaken belief. When a mom is riddled with guilt and feelings of inadequacy because she missed soccer practice, the laundry is stacked up, and the house is a mess, this is toxic guilt.

A cousin to toxic guilt is shame. Shame is the psyche's internalization of badness. Feeling not worthy, not good enough, and inadequate are all painful and related to carrying shame. Where guilt can sometimes be useful and effective to help us acknowledge our mistakes and realign with our own values, shame never has positive value. It is incredibly painful and keeps us hiding, disconnecting from others, and blocking the acceptance of others' love, including compassion for ourselves. When a mom blames herself for her children's imperfection or challenges and is convinced she has messed up her kids entirely, this is disproportionate guilt, and the shame she may feel from believing she is not a good enough mom can be crippling.

THE ANGER, RESENTMENT, OR RAGE MOM PART

When one part is working hard to push us to meet impossible standards, which includes suppressing our feelings and needs, it makes sense that another part (or parts) will rebel. The expectations of the intensive mother are all-consuming and impossible, especially without social and cultural structures and supports for her to accomplish all the things involved in parenting, running a household, and—the majority of moms—also working outside the home. Ideas that a good mother is selfless, always happy, and never complains are oppressive and unrealistic for any human. One or more parts within a mother's system will feel angry about this, resentful, and maybe even enraged that she is being suppressed and dismissed. Feeling disempowered very commonly leads to feelings of anger and can brew into simmering resentment.

At its most primary, anger is a healthy human emotion. We are hardwired to feel anger as a message to know when our boundaries or rights are being crossed or violated. Anger sparks energy and action in these moments—whether in social justice movements or on a personal level—and opens door for understanding and change.

When anger is felt, understood, and expressed with a positive solution or action toward change, the emotion has served its purpose; the person's need is met, and the energy is released. When anger isn't processed well or expressed in healthy and appropriate ways, or if it is stifled and suppressed—such as in gaslighting by the other person, invalidation, or backlash—anger gets repressed. Without healthy expression and processing, anger can simmer over time, transmuting into bitterness or resentment.

Webster's definition of "resentment" is a "feeling of indignant displeasure or persistent ill will at something regarded as wrong, insult or injury." You might say that resentment is the stewing, unpleasant emotion we carry when we feel unseen or unacknowledged or when there is residual pain and unprocessed anger. Resentment is typically unprocessed emotion and some perception of slight, injury, or invalidation.

We might feel resentment toward a partner who isn't doing their share or contributing enough to the childcare or household tasks. We can feel anger toward the broader system of inequality: Sexism in the workplace continues and, even with campaigns like #MeToo and #TimesUp, inequality for women persists. What can be even more painful is the emotional anguish of turning against ourselves. What's called fawning and people-pleasing are defensive strategies some parts take on to stay safe and avoid harm in a disempowered environment.

Women have survived eons of disempowerment by self-silencing, by being quiet and subversive, by taking care of others and subtly trying to exert power where it's possible. Yet the anger persists at being perceived as less than. Some women have found ways to let go, release perhaps, or find empowerment so that they don't feel like a victim or subjugated. But many moms have parts that carry anger and resentment.

Rage might be the accurate word for some moms. Minna Dubin's viral essay about her experience of mom rage led to her researching and publishing *Mom Rage: The Everyday Crisis of Modern Mother-hood* (2023). In it, she recounts various stories from moms across ranges of race, sexual orientation, and class who describe experiences of rage parts. Based on her research, she's determined that mom rage is "an international hidden emotion crisis." She states that "mom rage is the uncontrolled anger that's common for mothers to feel that stems from the impossible expectations of modern motherhood, combined with a deep lack of support from the societal structures and in the family systems."

Dubin argues that mom rage and anger come from carrying months or years of an unequal load and self-silencing. As Dubin points out, "Moms aren't supposed to get angry." Yet mom parts will simmer beneath the surface, feeling trapped with no outlet for empowerment, for only so long.

Our angry mom part feels an understandable reaction in response to the impossible standards she is being held to; she is exhausting herself every day to meet overwhelming demands and unrealistic expectations and often feels like she is failing. While one part feels inadequate, understandably she will have another inner-protector part who is pissed about this rigged system. Rightfully so! The truth is that moms and women have many reasons to feel angry at times. It's a valid emotion, but the myths of the good mother discount and gaslight it from being expressed or validated. The impossible model and representation of what our current culture and society bestow as a good mother means that mom manager parts are working exhaustively to meet an impossible goal. Self-sacrifice and self-silencing can only lead to parts rebelling, and anger at crossed boundaries is inevitably human.

One mama I interviewed put it this way: "I just have this anger because of this self-sacrificing loop I can get into. You know, I'll do and do and do all the things, and then over and over I eventually fill with rage. Then I wonder, *Why am I so mad?* It's like, is it the trash and mess or is it the exhaustion of trying to be everything all the time?"

Like a balloon being pushed down into water, anger will eventually rise. Our parts want to be heard. Stephanie described to me how her anger and rage show up:

"It's often expressed toward my partner. Because I grew up with a mom and a grandmother raising me where my mother internalized and my grandmother externalized all of her anger at us, and so I won't do that toward my son. It ends up coming out toward my partner."

Growing up in a home with constant yelling and fighting between my parents, I hated conflict and anger. A natural people-pleaser, I have parts that aim for harmony. So, one of the surprises of motherhood for me was how frequently I was angry, especially during COVID. I was miserable because I didn't want to be the angry mom. Hating anger and never seeing myself as an angry person, I found myself working hard daily to suppress and stifle anger and rage. "Mom is grumpy," my kids would say, but I knew it was anger from my sharp tone, inner heat, and tension all over my body. I hated seeing myself as the angry mother, but I lived the cycle day in and day out, trying to hide and shut down my simmering anger, only to feel more ashamed, more against myself, and stuck in how to feel better.

The anger or rage part might show up in words toward your kids or partner. It might feel like hot electricity coursing through your body that you manage by exercising or cleaning the house (I have a clean house when I'm angry!). My angry part is also the part that doesn't like parts of motherhood. This part gets angry when my kids don't listen the first time because it wants to be doing other things than telling people what to do. My thoughts will turn to frustration, annoyance, and irritation at circumstances that are totally normal for my kids' ages. And my part will be pissed that it feels duped and wasn't prepared for how demanding this motherhood gig is. Learning how to make sense of these reactions through IFS helped me drop the self-blame and shame that was blocking my joy in motherhood.

THE ROLE OF FIREFIGHTER PARTS IN THE MOTHERHOOD LEGACY BURDEN

Guilt and shame, fear and anxiety, and anger and rage can be incredibly difficult to experience, especially when and if we don't have nonjudgmental and compassionate support from people in our lives. When parts are believing that these emotions equal the truth, of course, it can feel like falling deep into the darkest, coldest, loneliest hole, sometimes almost too much to bear. It makes sense that other parts within our system will try to block this kind of emotional pain. This is where our firefighters come in to put out the flame of these yucky feelings at all costs.

The illustration of the motherhood legacy burden suggests several places where a firefighter part might show up to help moms buffer or tune out painful feelings of fear, shame, or anger, not to mention the exhaustion from trying to be perfect all the time. Chapter 6 expands on different mom firefighter parts, but just to note here that moms' firefighters have a number of ways to help them cope with the motherhood legacy burden: over- or undereating food, alcohol, drugs, social media, TV or movie binge-watching, shopping, sex, numbing out, or dissociating (zoning out and being taken over in a sense with lost sense of self for a period of moments).

The short-term ease we get from firefighters may be helpful; it might help us move on with life in difficult times when we don't have any other inner resource. It can provide a loophole from crippling shame that might knock us down into depression. That glass of chardonnay might temporarily give us a sense of relaxation and quiet the worry, but it also blocks us from being able to go to the exiled part that is believing an untruth—believing it's not good enough unless you're perfect—and so you stay stuck in this cycle, feeling far from your Self and feeling like motherhood could be so much better.

We can't be fully present in our lives when we're just surviving, instead of consciously responding to our world. When we are caught in this cycle of trying to be the perfect mother, we feel tossed around internally, always feeling like we're not quite there. We are surviving to meet social and cultural standards and are then missing our chance to live true to our authentic Selves.

SUMMARY OF THE MOTHERHOOD LEGACY BURDEN

Striving to meet the requirements of being Super Mom—following all the guidelines of the many myths, such as loving all aspects of motherhood (not being angry or showing anger), dutifully working hard on all things motherhood (physical tasks and invisible mental and emotional loads), and sacrificing herself selflessly with a smile—is impossible.

The part or parts that work tirelessly to be the perfect mom become exhausted and maybe even anxious, worried because inevitably they can't control everything or their children fully. Because of the myth that "a good mom has good kids," her reputation, perception, and belief that she's a good mom are highly dependent on things outside her control. This breeds anxiety.

The more mothers try to meet the impossible standards with an internal dialogue of multiple "shoulds" that are impossible to satisfy, the more frustration and anger are buried because moms aren't supposed to be angry. They're supposed to enjoy all aspects of motherhood and not question the patriarchy and the imbalance of systems that don't actually support them to be truly successful while juggling all the balls mostly on their own (due to the other myth that a mother can do it on her own).

Then the blowback to losing our cool is often shame and guilt. We feel terrible when our rage or angry part takes over and has its way for a time. We then sit in the shame-filled space of regret and pain, judging ourselves for losing our cool and knowing we did not in that moment show up as the parent we wanted to be.

This very uncomfortable emotion might lead us to unconsciously self-soothe through various coping mechanisms. Some may be considered healthy while others might reinforce more shame. From here, our critic will push us again to keep trying to get back on that hamster wheel to be a good mother—trying harder, working more, treading water so as not to drown. Caught in this cycle, moms feel more and more depleted and exhausted—and, if they have little or no safe supports around them, alone.

Rebecca explained how she felt caught in the cycle:

> So I had a painful realization that I didn't want to be home all
> the time with my children . . . and that I was absolutely burnt
> out from it. I think part of why I was burnt out from it was
> because the perfectionist cycle made it more tiring too, you
> know, like I was suffering through, which was so hard because
> I would beat myself up for the hard moments and how I
> responded [which included anger toward her husband and

kids]. And also I just genuinely enjoy working. I enjoy using
my mind and connecting with other adults.... And yeah, oh,
I can feel the sadness about it coming up right now, like [she
closes her eyes and "goes inside to see"], there's this.... I think
the feeling is shame.

When turning inward and getting curious about the part that
felt sadness and shame, Rebecca came to understand this part had
absorbed the messages of her critic, who was functioning from the
rules in the myth of the good mother, which is, according to her part,
that a good mother who loves her children is fully fulfilled by staying
home with them (which is what her mother had done).

A loving note, dear mama—

If you are feeling self-critical in any way, or grief or shame
or guilt, please trust that you have done way more good
than any human mistakes you've made as a parent. I'm
guessing you rarely celebrate how awesome you are as a mom.
And I know one thing for sure, even having not met you: You have
and are doing the best you can. Good moms read books about
breaking cycles. Good moms read self-help books so that they
can show up for their kids in the best way they can.

I promise you that if you experiment with the exercises in this
book and you begin to meet your parts with interest and curiosity,
you will be on your path to showing up for your kids the way your
heart desires. You are a change maker and a cycle-breaker. You
are putting a boundary on the abuses and wounds of your ancestors. You are doing the work that they could not. A—maz—ing.
Now take a pause and breathe that in.

THE COSTS OF THE MOTHERHOOD LEGACY BURDEN

Sometimes we can't slow ourselves down and turn inward with enough curiosity and courage to see what faulty assumptions and deep and painful misunderstandings are unconsciously guiding us in our lives. As they are passed down to us from prior generations, we seem to inevitably repeat the patterns of this cycle, with parts who cluster around still trying to meet society's expectations of a good mother.

Carrying the burdens of toxic guilt and shame is not only muddying the waters of motherhood where joy, delight, and bliss should live, but these burdens also taint present moments with growing babies, only to leave mamas riddled with regret or loss when children eventually move out of the nest to build their own adult lives.

Shame and guilt make us hide. They disconnect us from our Self, from our capacity to feel lightness, love, and joy. Our energy reserves are too busy shoving down the painful shame and guilt, managing our anxiety, and numbing us out in some way that then takes away from our present moments to be, to live, and to love ourselves and our children.

One of the most potent mistaken beliefs that I absorbed from the myths of the good mother was any difficulties or issues my children had were my fault—something I did or didn't do. If I were the sole person influencing them (myth: Good mothers don't need or want help!), then I would therefore be the one to blame when something went awry. This belief unknowingly pushed me toward ensuring they were happy, content, and comfortable at all times, which, as you may have come to know, is being touted as one of the biggest mistakes in present-day parenting. On her podcast, Dr. Becky talks often about ensuring that our children can face adversity, which is inevitable as part of this human journey. Therefore, the idea that my job was to shield them from difficulties was not only erroneous and getting in their way of building self-trust and inner resilience, but it was also setting me up to blame myself and feel bad when my children inevitably encountered challenges and hard times. Witnessing their low frustration tolerance seemed to provide direct evidence of my parenting mistakes.

Of course, I knew all this well and good on an intellectual and logical level, but my parts were functioning with their own agenda. Not until I discovered IFS and was able to connect with the parts that were carrying these beliefs could I truly experience some shifts by unburdening the myths and beliefs that were driving the parts in my system. Our parts take on these myths in very black-and-white ways, and they work their agendas subtly. They persist even when we have a more cognitive or logical part who knows this is inaccurate.

Honestly, it's still a work in progress for me to let go of the idea that I haven't messed up my kids. It's a practice, and I continue to connect with my parts regularly to ensure that they trust me—my Self—to lead in my relationship with them. It's possible that one or more of my parts will not fully relax and let me off the hook until my kids have grown into adults and they see tangible proof that I've done a good enough job to instill in them the skills and abilities needed to function as kind and civilized people in society. But the practice of going inside and getting curious about what parts I have that react during my motherhood journey has been a resounding anchor that I lean on to stay in Self as much as I can.

Having awareness of my protector parts who are trying to help me and negotiating with them when they get caught in this cycle is my way out of buying into the myths that say I'm not a good mom. The process of de-conditioning myself from these myths feels like the path to liberation. No longer led by self-protective parts, I can show up more fully as who I am—who I was always meant to be.

You may have resonated with my description of the motherhood legacy burden and the ways the perfectionist part shows up and is related to the fear-worry part, shame and guilt part, and angry mom part. You may have an inner critic who shows up in the way depicted here or in any number of ways. Or maybe this isn't something you've experienced at all. Perhaps you have other parts that are more dominant in your life, parts that pull you out of the present moment or lead you to feel like you're not fully your Self.

Tentativeness and sensitivity around our pregnancy stories, birth stories, and medical experiences can be traumatic. It can take years to process and understand the ways our parts take them on. Moms often don't have the time or the resources to truly process some of the emotions when we go through a traumatic reproductive experience. This may be true for you too.

Please know there is no right or wrong here. Whatever parts resonate with you, or the ones that feel different and unique to you—freedom is possible for you also! I don't offer these parts as models or proclaim them to be true for all moms. We are complex beings, and one mom's anger part is not necessarily another's. One mom's guilt is specific to her and her inner experience. I offer these few as examples based on some of the most common myths and the ways that parts accommodate to life as a mom today—as I and the many moms I've talked to and worked with have experienced. My understanding of the motherhood legacy burden is rooted in my own experiences as a white, cisgender, heterosexual mother, as well as in conversations with and the stories of mothers I've worked with and interviewed. I acknowledge that this perspective is limited and that BIPOC mothers and LGBTQIA+ mothers may experience cultural burdens that can look and feel very different.

The good news about being able to recognize this pattern or cluster of parts that arise and relate together is that the pattern can reveal an element of predictability, so it is possible to affect this cycle and change it. Even healing one part in the chain has the potential to transform the experience and power of how the motherhood legacy burden shows up in your life.

Stephanie puts it this way:

> The less and less room I give my rage parts to actually hear them, the more it's gonna come out sideways somewhere. So, when I take time out and hear them, if I sit with that part and get to know what's actually there, well, that part genuinely loves me and wants me to be treated well and wants me to treat myself well. But she also gets rage-y when I don't listen to her. And so yeah, it's been a process. But I'm getting more comfortable with her, and I can see that she is more trusting of me, which feels good.

HOW TO BREAK OUT OF THE MOTHERHOOD LEGACY BURDEN CYCLE

1. **Start Where You Are**

   Do you have any inner resistance to self-care? If any part of you has bought into the myth of the self-sacrificing mother or struggles with a lack of self-worth that might block any inner attention and care, you'll need to start here.

Many moms get stuck at this point—when it comes to being a good mother, they often sacrifice their own self-care or therapy needs, prioritizing their children or spouse instead, leaving little to no space for themselves.

If you experienced very punitive parenting as a child or negative or traumatic experiences when tending to your own needs when younger, then you may have developed a strong part that tries to block or resist any self-care or self-nurturance.

Here may be the place to remind yourself that the most important thing you can do for your children is to heal your own wounds. If you struggle to prioritize yourself and your own mental health, it might help to first look at it this way. *The best thing a parent can do for their children is to do their own healing. By helping yourself, you help your children.* In this case, you may need to spend some time with this part that numbed your own needs to self-protect. You may need to work on building your assertion that you deserve to do this important inner healing work.

2. **Appreciate Your Protectors**

   One by one, recognize the role that each protector plays in trying to help you in some way, even if it's causing inner or outer turmoil or pain. Offer this part a generous curiosity to understand what it is trying to accomplish for you. Then take some time to appreciate it. Doing so naturally opens the heart, fostering compassion, gratitude, and access to Self-energy that brings self-understanding.

3. **What Are Your Protectors Concerned About?**

   Often a protector part fears that an exile will take over, what's referred to as "flooding" the system. Or a protector part may be concerned about another protector part taking over, which is what happens when parts are polarized. Identify and hear the fear(s) of each part and see if you can assure them or address the fears in any way.

4. **Work Toward Negotiation and Collaboration**

Become a mediator to the parts, as you are the person to observe the different ones. With Self-energy and presence, you can witness as they each listen to one another around their intentions and their concerns or fears. Once offered a chance to speak and be heard, it's common that parts will soften naturally. Often two very polarized parts can find a common middle ground when they realize that ultimately they both want what's best for you—but they are just going about it differently, in ways that perhaps collide.

As each mother turns inward to get curious about the parts of her that have taken on and absorbed the many myths of the good mother, she opens up space, hope, and energy for all mothers. Each time we can include awareness of our own inner parts as we are parenting our children, we are bringing more consciousness, self-compassion, and attunement to our child, allowing a stronger relationship and less risk of disconnection.

This is the how-to of cycle-breaking. It's not for the faint of heart, but it's possible. It's not a one-off—it's a practice. By trying out the exercise that follows, you can see for yourself which parts of you are working hard to keep you in line *according to what others have decided a good mother is.*

EXERCISE: GET TO KNOW YOUR MOM PARTS MEDITATION

You can follow this meditation by reading along and pausing or you can access a guided audio of this meditation by going to: www.unburdeningmotherhood.com/guided-meditations.

Take some deep breaths as you find a comfortable position either sitting in a chair or lying down. Close your eyes or gaze softly toward the ground. Bring your attention inside. Invite in an energy of curiosity and openness. Just breathe and notice what's there.

Now imagine yourself at the head of a large table. It could be a round table or rectangular, whatever you'd like. It could be a circle of cushions on the floor, or benches: whatever feels right to you.

Next, invite in parts to join you at the table. Perhaps you noticed a reaction when reading this chapter—if so, you might invite that part to make itself known right now to join you at the table. If you didn't have any notable reaction when reading this chapter, then invite in now any parts that resonate with legacy burdens or parts that have absorbed the myths of the good mother. Invite them to take a seat, one by one.

Take a breath or two, and observe who's there. Check and see if you have any reaction to any of the parts at the table. If you notice any attitude or thoughts inside that are anything other than interest, curiosity, or neutrality, then ask this part that's taken a seat to step back and wait in a waiting room or to sit somewhere else in the room. It may want a seat at the table, and that's fine, but ask it to give you some space so that you can get to know these parts that show up for you around motherhood and parenting.

Now, gently invite one part connected to your experience of motherhood to come forward. It might be one that felt most activated if you just finished reading this chapter, or perhaps you're wanting to get to know a part that feels most present right now.

Turn toward this part with interest and curiosity. There's no judgment towards this part, just a curious and open care and desire to know it better. Let the part know you're there and get to know it by asking some questions.

Ask what role it plays in your life as a mom. It might show you in images or memories in your mind, or perhaps you'll sense this part somatically, as a sensation, mood, or emotion. Just stay attuned to it for what it wants you to know about itself.

Ask it what is it worried or concerned about? What is it afraid would happen if it didn't show up in your system in this way? How long has it been doing this? Do you sense this part started its job when you became a mom or was it there a long time ago, back into your childhood? Was this part carrying energy or beliefs that have been passed down from your mother, her mother, or other ancestors in your line? Just listen to what it wants to reveal to you.

As it reveals to you any information, let it know you're getting it. You're hearing it. Is it working really hard? Do you get a sense if its tired or exhausted? Let it know you're listening and that you get it.

Now, ask this part what it believes about its role in motherhood. Where did it learn that belief? Is it really true?

If it isn't, invite the part to release this old, mistaken belief to whatever feels right—air, earth, water, fire, or something else entirely. In your mind's eye allow it to give that belief away if it feels ready. If it is not, that's totally okay. It may need more time to be known and witnessed. For now, just keep listening and letting it know that you're getting it, and it is not alone anymore.

If it feels open and ready, invite in what you choose to believe instead —
a truer, more heart-aligned belief that is what you know in your heart and
you choose to believe from Self. What strength or belief about yourself
as a mom do you want to hold and know going forward? Notice how it
feels in your body to hold this new belief.

When you feel complete, thank this part for sharing with you. Let it know
you'll return again to spend more time together. Remind it that you are
here and committed to understanding it.

Take a few deep breaths into your whole body and slowly open your
eyes. Notice how you feel and offer yourself acknowledgment for turning
inward and caring for your inner system on this journey toward becoming
a Self-led mom.

CHAPTER 5

MOM MANAGER PARTS: RUNNING THE SHOW SO THAT YOU DON'T FALL APART

Letting go of control over our children is probably
the hardest spiritual task we face as parents.
—DR. SHEFALI TSABARY

I WOULDN'T HAVE ACCOMPLISHED what I have in my life were it not for my manager parts. My managers filled in during my childhood when my parents were too preoccupied with their own bad relationship and unhealed trauma histories to pay much attention to my brother and me. These same managers helped me, a common 1980s latchkey kid, become independent, rely on myself, travel abroad on my own, and eventually parent three kiddos while juggling graduate school and work.

Remember, our manager parts are the protective parts that help us feel secure by proactively controlling situations and circumstances as much as possible. They help us function in the busy day-to-day demands of life. They help us adapt to social demands and accommodate in ways that keep us safe, valued, and connected in our communities.

Part of our socialization in a culture requires that we adapt and learn how to survive: how to stay safe, avoid pain, and have our needs met. For many women, our profound need for belonging, love, and connection, and our desire to avoid harm mean learning traditionally gendered expectations of what it means to be female and feminine. In Western culture, the feminine traits that have historically been valued and enforced are qualities tied to nurturing, empathy (often meaning valuing others' feelings over one's own), gentleness, kindness (sometimes meaning passivity and deference), cooperativeness, compassion, modesty, and dependability.

Female socialization means we receive messages throughout our childhood that tell us what's expected of us. Our manager parts tune into these messages and guide us toward learning how to be a good girl, a good daughter, and then eventually a good mother.

Your manager parts have helped you get through childhood and adolescence, and they're also probably playing a big role in helping you run a household and parent. They function often by trying to control other people and the environment as best they can, including pleasing and caretaking. They are great analyzers and self-monitors and are generally involved in trying to understand the world and create stories or narratives about how we should live and act according to our family upbringing. Our managers observed the painful experiences we endured early on in life, and in the present they focus their energy on being preventative and proactive. The manager's mantra? "Never again!"

Manager parts can be so dominant that they believe they are you—and *you* believe they are you. This is where we mistake some of their thoughts—a common way managers communicate to us—to be our own thoughts. Often taking on their protective roles in our early childhood environments once painful experiences and lack of safety become evident, our managers take on their roles and work to continue to keep us safe and avoid harm. Until they learn that you are there, as Self, they will continue to forge ahead and function in your place, so to speak. Without time to pause, reflect, go inside, and notice—as in meditation, for example—most people are externally focused and so are unaware that they are living their life with a manager part at the wheel for most of their moments.

Our protectors work hard to suppress our unhealed exiles from rising to the surface and to keep any more emotional pain from happening. When unresolved wounds or unprocessed traumas are pushed down into our psyche, our protectors can become extreme. When in an extreme role, managers can polarize with other parts, creating a sense of turmoil or inner war in our system. For example, with dieting or when trying to lose weight, a manager part will be focused on the controlled and restricted eating and exercising: keeping the regime in place. But another part in the mom's system will eventually feel deprived and rebel, whether through binge eating or eating less healthy foods (hence the common experience of yo-yo dieting and why, in general, diets don't work for most people). The inner ping-ponging of parts trying to manage the system differently can feel like they're at war with each other; meanwhile, the exiled parts they're protecting never get the attention or the healing they desire.

Polarized manager parts can show up in parenting. For example, when my director-type manager part—feeling frustrated, reactive, and in need of taking control—gives my kids a consequence or directive (usually in an exasperated or angry tone and with tension throughout my body), another part will eventually take the wheel, and I'll feel guilty and think I was being too harsh. This has led to many moments of inconsistency as a parent because different parts are responding to my kids and trying to parent, but doing it very differently, hence the flip-flopping.

When I'm accessing more Self-energy, I'm not flip-flopping from polarized parts. I feel more integrated and have more clarity about the right action to take. I'm more calm and centered, so I'm not acting out of frustration. The decisions and directives I make from Self-energy are more aligned with the wisest part of me, so I don't need to change them or go back on them. I can stand in them with my open heart and presence, rather than the agendas of my protective manager parts.

A loving note, dear mama—

Remember, our managers are trying to protect us, so as you read the examples of parts listed here, I invite you to be curious and compassionate with yourself and any insights you may have about your own life and times when you have parented from manager parts. It is impossible to live fully in Self-energy, so we don't want to be critical of our manager parts. Bringing awareness and curiosity to our manager parts is the first step to becoming more aware, attuned, and able to negotiate with our parts so that we can have more Self-led parenting moments.

MOM MANAGER PARTS

Our manager parts are often very stoic, serious, and tunnel focused. They are staunch protectors that, when in extreme, can block us from creativity, awe, and playfulness. Let's get to know a few examples of what I've recognized and heard from other moms as common mom manager parts. These titles and names may not resonate with you, so focus instead on the description and the energy you sense as you read about each manager part. Also, know that these examples are far from exhaustive. There are plenty of different types of managers unique to each mom. Do any of these common mom manager parts reflect in some way your own parts and experience?

THE TASKMASTER

This manager part is the one that helps moms take care of shit. This part is organized, task focused, and action oriented. Much of the time she is remembering, planning, and scanning for what needs to be done, and generally less connected to feelings. She is the "What's next?" part that is competent in her role of ticking boxes off the to-do list.

Generally functional and helpful, this part's underside of strength is she may have a hard time letting go of her urge to have the house clean and all the items ticked off the list. She is unable to relax and get the rest that she needs. She may deny or ignore signs of exhaustion or depletion to meet her perception of the demands at hand. She can also become overcontrolling and, when dominant, prevent other parts that feel more creative, emotional, or joyous from taking space, ultimately leading to a dominant sense of being too serious, overworked, and out of touch with her tenderness.

THE ACHIEVER

The achiever is concerned with making goals and achieving them, whether in the workplace or the domestic domain. The achiever is future focused and energized by achievement. That might be projects at work, but it could also be losing weight, renovating a room or part of the house, or making dance or Halloween costumes. It might be baking or learning a new hobby. It might be organizing a community group. Anything related to setting and achieving goals could be classified as a type-A or achiever part, although they may want a different name.

The potential harm of an achiever part can be the tunnel vision that helps them accomplish things. If too extreme and hardworking to suppress more vulnerable exiled parts, the achiever will deny other needs in the system. It can become so focused on small details that it loses sight of the bigger picture. This can create new issues, such as internal conflict among parts with different goals, values, or intentions. It can also affect relationships by prioritizing a goal over the needs of others, potentially causing disconnection or strain. For example, the achiever's laser focus on accomplishing the goal might look like saying no to her child's invitations for play. Too many of these moments can lead to regret and a stifled level of vitality and joy in motherhood.

I have an achiever part that I call my "grad-student part." She helped me make the A's I needed to get into graduate school and earn my PhD while I also had three children. Other moms have described their achiever part as one that is their work or career personality. These parts are competent and professional. They are also action oriented, and they are concerned with appearing smart, capable, and successful. They try to do it all—at all costs.

THE CARETAKER

A caretaker part is one that works hard to keep you safe and connected by tending to other people's needs, sometimes at the expense of your own. Many women, moms especially, have a caretaker part that is highly influenced by the traditionally gendered socialization for females to be the caregivers for the children and elders in the world. Starting from early childhood years of playing with dolls and play babies, women are for the most part socialized as caretakers and nurturers.

If you're a mom, you have some aspect of your inner world that functions in a caretaker role. The very nature of being a mother requires it, and so as a mom, it's helpful that we can have a part that takes on this duty. It's not a bad thing; in fact, it is highly adaptive and helpful for our children and families that we take care of them in loving and motherly ways. However, when the part that is caring for others is too extreme, it may be taking on more than one's share—wanting to control or fix other people's emotions and lives, often becoming resentful in relationships when feeling like they give so much that might not be reciprocated or appreciated.

Our caretaker part likes to care. It feels pride, fulfillment, and a sense of connection from this role that can be rewarding. But when unbalanced, it can be at a cost to the mom's own emotions and needs. When the caretaker part's agenda is to cover an underlying belief established early on in life that they must earn love (e.g., an exile who feels and believes she is not worthy of love unless she cares for others and earns it), it can lead to burnout, resentment, and depletion for a mom. It can stifle her from establishing healthy boundaries with her family and rob her of feeling more free to relax, enjoy life instead of working so hard, and maybe even accept care from others—which is hard for caretaker parts.

THE PEOPLE-PLEASER

Similar to the caretaker manager is the people-pleaser part. A people-pleaser part is a chameleon who learned that she can stay safe and avoid harm by being the good girl or accommodating another person's wishes. Our part's intention to please others has likely served us well in our life before motherhood, and is a natural and seamless progression to becoming a mother and creating our own family. Our people-pleaser is highly attuned to others' needs and wants. Being the person (or part) that makes others happy is very adaptive and can help a woman receive what feels and seems like approval, keep the peace, or stay safe. It can also at times avoid judgment, negative feedback, and even harm.

The costs, however, of a dominant people-pleasing part can mean a disconnection from one's own feelings, needs, dreams, and wants. This part will deny our thoughts, feelings, and desires to prioritize what the husband, children, neighbors, or friends want or like. For many women, the resulting impact that I've heard in sessions is women not having a clue what they feel, need, or want in life. It can be a total self-denial and disconnection from Self.

Protections that helped you survive can become constraints in adulthood. They can lead to conflict avoidance and reluctance to assert one's rights, perspectives, and desires in the face of difference. People-pleasing parts feel very uncomfortable, scared, and unsafe in asking for what they need or want.

My people-pleasing part has not been super helpful in parenting. Feeling so uncomfortable with conflict, as my people-pleaser helped me coast through massive conflict and chaos in my home, too often I would choose to give in to my children's wants and wishes, at times when in hindsight I should have simply tolerated their complaints and discontent. Getting comfortable with other people's dissatisfaction or unhappiness is important in parenting, which can feel difficult if not threatening for a people-pleaser part.

THE MAMA BEAR

The colloquial understanding of the term *Mama Bear* is a good example of the implicit ways we all recognize our own multiplicity of selves (even if people don't know about IFS). Most moms I know identify with having a Mama Bear or "Fierce Mama" part. Again, whether biologically driven, socialized, or both, a Mama Bear takes on the fight energy of our fight-flee-freeze-fawn stress-response hardwiring. A fierce inner protector part, an activated Mama Bear part can be a bold force of protection for our children and our loved ones.

The Mama Bear part knows she needs to protect her offspring from harm for their own sake, but also because any harm that comes to her children will inevitably be harm to herself. She is attuned to potential harm and will act in service of keeping babies safe—and by proxy, her own sense of safety and security in a sometimes scary and potentially dangerous world. The Mama Bear is a strong ally and gift to our children when functioning as a balanced part of our system.

If out of balance and too extreme, however, the Mama Bear might cross lines or bulldoze others' boundaries in service of her mission to protect her cubs. Unintentional outcomes might include embarrassing her children ("Mom, you're so cringe!"), rupturing relationships with her child or others (including Other Mama Bear or Papa Bear), and behaving in extreme ways that other parts of the mom's system judges as shameful, problematic, or embarrassing. For example, the screaming hockey parent on the sidelines yelling at the ref or getting into altercations with parents on the opposing team might be an extreme Mama Bear part. Being overinvolved and meddling in her child's relationships with other kids, like calling other parents and principals rather than supporting from the home front and letting her child navigate and develop their own skills when developmentally appropriate, can indicate an overactive Mama Bear.

Many moms who have children with special needs have relied on the Mama Bear part to assert herself and advocate for her child's needs in the medical system, education system, legal system, or all of the above. When collaborating with Self, the Mama Bear is a strong and fierce ally to help her child feel protected and access the services they need and deserve. Qualities of clarity and courage are equated with Self-energy, and when accessed with intention can lead to positive changes and taking care of the child's needs and positive social change, as in, for example, the successful Mothers Against Drunk Driving campaign.

For example, when I perceived that my child's needs were not adequately understood or being met by his school, my Mama Bear was activated, and she felt angry; she wanted to be loud and domineering. She responded to e-mails with the school with a bit-too-terse tone, and she wrote a speech that I read at a school meeting that, while not untrue, was probably a bit too long and tainted by her angry energy.

When I calmed somewhat, I could access more Self-energy around issues with my child's educational experience. I was better able to have clarity and curiosity, and hold compassion for the teachers and the school team that I could better see were not trying to do a poor job for my child. I had a more expansive vision and could see (unlike Mama Bear tunnel vision) that they were trying and they wanted to be helpful; they maybe just didn't know enough or how to help. With Mama Bear as a sidekick working collaboratively with Self, I showed up with greater clarity, calm, and poise, which led to better reception from the school team and improved results for my child.

THE PERFECTIONIST

You met the perfectionist in the previous chapter as a contributing part to the motherhood legacy burden. The perfectionist part is doing all the things to meet the incredibly high standards our culture sets out for being Super Mom. Taking the cues from society and culture about what a good mother is and does, this inner manager drives a mom forward, aiming always for success. For some moms, the main goal is to have others simply view her as a good mom.

This part devotes most of her energy toward feeding the right food or decorating and hosting a child's birthday party that looks like it was photoshopped for a magazine, all while wearing a trendy outfit and hair and makeup that are right on point. She wears a mask of smiles as she presents herself as though she smoothly and effortlessly put the entire celebration together with a bit of magic, and she floats unbothered by the noise, mess, or chaos of toddlers tearing down her balloon art, because a perfect mom doesn't get angry. The image or perception of the perfectionist mom abounds on social media, with images of beautiful mothers with perfect hair and makeup happily enjoying nature or beautiful décor alongside their smiling, well-groomed children.

The perfectionist part is highly competent and functions like a well-oiled machine. She is organized, a multitasker, and often one to volunteer for all the boards and committees at school. She is the model against which many moms compare themselves and feel apart from, as on the outside this part exudes an air of joy in motherhood, accomplishment, and perfection.

Like the other managers, when too dominant, a perfectionist part can drive one to the point of exhaustion because no one can achieve perfection. It's a tiring marathon that will ultimately leave a mom feeling like she's missing the mark. Despite others' perceptions that she has all her shit together, on the inside the perfectionist mom can feel like a fraud, her insecurities hidden beneath an outer mask of confidence and control. Where there is a perfectionist, there will almost definitely be an inner critic driving this forward focus.

THE MEASURER

Related to the perfectionist part is one that is self-monitoring, intending to ensure that everyone's needs are being taken care of while trying to find balance and success as a good mother. One mom I interviewed, Rebecca, referred to this part as her "measurer" part. She described it this way:

> My measurer part has been like, *Oh God! We tipped out of balance!* It literally counts the hours when I'm with my kids and how much I'm working. As if it's counting on a calculator how many waking hours have they had with me or [my husband]? How many hours are they spending with other caregivers, and is that okay or not? And what does that mean about me as a parent? It's like a constant track in my head.

This protector part is working hard to help Rebecca meet the expectations of a good mother while also addressing the needs that emerge from her career. After feeling burnt out staying home and solely caring for her kids, she returned to work part-time and felt happier and more fulfilled. This clashed with a part of her that believed a good mother stays home with her kids, as her own mother modeled, so the measurer manager part adapted to try to navigate both worlds and not fail at her role of being a good mother. With her best intentions in mind to help her satisfy her own needs and the mother role, this part was helpful and also exhausting, as it kept her from truly feeling she was doing a good-enough job at both.

The measurer part—if you're wondering if you have one—is a monitor, a checker, and perhaps sometimes a judge. It is assessing, evaluating, and making sure you're on the right course of being a good mother. It is more neutral and softer than the harshness or the self-denigrating energy found in a critic.

THE CRITIC

A key player in the motherhood legacy burden, the critic was defined in the previous chapter, so hopefully it isn't new to you here. Inner critics help steer moms directly or subtly to meet the demands and expectations of what a mother should do and be like in the current culture.

Whenever you feel less than, ashamed, incompetent, inadequate, worthless, or down, most likely a manager part has taken on a critic's energy and style. You might mistake your inner critic for your own voice, or it may say things that your critical parent said to you while you were growing up.

For moms, it looks and sounds a lot like "You're not a good mom." It might feel like critical thoughts for not sticking with your career aspirations and then guilt-laden thoughts that you're away from your child too much when working (damned if you do, and damned if you don't!).

This is true for Tatiana, who described having a part that chides her for "not working enough" or "not setting good-enough boundaries with [her] daughter to get work done," yet at the same time, another critical manager tells her, "You're missing out on all this time with your daughter!," triggering feelings of guilt and stuckness—like she can't do it right, no matter what.

Tatiana also described how this critic that judges her has started to show up around how well her daughter, age five, does in school. It tells her that "[her daughter] has to be perfect." She shared her awareness of this part with me in session, and she said she sensed this part had been there "forever." She connected this to having a very critical father and a punishing mother who expected perfection from her. When our inner critic pushes us obviously or subtly toward perfection, it tends to show up the same way in our parenting and how we relate to our kids.

When clients I've worked with begin to name and acknowledge their inner critic, they will often say that part has been there as long as they can remember. It makes sense because often our critical part has taken on its role at an early age when many of our childhood needs went unmet or when we experienced difficult or traumatic experiences early in life, perhaps through the way we were reared—or even abuse. The critic morphed quickly with the aim to serve and protect us by preventing any further harm—doing whatever it could at the time. And, as in the case of Tatiana and many moms, until we get to understand and help our critic heal, soften, and trust us as Self to lead, it will keep doing its job the only way it knows how—by being harsh and critical. The painful reality is that our critic often projects onto our kids and shows up in our parenting.

A loving note, dear mama—

If a critic pops up here, please ask it to give you some space (and work with it in the exercise at the end of this chapter!). All of us parents can be critical of our children, me included. The good news is, using IFS steps we can get to know our critical part and understand what it's trying to do. We can negotiate with it so that it will adjust its manner and learn to trust us, as Self, to lead. Tremendous healing and change are possible, so have hope. Also know that we can always repair and heal our relationships with our children. This is the beautiful work of healing and becoming a Self-led mom. You got this!

UNDERSTANDING OUR CRITIC

I know it will seem radical or wrong, with something that sounds harsh and horrible, it's hard to imagine it might exist to help you, but, like all parts, your inner critic truly does have your best interests in mind. It just doesn't go about it in a very comfortable or healthy way.

This is good news, because once you understand your critic and its true intentions—the ways it is trying to protect you or support you—you can dialogue with it and collaborate to find a better way. You can help it understand how its manner so far has been harmful, which usually helps the critic consider an alternative way of playing its part in your system.

Some of the different intentions of critics might be

- Pushing you to meet high standards of what a good mother is to receive praise and acceptance (or avoid shame or criticism, perhaps similar to what you received as a child)
- Pushing you to control and suppress impulses or behaviors that might lead to social censure or criticism or

rejection—like overeating or bingeing, drinking or drug use, gambling, and so on—which are not aligned with what a good mother does

- Undermining your confidence so that you stay small and avoid harm by taking risks that might create conflict in the family home (i.e., with your spouse) or that seem in conflict with your children's needs
- Guilting you for actions and behaviors that it deems as wrong or outside the parameters or values of what was learned and believed to be what a good mother does and is
- Criticizing and molding you to conform to the cultural, familial, and societal norms and expectations of being a good mother

In essence, our critic is trying to keep us safe and avoid harm or to help us meet some unmet need of which we're usually not even aware; usually this takes the form of a young, exiled part that carries the pain from the unmet need. In this way, the critic is actually trying to stifle the deep and vulnerable pain from arising while finding a different way to rise above earlier pain and trauma and succeed in a complex, scary, and sometimes dark world.

I offer you hope, beautiful mama, because I speak from my own experience and I know that there is a way out. It might seem radical to consider that your inner critic is not actually a bully or inner tormentor you have to ignore or eliminate but is actually a part of you that belongs. But it's true—and trying to get rid of or ignore the critic doesn't work. In fact, trying to ignore the critic or shut it out can make it more reactive and dominant.[1]

Thousands of psychotherapy, self-help, and spiritual books have suggested that people try to replace or change their critical or negative thoughts to be more positive or encouraging. Thought replacement and positive affirmations are only somewhat effective. These strategies might be good for coping when we are really beaten down by our inner critics, but the strategies are only temporary. I'd feel somewhat better when I practiced, but if I forgot to practice or wasn't diligent with my positive self-talk (which is just trying to activate or bolster an inner coach or cheerleader part to counter the inner critic), I'd dive just as deeply down the rabbit hole of shame and self-blame the next time I messed up or judged myself as not good enough.

Having another part inside trying to argue or fight with the critic's energy only creates a sense of an inner war—like you're ping-ponging back and forth in your thoughts, feelings, and energy. That doesn't bring a sense of peace, well-being, or wholeness. True freedom and healing come from going to the source of the pain—the critic herself—and working to understand, dialogue with, and ultimately heal the vulnerable parts it's trying to protect. When we get to know and understand the intentions of our inner critics, something inevitably shifts.

Parts can't be sent away. The ongoing work becomes a connection with this inner part that plays a key role in your life. You want it to change its job from approaching you with harshness and judgment to keep you in line to being more collaborative and less extreme and rigid in your psyche. By making direct contact with your inner critic, you can help it update its belief system right at its core to dissolve and release the hold on the deeply ingrained myths of motherhood.

This connection offers less of an inner war and more of a relationship from Self to this part. It means better collaboration and integration in your inner system. This means being able to show up in your mothering in alignment with your intentions, your open heart, and your core values—your *conscious* values, not those you've absorbed from a broken and patriarchal culture.

HEALING AND COLLABORATING WITH THE CRITIC TO HELP IT CHANGE

Put simply, get to know your inner critic and understand its good intention. Update it about your strengths and what you've learned, and invite it to soften its approach and be more collaborative with all your parts. Since we can't get rid of our parts, the goal is to get to know our critic, to dialogue and negotiate with it to see if it will allow you—as Self—to respond and remain in the driver's seat as you move through life's interactions and demands.

Remember, your inner critic arose in response to your early life circumstances and situations that were painful and threatening. Even if no big-T trauma occurred, our critics form in response to slights, humiliations, criticisms, and rejections, most of which we experience either in our families, through school, or with peers. We learn what and who is deemed socially acceptable, and anything outside of that standard—which is a lot— becomes a potential threat to our childhood and adolescence.

But as a child, you didn't have a healthy adult Self to stand up to others for you, to validate your own feelings and experiences, and to protect and defend your needs for autonomy and acceptance. Little ones can't help but absorb the negative energies that surround them; they are defenseless to self-protect or rightly understand, for instance, that the adult's anger or frustration is about the adult, not them. Children's vulnerability and naiveté often cause them to misinterpret and misunderstand an adult's pain and trauma to be about or because of them. This is the pain that an inner critic suppresses and protects.

With this generous understanding of a critic's role, the first step is to get to know your critic and understand its good intentions. Once you learn that, thank it for trying to help you. Expressing gratitude to this part is itself incredibly powerful. Often the inner critic feels very alone inside—other parts don't like it. Then we turn to it and can genuinely see it has been trying to help us (and probably has helped us in many ways). When we thank it, a healing process begins. Then we can update the part and help it see that we are there, as Self, and have many capacities and resources that we didn't have as a child. This begins the negotiation process to invite the critic to take on a different role in our system: as a helper and adviser rather than a dictator.

I speak from experience. By following the steps in the IFS model, we can heal and transform an inner critic. Sometimes an IFS-trained therapist can help with this process, especially if the critic is particularly annihilating or harsh. I have been able to work with some of my critical parts on my own. For example, by following the steps that I share in the end-of-chapter exercise, I was able to transform what I initially experienced as a dark and sharp negative being within me into a small child for whom I held tremendous love and compassion.

When I invited in the critic to get to know it, I heard it say, *You won't succeed at starting a mothers' circle, 'cause you suck.* Then it said, *You're messing up your kids.* I could sense its sharpness. Listening to it, it continued to tell me how I'm not a good mom: *You don't play with them like you did when they were small. You're failing them around the screen time. . . . You're neglectful and lazy. You're a shitty mom.* Feeling the impact of this energy, I saw an image of some kind of being covered in black, sharp spikes. Then I heard the voice of the critical part loudly again: *You have no self-control. You're not getting it right. You should be better at this motherhood thing. You're making mistakes just like your mom did.*

I took a few conscious breaths and could feel myself sweating. Staying aware of my breath helped me stay in Self-energy—noticing this part but not being taken over by it. Still with my eyes closed, I asked this part, *If you didn't chide me, berate me, and put me down in these ways, what are you afraid would happen?* In the empty space of listening and waiting for an answer (not thinking), I *felt* a "knowing" all over my body that this part just wants me to "be good." *You'll make mistakes that you're gonna regret,* it said, so I see how it's trying to protect me from regret. It continued, *You only have these kids for so long, and then they're gonna be gone. So if you don't get it right now, there's no second chance!* Now I see again how it wants me to do a good job as a parent, to not have regrets, and also I sense the underlying value that the critic and I share. It's true that it *is* important to me to be a good parent to my kids. I let it know I get it, and then it showed me how it has helped me in the past—how it helped me achieve my goals, like getting into graduate school, which was highly competitive.

I helped you achieve goals! it said. With this, I began to understand more about its positive intent and the ways this part has helped me in my past. I felt a wave of gratitude and understanding. It had a point; it really did help me in my life in the past. But I wanted it to understand that I don't need it to push me so hard to be perfect— that getting into graduate school is different than parenting. I spoke to the part, saying, *I see how you've helped me, and I'm so grateful. And now, with my parenting, it's not as useful and it's really bringing me down.*

I updated this critic: *I'm forty-nine now. I have love in my life with my husband and kids, and things are good. I'm working on accepting and loving myself as I am, and I'm trying my best at being a good wife, mother, and therapist. I don't need to keep working so hard to make other people approve of me.* Hearing this, I immediately sensed the critic soften. It felt relieved, as it didn't want to keep working so hard. Its dark spikes fell like feathers, and it morphed into what looked like an eight-year-old child. I saw and sensed again that she has been playing this role for a long time, and she didn't know any better. She said, *I just felt so desperate and out of control, trying so hard to make things better for us. . . . I didn't realize the cost to me.*

I felt a strong sense of integration with this part. There was no more inner war or pulling. This inner bully was now my confidante and maybe eventually will be my friend. I felt hopeful.

I asked the part what new role it wanted in my system: *Instead of forcing me or putting me down with things, is there another way that you can help me that feels like we're together instead of separate? Would you like that?* She responded by saying she wants to be the one who helps me pause and helps me be deserving. She wants to be the one to point things out to me and ensure that I'm acting in line with our values. I let her know that I would appreciate that because I do get very distracted sometimes, so I'm not always doing things toward my best goals or intentions. We decided together that this would be her new role. I then watched this child part transform out of dark quills into a golden sparkly suit.

My body felt totally relaxed. I had an overall bodily sense of lightness. To integrate a part that internally was creating such a source of pain for me felt nothing short of amazing. My heart naturally bloomed love for this little part that just tried to help me out through hard times in my life. It's like taking a part that feels like an inner poison or a toxic spur and setting it free to transform. As it heals, it integrates into a feeling—an experience—of self-love.

EXERCISES: MEDITATION AND WRITING

I wish for you to experience the deep transformation that is possible from helping your protectors soften and find new roles in your system. The impact of this deep work is nothing short of true transformation. You may wish to try these exercises to know and work with your inner critic on your own, or you may prefer to work with an IFS therapist. I've also included a writing exercise for you to get to know one or more of your mom manager parts.

EXERCISE #1: MEDITATION: NEGOTIATION WITH THE CRITIC

(Adapted from Freedom from your Inner Critic: A Self-therapy Approach. Jay Earley, PhD, Bonnie Weiss, LCSW)

Begin by finding a comfortable position. Let your eyes close or soften and take a few slow, deep breaths—inhaling through the nose, exhaling gently through the mouth, allowing your body to settle. Allow your awareness to gently turn inward and let your breath return to its natural rhythm.

Now, invite in an attitude of openness and curiosity. Bring to mind the part of you that might have come up reading about *the critic*. If it helps, perhaps bring to mind some element of being a mom where you can be hard on yourself—where you point out where you should be different. See if you can sense or visualize this part. What image comes to mind? What does it look like, sound like, feel like?

[Take some time here to get an image or sense of contact with the critic part.]

Now, engage with this part of yourself. Ask the part or think about when it is most triggered. What kinds of situations or feelings awaken it? Note what it tells you and how it might be hard on you. Listen gently. What are its words, its tone? Let it speak freely, aware of your feet on the floor and that you are observing this part, and you are supported with awareness and Self-energy.

Then gently ask the part, *What are you trying to protect me from? What are you afraid would happen if you didn't do your job?* Stay open. Even if the answers surprise you, just listen.

Next, take a moment to offer this part an *update.* Let it know you're there and let it know what's different in your life now. Perhaps tell it how old you are. Notice if it is surprised by this news. Let it know why its fears may not be relevant anymore. Bring this part into the present and let it know what you've learned and how you are able to protect yourself and respond in your life, as a grown-up, as Self. Speak to this part kindly and firmly, as you would to someone who's been working hard to protect you.

Now bring to mind the strengths and resources you have today. Sense the qualities in yourself—like compassion, clarity, courage—and outer supports—like relationships, tools, knowledge, and boundaries. What do you have now that you didn't have earlier in your life? Think about how, having these resources, you might handle triggering situations differently now.

Let the part know that you appreciate all that it has tried to do to help you in your life. Let it know you're not wanting to get rid of it, and then ask it, *How would you like to help me now in a healthier way? Can you shift from criticism to wise discernment, or even encouragement?* What role might this part play that honors both its care and your growth?

If it is not sure just yet, that's fine. See if it is open to thinking about a new way to help you. Let it know you will come back to see what it comes up with. If it feels right, thank it for showing up and trying to protect you. Thank it for considering a new way of being and a new role.

Now, taking another deep breath in and out, exhaling slowly and fully. Gently bring your awareness back to the room, and when you feel ready, open your eyes. You may wish to write or journal about what came up for you. Remember also, if you said you would return, follow through. Doing what we promise to our parts builds trust. Each time we connect back with our parts, they'll feel more trusting of you, of Self, and you will experience greater softening and shifts within your system to be more Self-led.

EXERCISE #2: WRITING EXERCISE: GET TO KNOW YOUR MOM MANAGER PARTS

Feel free to use these questions as a guideline and write down what comes up for you when getting to know each of your mom protector parts:

This protector shows up as _____
[words, images, sensations, emotions, or a sense].

It wants to be called _____.

[Name] is trying to help me by _____.

[Name] has been there since _____.

I needed it/her/him/they then because _____.

[Name] is concerned that if it doesn't do its job, I will _____.
[Provide the part with an update on your age, your current strengths, and resources.]

Build trust with this protector by expressing the following:

* I understand now why you _____ [do your role].
  I can see how you were only trying to help me.

* I am thankful for your intentions and for working hard to help me.

* I appreciate you.

* I intend to _____
  [set an intention or promise to continue to know this part and help it
  shift as it will learn to trust you as Self].

CHAPTER 6
FIREFIGHTER MOM PARTS: PUTTING OUT EMOTIONAL FIRES

*What seems nonadaptive and self-harming
in the present was, at some point in our lives,
an adaptation to help us endure what
we then had to go through.*

—GABOR MATÉ

IT'S LIKELY THAT AS YOU READ about different parts, you realize that despite our many efforts to prevent bad feelings from happening in our lives, they're not totally avoidable. We are human after all, and despite our best efforts to avoid pain and seek pleasure, life includes many emotions that can be harder or more unpleasant to feel.

Where manager parts are dutifully working to prevent exiles from being triggered, firefighter parts are the protector parts that are activated automatically when, as will inevitably happen, an uncomfortable, painful, or vulnerable emotion has been set off. As firefighters respond to protect people from burning by putting out flames, our inner system is no different. As fast as possible, firefighters stomp out burning flames and the heat that threatens to lead to more pain, oftentimes creating wreckage in the process.

The firefighter parts use many methods to distract, numb out, or dissociate without any concern for the consequences, settling down only when the exiled pain has been put out (temporarily, of course). Some of the ways firefighters shut down our vulnerable emotions are through the common behaviors that we all do to some extent—social media scrolling and Netflix bingeing, overeating, having a few drinks, flirting, spacing out, smoking, increasing sexual activity, dieting, working, sleeping, overexercising, caffeinating, shopping, or daydreaming. Firefighters can also be extreme and intense in their goal to shut down pain at whatever cost. These include more significant efforts, such as self-harm, bingeing and purging, stealing, running away, affairs, abuse of alcohol or prescription or illegal drugs, as well as suicidal ideation or attempts, physical or sexual abuse, sexual compulsivity, or violence.

Though the milder forms of firefighting might seem different from the more extreme or damaging behaviors, they all serve the same function in a person's system: to shut down the vulnerable, emotional pain that's been triggered—to keep down the exile part and to not feel what's believed to be too hard, scary, or bad to feel.

Too many people experience great suffering because of not understanding that their inner parts are each trying their best to prevent painful wounds from coming to the surface; often it's pain they aren't yet able to cope with and understand. So firefighters do their job by shutting them down at all costs—sometimes in damaging and unhelpful ways. Without understanding the innate and adaptive ways that our psyche protects us in our childhoods by shutting down emotional experiences that are too painful or unsafe to process on our own as children, we end up caught in this self-blaming cycle, believing we lack willpower and we're just not strong enough to kick our "bad habit."

Beating ourselves up because we fell off the wagon again—whether the wagon is drinking, using drugs, or dieting—we misunderstand the part that seems to us like self-sabotage. Social media and screen addictions are rampant these days, including sex addiction and pornography use. Those who grapple with these habits are carrying shame, because without truly understanding what their firefighter parts are trying to suppress (i.e., underlying exiles and unprocessed trauma), the behaviors become the focus, and shame reinforces further attempts to numb and self-soothe. We berate ourselves for the ways we're trying to cope with the pain of being human.

MOTHERHOOD AND FIREFIGHTER PARTS

Tacking on the motherhood myths that moms are carrying around in their psyches on top of the intensive demands and current stress facing parents today creates a mix of potential firefighters. These parts help moms function in a culture that sets mothers up to face impossible standards without providing safe spaces of support or acknowledgment of matrescence. The busyness and stress of parenting mean that our early conditioning and ways of self-protecting and coping is often our default response mode. When moms are running on little sleep and possibly dealing with feeding challenges, health concerns, schooling issues, or financial strain, the parts that helped them survive childhood are primed to take over and lead. Far from exhaustive, the sections that follow detail some firefighter parts that many moms have described to me in our work together (and some I have myself).

Before reading the following, I encourage you to first take a deep breath and invite an energy of caring from your heart to your firefighter parts. Often the black sheep of the inner system, manager parts can be reactive and unkind toward these firefighter parts. The perfectionist and critic can berate and be cruel to parts that lead to what are often viewed as unsavory behaviors, such as overeating, getting drunk, numbing out on Netflix for hours, or flirting or cheating on one's partner, for example. Yet we all have firefighter parts, and in many ways we needed them to survive what was too difficult to bear in our childhoods. So, with this energy of openness, curiosity, and interest, consider your potential firefighters. They are your protectors. Like innocent children, they don't often know what damage or instability they might be creating in their efforts to help you cope with life's challenges.

A loving note, dear mama—

You may see some of yourself in these examples, or maybe not. You might have other parts that help you cope that come to your mind as you read about firefighter parts. The main takeaway I want for you here is to see the ways these parts are trying to help—the ways they helped you in the past. Though firefighter parts often create other problems or might even damage things, like work or relationships—trust that they've had good reasons and that they can change. This is not an exercise of self-critique. Rather it's seeing all parts with curiosity and a longing to understand. Deep breath, mama.

THE SCROLLER

The scroller is a common firefighter part, one most of us don't recognize as a part that helps us tamp down our emotion and vulnerability. Think of sitting in a waiting room on our handheld computers, which has become so commonplace. What we're really doing is numbing out of our own experience, which also creates a disconnect from others. Perhaps the worst outcome of the default to our devices is minutes of presence lost in our lives. But minutes add up to hours and weeks and months of our lives that, when we lie on our deathbed, we may look back and wonder, *Where did it all go?*

It's too easy and tempting to be instantaneously yanked from our own minds and emotions by simply looking at a device and getting lost in the scroll of images and videos. It can be especially tempting during the many monotonous activities of early motherhood. Feeling lonely and bored with our little ones at the park yet again, like every Groundhog Day, we can be compelled to open and scroll instead of sit with the discomfort, the boredom, perhaps loneliness or shame (e.g., from interpreting your unhappy-about-being-a-mom thoughts as wrong or bad, according to the myth of the good mother). As Gabor Mate has expressed, "Boredom, rooted in a fundamental discomfort with the self, is one of the least tolerable mental states." The ever-available plethora of platforms promises to take us out of our individual boredom or misery and captivate us, often by whatever they're trying to sell us.

THE NUMB-ER

While the scroller could also be considered an avoider, the numb-er (or avoider, dissociator, etc.) is a part that often enters unseen. Like one of the options in our stress response system—freeze— the numb-er has a way of shutting down the fumes of a flame we likely didn't even realize was triggered (that's how good some fire-fighters are!).

The numb-er might show up for a mom in resistance. Refusing to read parenting books (despite struggling with parenting), doing everything else except tune into her feelings, and, as the saying goes, putting her head in the sand are avoider-type behaviors.

My deer-in-the-headlights part I described earlier is a type of numb-er or dissociator. When a client is moving into vulnerable territory in our work and they say, "I lost it. . . . I don't know," this can mean a firefighter did its job shutting things down. It perceived we were getting too close to an exile, and it blocked the therapeutic process by numbing her out.

For example, when I was working with Joanne and she was getting to know a vulnerable mom part, she described a firefighter as a "blocker." We noticed it come into the session and block the process of her going to her emotions. Joanne noticed this less as a visual part but experienced it more like an internal shutdown. One minute she had somatic sensations of sadness, and suddenly she felt nothing inside. Her inner sense was that access to the vulnerability that was just there in her awareness was now unavailable because what she described as "the blocker" was playing its part.

I encourage you to be curious about the ways that you may have an avoider-type part and its unique way of tuning you out and shutting off the fumes of what feels threatening to your system. If you ever question your motivation, perhaps noticing it wane despite its initial energy, you may be seeing the nuanced actions of a numbing or avoiding part. These types of firefighters are subtle. They enter through the back door of our consciousness, often so that we don't realize we are being cut off. *Dissociation* is the clinical term to describe a state of disconnection. In its most extreme form, dissociation results in a loss of memory or awareness from one state to the next. The avoider I'm referring to here is a milder version of this, which I heard many moms describe during our interviews about what parts they notice along their motherhood journeys.

SHOPPER

Our mass-consumer culture, where we're bombarded daily by thousands of ads and images trying to sell their products to us, creates a rich territory for a firefighter part that can use buying things as a way to put out the fires of uncomfortable emotion. One mom I spoke with described having a part that used gift-giving for her children to ease her own uncomfortable feelings. She admitted that this part may have been compensating for her perceived parenting mistakes, or when trying to get her kids out of their uncomfortable feelings. Lisa described it this way:

> I think it was tied into "let me make it up to you" for any time that I was controlling or like Sergeant Mom (a manager part). Spoiling Mom might go a little overboard in the other direction. . . . But it's more than just the guilt, it was like, I'm gonna buy your happiness for you, if I thought the kids were struggling. I can't fix other things in your life, you know, but I can buy you something that might make you happy temporarily, so I'd get them a new pair of sneakers—kind of like retail therapy! Yeah, that's definitely what that part's about. Shopping is like a firefighter.

It could be buying things for your children, like Lisa did, or it could be shopping for you or anyone really. The point is to be distracted from our emotions and get lost in the world of shiny things that temporarily take us out of worries, stress, sadness, or loneliness.

THE SNACKER OR BINGE EATER

Overeater, snacker, binger, junk-food eater—any of these terms might apply if food is a source of coping or comfort or a means for your firefighter to shut down emotional discomfort quickly and halt the impending threat of an exile surfacing. Food, especially food high in sugar and carbohydrates, quickly shifts our dopamine levels and carries notable physiological impacts. I'm not a food scientist or dietitian, but I have been a therapist for many young women who struggle with disordered eating, and I too have had a potent firefighter part that used food to help me cope with the impacts of trauma.

Firefighters who use food can be extreme, as in bingeing and purging, or they may tune out with extra bites or a sweet tooth. Recall Milena from Chapter 1, who had a very young exile from being separated from her mother her first day after birth. She described how eating is one of her firefighter's ways of coping with the nonstop demands of motherhood life with a baby:

> I feel like the strongest firefighter part of mine is binge eating. Anytime I'm out of resources and feeling angry, or even before any similar hard emotion comes up, I feel this urge to eat. I usually go for it, you know, because I'm tired and I don't have enough resources to do it differently. I feel like it's all about those difficult emotions and, yeah, not managing them. And it's very difficult by yourself, alone.

Eating behaviors for women can land somewhere on a spectrum, from on one end, food used simply for nutrition to the opposite end, eating disorders. Most women fall somewhere in between and can shift along at different times in their lives. I no longer have a firefighter that relies on food, but for many years I did. Starting as a toddler, I have memories of wanting to eat at my friend's house because my house didn't have such delicious food. My mom hated cooking, and I seemed to find food soothing.

Though it took me years (and lots of self-blame and shame) to realize it, in my adolescence my firefighter ramped up and drove me to eat compulsively for a few years, which I later realized was a way to self-protect. I gained weight during key teen years, when I had no assertiveness skills or capacities to protect myself and had encountered coercive and pressured sexual experiences I didn't know how to navigate. In hindsight much later, I realized that my firefighter part was trying to help me by making my body less attractive to men as a strategy of self-protection. Not surprisingly, the extra weight and desire to binge subsided alongside my ability to speak up for myself and better know how to respond to unwanted sexual advancements from men.

Snackers can show up in more subtle ways. Perhaps the delicious, savored flavor of that vanilla iced coffee or the four squares of chocolate every afternoon with your coffee are the ways your firefighter helps create a temporary bubble. Just you and the coffee. Just you and the creamy chocolate, even for a few moments. The frustration, the loneliness, the emptiness, or the isolation subsides as you taste the sweets. This is a firefighter doing its thing.

Lisa, mom of two kids now in their twenties, recalled how food and TV were her combo firefighters, calling them her "Netflix and Ben and Jerry's mom part":

> I think that's one of my firefighters in general, but, when I got
> the kids to bed, I couldn't wait to finally go upstairs and watch
> my show and eat my Ben and Jerry's and drink tea. I'd have to,

and I'd sit and watch my show, and it was like, I'm done. I'm so done.

THE (WINE) DRINKER

In Western mainstream culture, many firefighter parts use the socially sanctioned drinking of alcohol to ward off the vulnerable exiles and keep them suppressed. In fact, one recent study by the National Institute on Alcohol Abuse and Alcoholism showed that women are consuming alcohol more than ever, with mothers using alcohol to chase away the boredom from the many mundane aspects of motherhood, to cope with the burdens and stress of "momming," or to reward themselves for making it through yet another day of selflessness and depletion.

Rebecca described how her wine drinking feels like a firefighter for her in motherhood, in both looking for a way to relax and to quell her resentment toward her husband:

It's like, at the end of the day after wrestling the kids down to bed, I'm so out of Self-energy—and sometimes I'm mad at my husband, because he's been on his phone through bedtime, or I feel like I have to do the whole thing myself. I want to just watch TV with him for an hour and smooth out. Zoning out with a glass of wine and TV is a smoother. I'm not wanting to address my annoyance with him right then because neither of us are at our best. I just want to watch TV for an hour and go to bed. And so it smooths those interactions between us, and it feels like this reward for getting through all of the difficult parts of the day. I want to be relaxed—and so there's a part that just wants something pleasurable.

Alcohol was never tempting for me in adolescence or young adulthood. It was when I was home on maternity leave with three children under age five that I noticed a pattern of happy-hour wine drinking. I got curious about this since it wasn't like me to have much interest in alcohol. It was clear that I was treating myself with a glass of wine while I made dinner. I hated making dinner. I was sick of having to feed other people every single day, and at the time, I wouldn't admit to myself just how much.

I avoided owning this feeling and expressing it because, as a mom, keeping people fed was such a big part of my job. Admitting I hated it might make it worse—it might bring up a trapped feeling because there was no other choice. So I drank wine to not hate the task so much. The little buzz I got from the wine temporarily made preparing dinner seem not so bad. After a day of taking care of others, by 4:00 PM I needed something for me, but what could that be? I couldn't hide away in my room to meditate or go to the gym to work out (things I did before kids). But I could easily savor a glass of wine while still cooking and watching my kids play.

Moms are marketed to in ways that seem to make wine drinking a permissible strategy to cope with the demands and stresses of motherhood, which kinda drives me nuts. Jokes on dinner napkins with women dressed in retro-fifties style, holding a glass of wine and saying things like "I cook with wine. I sometimes add it to the food," or wine glasses encrypted with quotes like "Mom's Reason to Wine: 1. Jane, 2. John," point to how hard it is being a mom while simultaneously selling permission to drink the strife away.

This humorous take on moms drinking to cope with life whitewashes not only the challenges of motherhood and the patriarchy-infused constraints on women, but it silences women from identifying and addressing any problematic drinking behavior that they may be struggling with in confusion, self-blame, shame, and isolation.

Wine drinking is romanticized and minimized, leaving moms to feel even more afraid to share their struggles for fear of others' perceptions and judgment or having to proclaim themselves "an alcoholic." There's little room in our culture for healthy discernment and open conversation about the role alcohol plays in our social and personal lives. Seeing that drinking is a way to stifle valid pain is a huge omission in our culture that leaves moms to blame themselves and maybe struggle alone.

The medical disease model of alcoholism leads people to feel they either have it or they don't, silencing them from sharing their struggles in the gray area, which contemplates: How healthy is one's relationship with drinking alcohol? How clear and unburdened is it really? How much is drinking a firefighter behavior—a sign of a part trying its best to quell and contain a volcano of pain or unprocessed heartache or coping with stress?

It may be a firefighter part trying to keep unpleasant and vulnerable exiles at bay, or it may be a manager part leaning on the socialized normalcy of sharing a glass of wine to help a mom feel close to others and less alone—providing a sense of connection she is longing for but missing in her life. Understanding multiplicity and that drinking is commonly a firefighter part trying to cope with or manage the inner system in need of change and healing is the first step toward deeper self-understanding and change.

THE LAST-RESORT PROTECTOR

At its most extreme and desperate, a mom's firefighter part can drive overwhelming thoughts—self-harm and suicidal thoughts or actions—to stop the pain. When it feels like no needs can be met, the firefighter may push toward the ultimate escape: getting out alto-gether. Tragically, as the Centers for Disease Control and prevention note, suicide is the leading cause of maternal death in the first year postpartum—an illustration of inner coping attempts when every-thing else feels impossible.

There are varying degrees of intensity, and the firefighter always aims to stop and manage the pain or stress in some way. Firefighters need to be heard. They play a role in trying to put out fires, and they'll do it at any cost. For example, when exploring the parts that come up in the motherhood legacy burden, Milena identified a part that was angry, and it wanted to be known. Probing a little more, Milena learned that this part gives her scary thoughts that she might take her anger out on the baby.

She realized that because of her deep-rooted belief—which she learned from her mother and maternal lineage: that being a good mom meant being the only one to always take care of her son, and that she shouldn't get a break—she was pushing herself too hard. Getting curious about this part that thinks in the extreme helped Milena see that its role is to give her these thoughts so that she'll take a break. She realized that the only time she would allow herself a break to rest and to have her husband watch the baby was when these thoughts would come up that showed her total exhaustion and concern about how she was managing. Here is an excerpt from our session:

> Milena: I have the feeling that this hour and a half is
> so difficult that I don't want to make [my husband] do
> that because he'll be tired. So I should do that. I should
> do that all. And so that's why this part makes me angry
> at the baby. So I'm scared, and I've eventually asked for
> help.

> *Angele: What does that part say? What is it that it says that makes you realize, Oh, I need to ask for help?*
>
> *Milena: It's kind of like not even saying something, but it's this angry energy. . . . I feel this really destructive energy. Yeah, like I would shout at my baby, or something, or shake him, for example. . . . Those are the thoughts.*

Getting to know this angry part and the role it was playing was helpful and healing for Milena. She was able to appreciate this part and see its role, which allowed the beginning of a dialogue and negotiation so that this firefighter could still help her know when she needs a break, but not in such extreme ways—giving her thoughts that caused her shame. Her self-judgment also lessened in realizing this part was just trying to help her get the rest she needs.

> *Angele: Seeing the kind of role that it's playing, the job that it's doing, how do you feel? What's coming up for you?*
>
> *Milena: This is the first time I understand that pattern— and I even feel like I'm crying. And someone is very moved. I think this angry part is crying . . . like, it's the first time it's heard and understood.*
>
> *Angele: And so it's really touched and moved that it's not alone anymore. . . . Great. So let it know you really get that and you are listening. So let it know it doesn't need to be alone.*

[Pause for some moments with Milena's attention inside connecting with her part.]

Milena: I was very angry at it, and now I feel like it really helped me a lot to get some rest.

Angele: Yeah, right? So, there's another part inside that judges it. It doesn't think that's the right way to be, or that other part is concerned about it, or—?

Milena: Yeah, like, it's not okay to act like that. But, actually, I now understand that it was the only way I would ask for this help, so nothing else would work.

Angele: How do you think that would be different for you now, if you imagine yourself in one of those moments?

Milena: Yeah. Great question, because I feel like, when I understand it better, now, I can—first of all—I can get some space from it. Observe when it's happening and then negotiate, because I cannot promise that there won't be situations I will not have time or I'll be out of my resources, and there will be no one, so it's not that black and white. But yeah, when it happens, maybe I can negotiate with this part, you know. When I'm sure I can take rest, or to think more about how can I get more rest . . . Or maybe we can think of some things beforehand—like what I can do every day, you know, to just recharge.

This example with Milena demonstrates how turning inward and getting curious about the parts that we might judge as wrong or feel embarrassed by can be a gateway to deeper self-understanding and wisdom, and a new way to move forward with greater inner balance, collaboration, and self-compassion.

If you're experiencing extreme thoughts or self-harm or suicide, reach out for help. National Crisis lines include: Dial 988 for National Suicide Prevention Hotline or text HOME to 741741 anywhere in the USA. Text Help to 800-944-4773 to contact Postpartum Support International.

CHANGING YOUR RELATIONSHIP WITH YOUR FIREFIGHTER PARTS—AN EXERCISE

It is possible to change our behaviors and habits, but rather than coming from an external, behavioral, "habit-focused" approach, we make the U-turn, go inside, and try to understand what this firefighter part is trying to accomplish. We effect change from the inside out.

Start by finding a quiet place in an environment that feels grounded and supportive. You may wish to have a journal or paper and a pen to write down what comes up, or you might wish to record yourself. Neither is necessary, but they are options for you if you feel that sitting quietly and going inside alone need something more.

Taking a few deep breaths, invite in the part that you suspect is a firefighter. Perhaps while reading this chapter, you resonated with a part, or a different firefighter popped up in your mind with a newfound awareness that it might be working to put out the flames of unpleasant emotion in your system. Parts can show up in many ways, and none are right or wrong: Just notice. The firefighter might arise as thoughts or a voice in your mind, or it could produce an image or picture in your mind. A notion that it is close to your body is also possible, perhaps a bodily sensation.

If you notice something, focus your attention on the way it shows up and begin to get to know it. Ask it the following questions and listen to its responses with an open heart, as best as you can. If you find yourself becoming close-hearted or judgmental in any way during the interview, this is likely another part (critical manager part) popping in. Just let this part know that right now you are only trying to get to know this firefighter, and you will make sure it does not overwhelm you or take over (often a manager fears the firefighter will take over). Ask this manager part to give you some space for a few minutes. Notice if this part agrees. Even if it agrees to only step back a bit for a few moments, this is fine and very helpful.

Then, turning toward this firefighter part with interest and curiosity, ask the following questions, listening to its responses without judgment or interpretation—just allowing openhearted witnessing:

- What would you like me to know about you?
- What do you do or say inside (if anything)?
- How are you trying to help me?
- What are you afraid would happen if you didn't do this?
- When did you take on this job?
- What was happening then that you had to start doing this?
- How old do you think I am? [This helps give the protector part a sense that you are no longer a child and help it realize the strengths and resources you now have. Provide it with an update. Show or tell this part how old you are now and all the things you've accomplished and been able to handle. Explain to the part how you have more resources and might not need to get shut down now the way it had protected the vulnerable part(s) inside earlier.]

[Pause here to let this part take in this new information and see how it receives it.]

- If it is possible for you not to have to keep down the vulnerable parts you're trying to protect, would that interest you? If you knew I (as Self) could handle it, would you want a different role in my system?
- Would you like an easier way for me to hear you? [Here, you may be able to negotiate a new way of communication or dialogue with this part.]

Before you end this dialogue with this part of you, thank it for showing itself to you and helping you understand its history and function in your system. If it feels sincere to you, thank the firefighter part for the ways it has tried to help you, despite any of the harm or destruction it caused, because you appreciate its pure intentions. Let the part know how you now see it through the eyes of compassion.

You may not get to this place in a first dialogue. You may need to come back and revisit. If you can see this part and understand its intention to help protect you and how it evolved in your lifetime from previous troubled times, this can be a profound shift in your self-understanding. Setting an intention to come back to this part regularly is important and helps to build trust with your Self. The more you do this, the more this part may begin to trust you and communicate differently in your system rather than functioning as a silo.

Working directly with our firefighter parts might be challenging because of other manager parts in our system that feel threatened by our opening to the firefighter. If it becomes difficult to work directly with your firefighter because of this, you may want to find an IFS therapist in your area who can help guide and support you. (The IFS Institute has a directory on their website).

Still, even a shift in seeing the good intentions of our firefighter parts can go a long way in easing some of the distress and shame we carry because of firefighter behaviors. Understanding that we all have firefighters that aim to help us cope within an incredibly broken and sometimes traumatizing world (and childhood) can help us begin to see ourselves in a new light: one that offers kindness, understanding, compassion, and even love.

To become a conscious mom and show up the way you want to in your life and for your kids, you may need to give your firefighters some time and attention. Going inside to check to see what parts are there and what they need becomes the directive rather than trying one more external goal or program that will test your willpower. Befriending our protectors and showing up more in our lives with Self-energy is the pathway to developing a new experience of our inner landscape—one that is more inquisitive, compassionate, and collaborative. In other words, changing our life on the outside is an inside job. Once our protector parts are more trusting of us in Self, then we can move toward getting their permission to heal the vulnerable parts that have been carrying the wounds and pain and unburden them, so they no longer need to remain in their protector post.

EXERCISE: UNDERSTANDING AND BEFRIENDING YOUR MOM FIREFIGHTER PARTS

Befriending and appreciating our firefighter parts can offer a profound movement toward integration and inner harmony that can manifest as healthier coping and functioning in life. Write in your journal or follow the guidance on working with your firefighter parts, and notice what comes up for you as you get to know and begin a more trusting relationship with one of your firefighter parts.

This protector shows up as _____
[words, images, sensations, emotions, or a sense].

It wants to be called _____.

[Name] is trying to help me by _____.

[Name] has been there since _____.

I needed it/her/him/they then because _____.

[Name] is concerned that if it doesn't do its job, I will _____.

[Provide the part an update on your age, your current strengths, and resources.]

Build trust with this protector by expressing to it:

- I understand now why you _____ [do your role]. I can see how you were only trying to help me.

- I am thankful for your intentions and for working hard to help me.

- I appreciate you.

Now, set an intention to continue to know this part and help it shift as it will learn to trust you—Self.

CHAPTER 7

MOM EXILES

*Perhaps everything that frightens us is,
in its deepest essence, something helpless that
wants our love. So you mustn't be frightened if
a sadness rises in front of you, larger than any
you have ever seen; if an anxiety, like light and
cloud-shadows, moves over your hands and
over everything you do. You must realize that
something is happening to you, that life
has not forgotten you, that it holds you
in its hand and will not let you fall.*

—RAINER MARIA RILKE

NOW THAT YOU HAVE A GOOD UNDERSTANDING of the value and the roles of protector parts in the system, we can get to know better the parts they are protecting: the exiles. Our exiled parts are often the young, most vulnerable parts that have experienced wounds and attachment injuries, trauma, or painful experiences that were too difficult to process at the time (e.g., children without safe adults on whom they could rely for support). Hiding deep inside as though locked in the trunk of the car, exiled parts are carrying the strong emotions and beliefs tied to early experiences of pain and trauma.

Little-t and big-T traumas are experiences that lead to burdening and suppression of parts, but even somewhat commonplace experiences of embarrassment or humiliation, punishment, shaming or criticism, or judgment by others when being playful, gregarious, and excitable, or curious and questioning, can cause an exile to shrink and hide.

We learn quickly what's considered acceptable or unacceptable, not only in our family but also in school, in a faith community, in peer groups, through the media, and in social and cultural institutions of all kinds. Systems of oppression and power pass on patriarchal, white supremacist, classist, ableist, ageist, and sizeist standards by which we all feel compared and valued.

Our parts internalize and absorb these broader macro-level messages, as well as those impactful micro-moments in our daily lives when we may be shamed, criticized, or judged, or being told we're "too _____" [loud, sensitive, hyper, silly, loud, braggy, sassy, etc.]. Our parts pick up on these cues, suppress the behavior, and it becomes exiled. Unable to process this pain, the part is pushed down by protectors as a way to avoid feeling what can be painful, terrifying, or excruciating. What was once a free, clear energy gets burdened by negative emotions and beliefs, hidden away to learn the rules of the outside world, leading to less pain but possibly more shame and self-rejection.

Exile parts can also carry burdens that are misunderstandings. Children are not good interpreters. So when bad things happen in the environment, and a child's needs for being seen, understood, safe, and secure are not met, the child can internalize the experience in a way that somehow they are responsible for it. A simple example is a child who believes that her parents' divorce or a parent's leaving happened because the child herself wasn't good enough for the parent to stay. Confused and without any capacity to protect themselves or to have the circumstance explained clearly, these young parts absorb and internalize beliefs about their worth alongside the intense, painful emotions that accompanied the injury, such as shame, fear or terror, powerlessness, sadness, and hurt. Other traits that describe exile parts include feeling empty, fragile, frozen, hopeless or helpless, abandoned, angry, or unlovable.

Exile parts long to be heard, witnessed, and healed. Though they hide and are locked in by protector parts, they desperately want to be seen and understood and to come out of isolation. Their stories and the burdens they carry need to be witnessed by us, perhaps by another person, and by Self to begin healing.

Carrying the burdens from an injury, misunderstanding, or trauma, the natural gifts and energy that exiled parts came into the world with are suppressed. In their unburdened state, these young parts often hold energies of tenderness, playfulness, curiosity, trust, sensitivity, awe, warmth, and innocence. Through unburdening and healing these tender parts of us that have been hidden away, their natural essence is transformed and released, allowing a return of joy, lightness, vitality, wonder, and awe. By healing our burdens, we free our parts to return to their natural states. In other words, by doing our inner work and unburdening our parts, we become the person we were always meant to be, and truly are, when we no longer need to live in self-protection mode. We can live with an open heart and experience more of the beauty and gifts that are possible to experience in this lifetime.

Until the unburdening process is facilitated, however, the exile parts that are carrying the emotional pain from injuries and traumas will pop up and be triggered at times when an opportunity for their expression is made possible. Perhaps an interaction or a relationship that feels similar in some way to an original wound can open a window for the exile. Sometimes it's a reminder in the form of a person, place, or thing, or it can be given space in times when protectors are less vigilant, like when consuming alcohol. I've noticed that being ill (e.g., with a cold or flu), suffering chronic pain, or during menstruation and other hormonal fluctuations, exile parts can be activated temporarily escape from the trunk, so to speak.

Exile parts can be accessed in therapy with a goal of healing—either on one's own or with the support and guidance of a therapist—or exiles may be spontaneously triggered in life. Without understanding what's happening, the latter can feel very destabilizing. The intensity of emotional pain can often trip us up, leading to confusion and even self-blame, added self-judgment, or shame. In our culture, tears, sadness, and crying are associated with weakness, so it's common that these tender emotions that have been suppressed face judgment and inner criticism when they surface.

But once we understand that we are made up of a system of parts, we can recognize these emotions as clues to the parts that are calling for our attention. These strong reactions—what in IFS we call "trailheads"—can offer us critical openings where, if we can accept this invitation and turn inward, we can begin to understand ourselves and what is asking for attention. By turning toward our inner landscape with kindness and care, we begin to create a trusting and secure relationship from Self.

We know that in matrescence, a mother's old wounds, traumas, and unprocessed pain will be triggered. Knowing this and having the tools and map to know how to respond to ourselves when this happens are the stepping stones for healing and being able to show up as the mom you want to be.

> ## A loving note, dear mama—
>
> It's very human and normal to not want to feel hard feelings. As we learned in the last chapter, our firefighters have worked hard to shut down our painful or bad feelings to help us survive. But true resilience and openhearted living means feeling all our feelings—the joys *and* the sorrows. At our own pace, we can build the trust and confidence in Self to know that we can go through tough stuff, and that by doing the inner work, we end up feeling much better than we imagined. We feel relief, spaciousness, love, compassion, confidence, and self-trust. We also give ourselves grace as we respect the pace of this work, and we recognize and honor our protector parts first and foremost.

RELATING AND RESPONDING TO AN EXILE

Because exiles often carry heavy burdens, they can be felt as overwhelming or too intense when they are triggered. They can become blended with us, and too much to make sense of or even understand. For that reason, we need a bit of space from our vulnerable part, and we need to have enough Self-energy to be grounded and witness the story the part wants us to know and redeem.

Remember, there's a reason, after all, that we have many strong protector parts who have worked hard for us for years to prevent the exiles from surfacing. They are terrified and rightfully concerned about being hurt again or overwhelmed. Because of this concern, the work of healing and unburdening exiles is often only possible with the help of an IFS therapist, trained coach, or practitioner. Authors and master trainers, like Jay Earley and Bonnie Weiss, promote the potential to do "self-therapy" (the name of Earley's book), and I can attest it is possible. I have been able to go to many of my exiled parts, witness their pain, and help them heal and fully unburden.

Experiencing for myself the transformation of what felt like painful "dark energies" (burdens that included beliefs that I am not loveable) into feeling lightness, love, and joy as my parts reclaimed their gifts of positive energy and released mistaken beliefs and shame was nothing short of a miracle for me. It's the reason I decided to train in IFS. Experiencing how effective it can be and how this map offers us a pathway to heal, even on our own, inspired me to shift my career course to train in IFS, so that I could help moms experience the same healing—without necessarily having to go through months or years of talking in circles as in some popular talk-therapy models.

All that to say, in my conversations with Dick Schwartz, he said my capacity to unburden exiles by myself is rare, as unburdening exiles on our own isn't common. It's true that while I have been able to unburden some of my exiles on my own, I also found that some of my exiled parts, as well as some strong protector parts—like fire-fighters and managers—that were quite polarized required the help and guidance of a skilled IFS therapist.

Another risk is that if you try to unburden or heal an exiled part without the full permission of protector parts, you can experience backlash. What might feel like one step forward in healing can be sabotaged as parts in the person's system, who were not permitting this or trusting of Self, set the course backward or even create more suffering or harm. For this reason, working with our exiled parts should be done with the help of an IFS-trained therapist or certified practitioner (see the IFSI online directory to find someone near you).

Even if you can't fully unburden and heal an exiled part on your own, you can create a safer and more harmonious relationship with these vulnerable parts, which can do wonders to improve your daily life and life through matrescence. The more you go inside and build a supportive and trusting relationship with your protector parts, the more likely that they will eventually permit you the space to contact and work with your exiles. Once you begin to create a safe and trusting relationship with your vulnerable exile parts, the protectors will feel more capacity to soften, creating a generally more settled and harmonious experience in your system and in your life.

Some of the hardest moments in parenting are when my exile parts are triggered and I become blended with these parts that carry strong, painful, and vulnerable emotions. It can feel like a tsunami of intense emotions as sadness, shame, or fear takes over completely. As hard as I try at these times, I can't keep back the tears. I remember once on a family trip, an exile that felt unloved and sad was activated in a discussion with my husband. I couldn't help the tears that poured down my face while the five of us were stuck in a cab driving through London. My daughter automatically reached over to soothe and comfort me. While I didn't have enough Self-energy to help the exile move to a safe place in my mind right away or to hide the strong emotion I was feeling and be more regulated and present, I had enough awareness and degrees of Self-energy to know that I didn't want my daughter to feel responsible for taking care of my emotions, or for any of my kids to feel unsafe or upset because I was clearly upset. With a few deep breaths, I assured my daughter that I was okay, that I was just feeling sad about something else, but that I could take care of it. The look on her face told me that she felt relief, and a few minutes later I was calmer and more grounded.

Learning how to attend to your exiles when they're triggered in life (especially in parenting) is extremely helpful. It can be tricky when an exile is triggered in busy day-to-day parenting moments. The following suggestions on how to connect with an exile may help build a safer and more grounded experience that over time will help you feel more confident, resourced, and capable of showing up as a mom the way you want to be.

AWARENESS AND ACCESSING SELF

When you are fully blended with an exile, you're usually not aware that it is happening. You might be flooded with strong and intense emotion. You might find yourself weeping uncontrollably, enraged, or anxious and terrified—it's like the emotion is a tidal wave that's carrying you with it.

All you need is a small degree of Self (awareness that this is happening) to begin to shift and become more calm and regulated. Many therapists recommend grounding strategies for that time, like "box breathing" or noticing five things you see, five things you can touch, and saying them out loud. These actions engage higher-level brain networks, helping you reclaim control from what neuropsychologists call the reptilian brain-centered in the amygdala, the brain's primary emotion and threat-detection hub.

These strategies can be helpful, but in IFS, we prefer to engage directly with our parts. Mindfulness practice, such as noting and describing what you are experiencing, can help you access degrees of Self-energy. For example, when I'm crying because an exiled part that feels deep shame has taken over, I start by trying to breathe deeply and slowly. I may at this point just become aware of the thoughts that accompany this exile, like *I'm so dumb, I'm so useless, I can't do anything*. . . . These thoughts do reinforce the tears, but rather than try to stop or change the thoughts, as in other therapeutic models, I just note to myself, *A vulnerable part is here.*

As soon as we can be the observer of the experience (the tears, the sensations in the body, the thoughts that are like voices in the mind), this is where we start to be less identified with the exile; we become *less blended.* Learning to unblend is a key tool for a mother's toolbox in her journey to care for herself and heal while she's caring for and raising her own kids.

COMMUNICATE TO THE EXILE

Speaking to your part can be helpful. Letting it know you—as Self—are there and it's not alone can sometimes help it lessen in intensity. I find placing a hand on my chest while whispering to the part, "I'm here. . . . I care about you," can be helpful. You might ask the part to give you some space if the emotion feels too intense. For example: "Would you please give me some space so I can understand better?" Let it know that what it's feeling is important, and it's easier for you to understand its feelings and needs if the part wouldn't be so intense and overwhelming to you. You may communicate through whispering, like me, or maybe a simple gesture. Any way that you can convey your attention so that the exile knows you are there with it is helpful.

Communication may help you have a little more awareness and ability to feel more emotionally regulated, although it still may feel quite intense as exiles hold deep and painful emotions. I have found that being able to turn toward the part inside and let it know you're there begins to help it calm a bit. This is an example of Self-to-part relating that is the foundation of IFS practice.

EXPAND YOUR SENSE OF SELF

Another option is to try to expand your Self-energy. These strategies are detailed in Chapter 8, but I note here that inviting in something greater—that can hold you and the painful feelings you're experiencing—is another way to be with the exiled part that's risen. This could be expanding your attention to include listening to music, or looking up and imagining the sky—or water, trees, or your favorite natural element—holding it all. Another helpful option for steadying and grounding yourself when an exile has surfaced is using prayer or some other resource to expand your sense of Self to enable you to be with the exile.

Sometimes I'll place my hand on my heart, and as I begin to get a bit more Self-energy, I can then send kind energy to this exile. Without trying to judge or change it, you might express your care to this part and send loving energy toward it. If another protector part (perhaps critical or judgmental) tries to come in, see it as concerned and ask it to step back and give you some room with this one part. With enough Self-energy, you can assure the protector, "I've got this," and you'll make sure this part doesn't take over and or get hurt again.

COMMIT TO RETURN AND CHOOSE A SAFE PLACE

If you can't fully get to know the exiled part, depending on when it was triggered and your circumstances, you can let it know you see it, that it matters to you very much, and then make a commitment to return to it later. Following up is very important as you will only build trust within your system if you do so. Otherwise, it's only a matter of time before this exile finds its way back into "randomly" blending with you again at the next opportunity.

As you are inviting the exiled part to subside for now, you might ask it where it would like to stay while it waits for its time with you. You might imagine a cozy and safe room in your mind where you can offer this part a stuffed toy, a pet, some blankets, or anything or anyone else it wants. For example, when I started using IFS and experienced unburdening exiled parts, I imagined them in a beautiful cottage on the ocean. For me, the beach is a safe, cozy place—a replica of where I lived for a while on the west coast of Canada many years ago. You might think of a place you've been or it can be somewhere you imagine. There are no limits. Allow your mind to come up with whatever the part wants.

Then notice how you feel in your body. If you can, you might make a few notes about what you have noticed already about this part, what was happening that led to it arising, what it said, and what feelings it carried. Take some deep breaths. If you're able to communicate in this way with your exiled part, you'll likely find you feel a bit more grounded and centered. Write in your calendar when you will go back to this part, either on your own if you feel comfortable doing so or with the support of an IFS therapist.

In a recent moment of an exile being activated, I found myself caught in a shame spiral part and was taken over by a mix of sadness and anger, feeling just plain awful about myself. I felt hurt and alone because I was the only parent at home. These moments are some of the most challenging for moms—when you can't take space or time for yourself and you've got to get it together ASAP for the sake of your kids. You want to be the sturdy leader, but you're blended with a part of you that feels small, weak, and awful.

I locked myself in my washroom and started to repeat to myself, "I'm sorry that you're hurting. . . . I'm sorry that you're hurting. . . ." It was as if whispering these words and imagining sending them directly to the part that was taking me over with emotional anguish was directly acknowledging and calming this part. Within a few moments, I was much more calm and felt completely regulated.

The more we can turn to our hurt parts and get curious, listen, and offer them Self-attunement and compassion, the more we build inner trust with our own vulnerabilities and wounded parts. Healing them through befriending and unburdening builds not only more peace and integration in our bodies, minds, and hearts, but it gives way for us to be able to stand steadier, firmer, and more courageously to witness and support our children through their journeys that will also include heartbreak, pain, and adversity.

Healing ourselves through caring for all of our parts allows us to parent with more consciousness and authenticity. Releasing what we've been carrying from our own lives—and sometimes even past generations—frees us up with more energy, zest, creativity, presence, and love to give our kids. Emma described it this way:

> So, when I could do the healing . . . when I was healed, I went to those parts that held the big-T trauma, the abuse. . . . I went to the parts that held the attachment little-t trauma of holding the beliefs from hearing, "You're too much! What's wrong with you?" and gave myself what I needed. It really helped expand my capacity to be with and be present for my child and his tantrums and his emotions.

It is absolutely possible to heal ourselves alongside the raising of our children. In my opinion, based on my own experience, it's the best pathway to repair, thrive, and feel connected with our children. Recommendations on what to say and do in certain situations that are found in "expert" parenting books have been helpful here and there, but above all else, the most impactful improvements I have experienced in my relationships with my kids and as a mom came through getting to understand, know, and heal my inner parts.

So while I recommend that you work to know and heal your exiles with the help of an IFS-trained therapist, I know that getting to know your mom protector parts will help you feel huge shifts in your life and in motherhood. If you're interested to learn more about what an IFS session is like and what the process of unburdening an exiled part looks like (perhaps your protector parts are feeling curious if this is brand-new to you), then I invite you to read an excerpt below from a session I had with Dick Schwartz.

AN EXAMPLE OF UNBURDENING AN EXILE

To set the context, the session started out with me focusing on one part that was feeling resentment toward my kids. This is a part, we realized, that had been pushed down by other parts, as there's no permission to think this way or feel this way in motherhood, so it had been rejected inside for a long time. Specifically, I expressed that this part "hated being a mom." Given this opportunity to share and speak its story, we came to understand this was a protector part that was protecting a more vulnerable part that was also being triggered in parenting. Dr. Schwartz facilitated a powerful conversation and a moving unburdening process with this exiled part.

Dick: So maybe just see if there's something she can have while you got the kids, if there's anything that would make her feel better. Can she do something creative with the kids?

Angele: Yeah, okay. [I turn inward to check with the part.]

Dick: But just be open to the answer, don't be judgmental.

Angele: She's like, I've tried—which is true, you know—but they take over and they ruin things. There's this like feeling that she thinks they make me feel bad, so she just wants to get away from them.

Dick: Is it true that [the kids] make you feel bad?

Angele: Well, Sometimes . . . yeah, being a mom.

Dick: Yeah, so let her know she's got a point. She's trying to protect you from feeling bad. Ask her if they didn't make you feel bad the way they do, would she be as upset with them?

Angele: She says no, like if they would just get along—

Dick: [chuckles] Oh, that's not what's gonna happen [laughing], but—

Angele: —that would be great. We can all just make art! [laughing]

Dick: If we can go to the parts that feel so bad when they don't get along and heal them, so they weren't so triggered by the kids, how would that be for this one?

Angele: Ok, yeah. [Goes inside to see.] She's open to that. She said that it would be different.

Dick: So, does she give us permission to go to those parts?

Angele: Yeah, she said it would be fine if these other parts aren't getting in the way.

Dick: So, do you know, or she can point to the part she wants us to heal?

Angele: [Connecting with the exile.] Yeah, so she points right away to this part and it's a little part—and this is a part that comes up a lot with my kids because it feels like I am a kid, it's like, What the hell am I doing? I have no idea what I'm doing!

Dick: So, where do you find this one in your body, around your body?

Angele: Just kind of like sitting right here, heavy, like a big lump.

Dick: How do you feel toward it?

Angele: Well, I feel bad for it. I feel sad for it.

Dick: So, let it know and see how it reacts.

Angele: [Going inside to listen to the part.] It's just, so—it's giving me a feeling of, like, I don't know what's right or wrong—like how am I supposed to decide and it feels like there's a lot of pressure.

Dick: How do you feel toward it?

Angele: Kinda feel like I want to save it, like that sounds tough to live under that pressure.

Dick: Ask it why it thinks it's the one that has to decide and do these grown-up things.

Angele: Right. It just says, I'm just here. I don't know why I'm here, but I'm here.

Dick: Okay. But would it like to do something else? Would it like to be relieved of all this responsibility?

Angele: Yes, definitely.

Dick: Okay, so we can do that. So ask if it needs to show you anything about being stuck in the past, first.

Angele: So, I don't know, but suddenly I'm seeing myself walk to school like this where I grew up, this route I used to walk every day, it's showing me that.

Dick: Yeah. Stay with it, whatever it wants to show you about that.

Angele: The words "there's nobody else." It said, "There's nobody else."

Dick: Do you know what it means by that?

Angele: Just like, I'm by myself—so I think there's, like, like I would walk to school, then I'd have to go home for lunch. There was just a lot of me by myself 'cause both my parents worked, and—I mean, I had an older brother, but he was older and doing his own thing so there was this like—I feel like this is the part showing me like I kinda grew up too fast like just was by herself a lot, did things on her own a lot because there was nobody else.

Dick: Does that make sense?

Angele: Yeah, it does.

Dick: So let the part know you get that and because of that it had to take on all this responsibility before it was really ready, and it wasn't fair.

Angele: Uh-hmmm . . .

Dick: See how it reacts to being seen for that.

Angele: It just like gave me a huge hug and is, like, "I'm so lonely. Yeah, I don't wanna be doing this."

Dick: Yeah, so go into that time period and be with it the way it needed it at the time.

Angele: [Long pause while connecting with this little girl part] It's kind of like this fast-forward montage of just being with her a lot, walking her to school and asking her about her day—and just those little things [tears].

Dick: That's right, that's all she needed. And how is she reacting?

Angele: She's really happy about it and just very sweet and thankful. There's no anger or resentment in this part, just like an innocent little kid, happy to have some attention—and there's relief, I guess.

Dick: Yeah, to not be alone. See if she'd like to leave that time and place with you and come where you can take care of her.

Angele: Yeah, she does for sure.

Dick: Does she want to come to the present here, or your house, or to a fancy place of her choice? Wherever she wants to be—

Angele: She wants to—I'll put her at the cottage at the beach with the other parts. None of them want to be alone.

Dick: Good. So how are the other ones greeting her?

Angele: It's like a wonderful reunion.

Dick: That's great. Tell her, she can just stay there and you can look after her. And see if now she's ready to unload all the responsibilities and loneliness and all of the feelings she got from those times.

Angele: Yeah, she's like, "I don't want that anymore. I don't need that." She's happy to be with the other little kids.

Dick: What would she like to give it up to: light, water, fire, earth, anything else?

Angele: She liked when you said light, that got a little ding.

Dick: Okay, so invite the light to come and shine on her and tell her to let it just all go into the light and let it take it away until it's all gone.

Angele: It's wild—like I can see it beautifully, like a painting almost—and then when I checked into my body the sensation was gone out of my body.

Dick: So how's she doing?

> Angele: She's awesome! [Feeling light, warmth, relaxed, and almost effervescent.]
>
> Dick: And let her know she can trust you to make these big decisions and handle your life. She can just be a kid on the beach.
>
> Angele: There's a feeling of hopefulness and—what is the right word?—optimism. Like she's happy with it. Feels like there's maybe some potential. Not feeling so trapped anymore.
>
> Dick: Good. That was good.
>
> Angele: That was great! Wow.

You have an essence within you that knows the right way. It is ready to help you open your heart to yourself. It's the core in which you can feel calm and confident, where you access your courage, where you find clarity and purpose, and where you can parent your children with sturdy feet and an open heart. This journey of mother-becoming—matrescence—is a journey to know your Self. Let's shift now to explore the different ways you can reconnect with the you that's never been broken, that flows with life, and that holds the wisdom you seek. In the famous words of Dorothy in *The Wizard of Oz*, "There's no place like home." You need only look inside.

EXERCISE: MEETING AN EXILE WITH CARE AND COMPASSION

This is an introductory exercise if you feel comfortable turning toward a part that you think is an exiled part. As mentioned earlier, I recommend working with an IFS therapist to unburden exiled parts. These young, vulnerable, and often emotional parts can get activated in motherhood, and I think it's helpful to have a sense of your exiles and begin to meet them with care and compassion. This way of relating to your inner vulnerability may be different for you, and it can offer significant shifts in our inner landscape and in our life.

I invite you to spend some time where you can write and sit for ten to fifteen minutes. Take a few deep breaths and settle into your body by inviting presence and awareness of your body and mind. Invite a gentle intention to know a part that you may not have come to be aware of earlier. Follow these instructions:

1. Write in your journal or notepad parts you suspect may be exiled in your system. Think of times when you feel triggered in your parenting and a part seems to take over with strong emotion—anger, shame, guilt, sadness, or fear.

2. Write what part(s) you suspect might be protecting them. You may glean, for example, a protector part like a bodyguard of sorts, standing in front of the exile, or, as you move toward the exile in your mind's eye, a protector part might jump in front. Parts could either be protecting by managing or firefighting. The exile is the one that is more vulnerable. It might feel young, helpless, and small.

3. Write down when you've noticed that this exiled part is triggered. What contexts? People or situations? You might write with words, draw, or color what comes up.

4. Now, take a breath or two and speak to this part inside right now. Let it know you see it was trying to communicate with you and that you are starting to understand. You might tell it you're learning IFS and you didn't realize it was just trying to get your

attention. Let it know you're listening now and you will find a time when it works to get to understand it and help it. Send it some loving energy and care.

5. Ask the part if it wants to go somewhere or to stay in a safe place, as in the guidance above.

6. Open your eyes with a few deep breaths and move back outward into your day. Make an appointment in your calendar to come back to get to know this part (ideally with a trusted IFS therapist).

CHAPTER 8

BECOMING A SELF-LED MOTHER

*And that is the most important sign of a
"good mom" that there could be. One who
can mother themselves. One who can hold the
terrified crying child inside and allow her to
rage and shout. . . . Because we are all seeking
only that—our own inner parent
to love and accept us as we are.*

—RACHEL PLATTEN

WHAT DOES IT MEAN to be a Self-led mom? We all have a Self, the word Dick Schwartz uses to describe the essence within each of us that is not a part but is our core energy that is itself a healing agent for our change and transformation.

Self helps us heal and live more consciously. It's never damaged or broken, no matter what we've experienced in life. It is never bitter or judgmental, abusive or jealous. Self is the essence of our Divine energy. You might want to call it something other than Self, and that's totally fine. Many traditions and contemplative practices have words to describe what I perceive as the same thing: Buddha-nature, Allah, God, Spirit, the Divine. I think the "Soul" (or as Liz Gilbert points out to her Substack followers, "The Spirit of Unconditional Love") fits nicely, and I use it interchangeably with Self. In IFS, we also say the degree a person has "Self-energy," because the reality is we are rarely, if ever, fully in Self. Rather, because we are made of many parts that help us function and take on different roles in our lives, it's usually a matter of how much Self-energy you have rather than being either in Self or in parts. Feel free to use these words or whatever word fits for you as you come to recognize and know this essence within yourself.

As one IFS lead trainer and author Jeanne Catanzaro put it, "Our parts are to the Self as the clouds are to the sun," meaning that our Self is always there, only obstructed when our parts blend with us and take over the wheel of our experience. When blended with our protector parts, we are cut off from the core wisdom that is within Self-energy. When in Self, we experience flow, ease, and access to the wisest part of our being.

THE 8 CS OF SELF FROM INTERNAL FAMILY SYSTEMS

How do you know when you're in Self-energy? According to Dick and his decades of developing IFS, there are eight key qualities or characteristics that help identify and characterize Self. They're known as "the 8 Cs" (from *Internal Family Systems*, 2nd ed.).

Curiosity. There is no room for judgment and protection when we are curious. Curiosity opens possibilities and allows for safety and invitation to what's more vulnerable—to what might be hiding or feeling too scared to reveal itself. Curiosity carries no judgment and genuinely wants to understand a part or another person's parts and experience.

Calm. Self is a state of true equanimity, able to tolerate the ups and downs or inner stormy seas of emotions—riding the waves, if you will—with a deep trust and knowing that this too shall pass. The Self can flow with life with a deeper sense that "all is okay." Calmness is grounded and centered, having a gentle and strong presence and steadiness in all situations.

Clarity. Self carries clarity of view because it's not tainted by the extreme beliefs and emotions of protector parts. Distorted perceptions arise from inner protectors; therefore, when we are in Self-energy, we are better able to see our own and others' strong reactions as just that: frightened inner children.

Compassion. The natural arising of the energy of the heart that is compassion comes when we're able to accept and get some space from our inner protector parts, the ones that feel angry or frightened. "I feel bad for" the little exiled part is a common expression when going inside to connect with our parts. According to Dick, compassion isn't something we need to train in; rather, it is a natural state and energy within each of us. Seeing the oneness in each of us and our parts facilitates this opening of compassion. We feel for and long to ease the suffering of ourselves—our parts and others in Self.

Creativity. Artists and athletes speak of being in flow. Noting how some of the greatest ideas come out of mental quiet and spaciousness that can only occur in the suspension of fear, worthlessness, and shame (our burdens) speaks to the aspect of creativity that arises from Self. When the inner protectors are quieted, there is often the arising of creative and innovative ideas and inspiration, or knowing what's the right next step, better than any inner achieving part can strive for or hustle to reach.

Connected. Awareness of our interconnectedness—that we are one—arises from Self. This is where IFS has what some describe as "spirituality" or "spiritual elements" within the model. Some might use words like the Divine, Loving Awareness, Universe, or Spirit, but it's the awareness of yourself as not a separate individual but connected to the larger world in which you live. Tapping into the Great Mystery will embolden you, ground you into something larger and more resourced than yourself, and from there, you will access your power to mother from your deep wisdom.

Courage. The courage aspect of Self-energy emulates our inner strength—our capacity to assert and protect in a healthy way in the face of injustice. Courageous energy from Self allows us to face our fears and forge ahead with dignity and integrity, not from a controlling or aggressive place that can arise out of fear that our inner protectors carry. We have the capacity to redefine what it means to be strong. Strong does not mean suppressing our vulnerability—quite the opposite. When we meet our exiles in their darkest and most vulnerable places and help release them and heal, we are courageous. We are rewarded with greater courage in showing up for ourselves in this way. We begin to live as our own inner champion.

Confidence. Confidence arises in Self-energy, as from this place the slights, reactivities, and bitter resentments of inner protectors are calmed while the deep and vulnerable pain that exiles carry is witnessed, validated, and unburdened. This process provides confidence within from our inner protectors to trust the Self to lead and respond. With each expanding sense of trust in the Self to lead, we find more ease, centeredness, sturdiness, and alignment with our heart's intentions.

Each of the Cs is interrelated and connected, and each one can itself be a gateway into more Self-energy in your system. For instance, if I do some breathwork practice, this will likely help my body shift into homeostasis, relaxing my nervous system and allowing me to experience more calm. From there, I am likely more receptive to gaining clarity on something, getting some space from some of the louder inner protectors, getting curious about my experience or the person I'm interacting with, and perhaps even feeling my heart open with more compassion.

In her book *Beyond Anxiety*, Martha Beck encourages that the antidote for a fear-based mindset and experience of anxiety is to focus on creativity and curiosity. Using the language of IFS, Beck's theory is about accessing Self-energy to help us shift out of anxious states (or parts), as curiosity and creativity are both C words to describe Self.

Of course, there are more qualities and adjectives to describe Self-energy, such as perspective, joy, patience, kindness, gratitude, playfulness, equanimity, and certainly love. The 8 Cs were created as a mnemonic as part of the IFS model to help us all learn and access Self-energy more easily.

Realistically, the degree to which we can live from this energy of the 8 Cs may be only possible by living as a monk in a hermitage far away (and even then, maybe it's not so easy). Daily life, parenting life especially, is incredibly demanding. The hustle and busyness of our modern schedules with kids usually mean living from our competent inner-manager parts who are skilled at getting shit done and staying on course to either survive or hopefully thrive.

I believe one of the main reasons parenting is the hardest job is that we feel tossed around internally; we are emotionally triggered and activated by our unresolved wounds and traumas. We are driven by protectors who've taken on unrealistic standards inspired by myths that are impossible to meet while being tasked with a never-ending to-do list ranging from the mundane to important responsibilities and roles. Our many managerial parts help us function in the busyness of daily tasks, so slowing down, having an awareness of our inner world as we interact with our outer world, and being more conscious and intentional with our parenting can be hard.

Each of us wants to be a calm, collected parent. We'd love to have time for our creativity to arise and evolve, and we strive to be a courageous leader—or, as Dr. Becky Kennedy says, a "sturdy leader"—in those tough moments, infused with deep clarity, confidence, and calm. We know we have compassion somewhere in there if we only had the time to stop and reflect on our moments with curiosity. But often, in the context of our overscheduled, digitized, noisy modern world, we are racing from one to-do to the next, and our energy is conserved unconsciously by our inner worker parts that have taken us this far in life.

I'm not saying it's easy or that it won't require some intention and reprioritizing of your time and how you value your emotional and psychological health, but you don't need to wait until your kids are out of the house (or at least way more self-sufficient) to do some healing and to access more Self-energy in your life. I know it's possible because I've done it. I'm grateful that I prioritized my healing. I'll have fewer regrets to contend with down the road because I've begun the healing work of turning inward to get to know my parts and develop a relationship with them from Self.

My relationships with my kids improved tremendously when I began practicing IFS, and my understanding of my inner reactivity along the journey of motherhood helped me find acceptance and self-compassion in ways that calmed the inner turmoil I was feeling that was making me resent and—at times—hate motherhood.

You don't need massive chunks of time to begin to tend to your-self. Start now, right where you are, and you will quickly see the benefits of understanding and connecting with your inner system in this way. You will never regret taking time for your own healing, which we know can only benefit your children and your family. In the words of author and podcast host Erica Djossa, "The best thing you can do for your children is do your own healing."

HOW DO WE PARENT FROM SELF?

In a nutshell: The more we heal and unburden our exiled parts, allowing our protector parts to step out of their extreme roles, the more space we create to live in harmony with all our parts working together. This brings us more fully into our bodies, deepens our con-nection to our inner wisdom, and aligns us with the truth of who we really are.

The more we do our inner healing work and unburden our exiles that carry the burdens and pain in our psyche, the more our pro-tectors trust us to live from Self—the wisest, purest essence of our true Self unburdened by traumas, wounds, and needs for armoring in self-protection. When we heal and release our exiled parts, our precious protectors can also unburden and unhook from their rigid roles to enliven their natural gifts and talents. We no longer react from child parts, and we have more energy freed up that is aligned with our natural gifts and talents. We are healthier, less reactive, and whole.

And this healing work is a journey. There is a map informed by the IFS process, and there is also spaciousness and room for our own inner wise woman to intuit what she needs for healing. We come at the work in many ways with many tools we can resource ourselves along the healing journey. It is a uniquely personal deconditioning and transformation process.

The following suggestions include IFS-informed methods that can help you mother from Self as well as other practices, tools, and approaches that I personally found helpful. There is no one way, but hopefully you will find something here to help you begin—from wherever you are on your healing journey.

STOP AND U-TURN

I hope that by now you have a sense of how the IFS process works to help you change your relationship with your inner protectors to create more self-understanding, more inner trust and confidence, and more compassion both for yourself and your kiddos.

We don't need to live in self-protection mode for our entire life. It's possible to live with more consciousness and with more Self-energy: We need only begin to turn inward, and regularly, to get to know the inner parts that are taking over the wheel in our life. We can't push away our parts, but we can get to know them. They are waiting for us to try. They are excited to relinquish their roles and be freed up to express and live as they were meant to—if they hadn't needed to brace for the traumas of life.

Building a consistent and trusting relationship with your parts, like all relationships, happens by following through with attention, interest, and commitment. As you learn about your parts, regularly checking in with them and assuring them you care and that you're listening and validating them will give you the inner building blocks to gain their trust. A daily morning meditation to connect with your inner system can be tremendously helpful here.

I also recommend practicing the four steps I've found to be the quickest and best way to check yourself. They're explained in a short acronym: **HEAL: Halt** and go inward, **Explore** what part(s) is here, **Ask** what it's afraid of or concerned about, and **Let** Self lead.

HEAL: 4 STEPS TO SELF

There are many day-to-day moments of parenting when life and kids will trigger you. The HEAL acronym is a helpful way to remember the steps to reconnect with Self in those times so that you can live and parent with more Self-energy.

The first step is always to notice your own inner system, which is only possible by pausing and having an awareness of what's happening for you on the inside. With practice and getting to know your inner parts, you may be able to have what's called a "dual awareness," meaning you can connect with your inner parts even when you are in an interaction with your child. Or, if you become very blended with a strong part, you may need to step away from the interaction. Tell your child you'll be back, but you need a minute or two to get space to practice HEAL and then return.

By following the steps of HEAL over and over, you'll shift the dynamics within your Self, which can positively impact your automatic reactivity. You will access more self-control, regulation, and conscious space to mindfully choose your responses in your life with the people who matter most to you, your children. Here are the four steps of HEAL:

H: Halt and go inside (do a U-turn—turn your attention inward, with eyes open or closed). In IFS, a U-turn, or *You-turn*, refers to the act of focusing on what is coming up for you inside your body and mind rather than focusing on what the other person is doing or what the external situation is. A mentor of mine describes the U-turn as a way of "reclaiming your psychological center of gravity." By turning our attention inward instead of what we usually do—which is focus on the other person and what they're doing, often blaming our reactions on their behavior and wanting them to change—we tune into what is coming up inside us, with curiosity and accountability. This is a freeing process of learning how to be okay without needing other people to be a certain way.

E: Explore what parts are active. This means to scan your body as you take a few conscious breaths and get curious to see what parts might be showing up. It may be an exile, but most often it will be a protector part that is activated. With an attitude of interest and openness, observe if any part is coming through in your thoughts, like a voice in your head, or it may be a strong or notable sensory sensation (e.g., tight throat, jitteriness all over your body, shaking knees). It may be a strong feeling or emotion that is coming through your body like a wave of energy. Sometimes we can sense a part outside our body, like sitting above our head or on our shoulder to the left or right (e.g., think of the popular notion of the angel and the devil on your shoulders). Just note who is there and listen for a moment as the observer of your part or parts.

A: Ask the part(s) what it is afraid of or concerned about that is being triggered in the current moment. For example, mornings in my household have been challenging this year with three teens. No one seems to want to get out of bed and get to school on time. I am familiar with a manager part that becomes very frustrated. I notice that with each additional "Wake up!" my tone gets sharper with my kids, and sometimes I start uttering desperate threats. When I do HEAL, I quickly check in with the manager part and see why she's getting so riled up. She will let me know she is frustrated because if these kids keep being late, that means they're not self-disciplined enough and not likely to function well enough and this lands on being my fault. Quickly I can see how this manager part is invested in my reputation and not wanting to feel like I'm not doing a good enough job as a mom (both wanting to know my kids have life skills and to be honest also wondering why I can't seem to get them to school on time and other moms can).

Our parts may have a fear similar or different to mine in this example. There can be many fears. Another way to find out what your part is concerned with is to ask what you are afraid might happen if you don't keep doing what you're doing (whether that's raising your voice, nagging, or whatever you think this part is doing or how it's showing up in this parenting moment).

L: Let Self be in the lead. After validating the part's concerns, you will be able to address its fears. Usually what they're fearing is something based on your past experience, such as in childhood, and is not relevant in the moment. What do they need from you to give space and let Self lead? You might let it know, "I see you and I get it. But right now, I got this." Or you may ask it, "Can you give me some room to do this a different way, with more Self?" Offer a commitment to return when you have more time.

WHEN HEAL(ING) IS HARD

Understanding how HEAL can be helpful is easy and probably seems like common sense. Doing HEAL is not necessarily easy. Like creating habits in general, developing the habit of practicing HEAL will require many rounds and repetitions.

I want to make a note about what can feel like incongruence between the recommendation to use HEAL and the reality of doing it in your very busy daily life. When protector parts are active, they can be compelling. Like the energy of a Mama Bear who won't back down, this intensity and rigidity—the tunnel vision of a protector part—can be difficult to sway. For HEAL to work, for instance, you need first to halt. Sometimes stopping your mouth from moving can be the hardest part.

It can almost feel like we're trying to do the opposite action. Like when we're angry at someone, the last thing we want to do is give that person a hug. It feels too contradictory and almost unnatural. This is what it can feel like when a powerful manager or firefighter part is at the helm. They don't want to give up the wheel—because protector parts come from the mindset that they alone are the median between safety-survival and potential destruction-devastation. It feels like do-or-die to a protector, and if they haven't yet met Self and learned that you're there and willing and able to take over the helm, they will stand firm and strong at their post.

Practicing HEAL in the rubber-meets-the-road moments with your kids will be easier the more often you regularly take time each day to connect with your parts. A daily parts meditation helps build a foundation with your internal system so that when tricky parenting moments arise, it'll be easier to HEAL. This may only be a five- to ten-minute meditation, or perhaps one minute three times each day to make the U-turn to pivot your attention inward and say, *Hey, who's there? I see you, I'm here. I love you* (if you're able to say that to the part).

Another huge challenge for moms in doing their healing in the busy, task-filled days of modern-day parenting. Rushed from one activity to the next, filling the spare moments with laundry and meal prep, school e-mails, phone calls, and errands make it difficult to slow down and go inside. It's then typically from this hustle-bustle energy that we respond to our children and their expressions of need.

A loving note, dear mama—

You might be thinking, *Yeah right! I'd love to have the privilege of time to sit and meditate or write in my journal. What a luxury I can only dream of now with one, two, or five kids at my toes!* I get it. And I also know that almost all of us can revisit how and where we spend our time and energy and find some time to devote to our inner healing. We may have resistant parts or firefighter parts that would rather zone out on television or social media. But be truly honest with yourself: Can you reconfigure even five to ten minutes each day for your emotional healing—to make even one small change in your life that can have profound ripple effects?

If HEAL seems too long or like too many steps in those tough moments, remember this: Dick Schwartz simply asks his parts, "Will you please let me [i.e., Self] do this? It always works out better when you do!" Asking permission from our protectors is a good and quick way to access more Self-energy. The more you practice, the more you connect with your parts, the easier this will become for you in these tricky parenting moments.

I've had many situations when I've tried to invite my protector parts to give me space. Sometimes the hardest moments for me have been when I become blended with an exiled part. I remember a recent visit with my mother, which is always fertile ground for triggers of deep attachment wounds. I was walking upstairs and trying to hold back the tears that were rising up like a fountain. With each step I took, I focused on my breath. I placed my hand on my heart and invited in the little exiled part that was flooded with sadness and just wanted to cry and sit on a swing for a while. That's it. Just like that, she knew I (Self) was there, and she was happy to swing for a while. Rather than unconsciously blocking or a firefighter jumping in to try to shut down the exile's pain, I could lovingly send her my care and kindness, inviting her to find a place to wait where she could safely hang out until I had more time and space to tend to her. By the time I was at the top of the staircase, I felt calm, centered, and more resourced to continue with my family visit and show up with more Self-energy for my kids.

Maybe some days you'll find the time to attend a therapy or coaching session. Maybe you can do it when you walk your dog, which you need to do anyway. Or maybe while you lay with your little one to support them getting to sleep at night. It's not easy and it may not be every day, but I guarantee that the attention you give to your inner system will pay you back tenfold. The energy that you will free up by befriending your inner protectors will open up new perspectives and strengths you didn't realize you had available. It doesn't have to be huge chunks of time to benefit. Start small. Start with one thing and, like with watering a bud, watch it grow.

PARTS MAPPING

Parts mapping is an exercise in writing down or drawing in any form of representation or medium what parts are here in the moment. You may close your eyes for a moment or two and then write out in words, images, symbols, or colors how your parts are speaking to you and revealing themselves.

I've found that parts mapping helps my parts feel acknowledged, and through the exercise I can very quickly feel more grounded. I often gain clarity in seeing the names my parts choose, and I can draw lines and arrows and see their interactions. For me, it can feel as though I've gained access to spaciousness simply by acknowledging and naming the parts that are inside by representing them on the page.

Not everyone will have the same experience. When I suggested parts mapping to one mom I worked with, Juliana, a married mom of three small kids with no family support, she expressed a fear of "putting things down" and seeing them in black and white. Grief from her father's death and many problematic family dynamics were exacerbating her already difficult phase of motherhood. I assured her to respect this part and listen to it. Sometimes there is a fear that exiles might flood through in such an exercise: These protectors may require more time and attention before venturing into an exercise that speaks or spells out emotions and thoughts. Trust your own pace and what's right for you. Experiment and see for yourself.

REPAIR

Dr. Becky Kennedy's 2023 TED Talk on the single most important parenting strategy, which has 2.4 million–plus views, focuses on repair. I've found that repairing with my kids can be a gateway to Self. Doing a repair means revisiting a disconnection that occurred, taking responsibility for your actions and behavior, and acknowledging the impact it may have had on the other person. Repairing is not only a gateway to connection, but when we demonstrate taking responsibility and offering a heartfelt and humble apology to our children when we react and act from our parts, it models how to speak *for* our parts rather than *from* them and how to be in Self. Repairing also helps us align with this energy to heal a rupture in our relationship with our kids.

A repair might sound like, "Sorry that I raised my voice there. That wasn't cool," or "I need to apologize for reacting like that. I shouldn't have done that. I'm sorry." I often use parts language with my kids to model this understanding of ourselves to them: With a calm voice from Self, I might say, "You know, I'm really sorry that I raised my voice. I had a very frustrated part that was feeling annoyed and trying to get some control. What was that like for you?"

When I've gone to my kids to admit I didn't do my best, they always seem happy to forgive me quickly. I can literally see their bodies soften and relax. They feel relieved. We both feel closer to each other and connected.

When I can repair, I take my child out of the murky territory where they might blame themselves for the issue or rupture. Kids are not good interpreters. They will often internalize whatever disconnection or argument happened: It must be because they did something wrong, or they're bad or unlovable. This is how our parts take on burdens in our childhood environments. It feels better to internalize and assume one's blame, giving a glimmer of hope for change and it's not Mom and Dad or the world that is unsafe and awful.

Noelle, one mom I interviewed, described how repair is her most valuable parenting intervention and helps her own parts in difficult moments:

> I take a step away from the situation so I can breathe, and I can access my Self, and I'm here now to at least then do the work … and maybe it doesn't get as internalized for them. When I can say, "I'm so sorry, it is my responsibility to work on it—and I'm trying to raise my voice less," or whatever it is I'm working on. When I'm open about it and I tell my kids, then that helps my perfect parts or my critical parts ease up a bit, because they're like, okay, if anything, you are able to repair so that maybe things aren't internalized as deeply that they can make another narrative out of it.

Repairing with our kids shows a model of accountability and imperfection. It demonstrates to our kiddos that we aren't perfect, showing them that it's okay that they also make mistakes—they too can learn the art and magic of repair. No one needs to carry shame and feelings of unworthiness because of acting out from their parts. We can help our protectors disarm and connect again with one another from Self.

I love Noelle's explanation to her three kids that she shared with me that models what I'm talking about. She said when she realized she was carrying her resentments and frustrations with her husband over into parenting her kids, she recognized it and simply said to them, "I'm gonna do better. There are things that make me frustrated, and they have absolutely nothing to do with you. So, you shouldn't have to receive that from me. I'm going to do better."

I've gotten pretty good at apologizing to my kids, and honestly, it's saved me many times from going down the shame spiral. I don't overapologize. I'm not suggesting you apologize from a part that feels unworthy and diminished. What I'm talking about is an apology that occurs after you've calmed down some, after gaining clarity about being taken over by a part that had a strong reaction. You can see that a part inside snapped or yelled, was critical, or shamed your child in a way that was not intentional or conscious, but you were triggered and blended. An inner protector swooped in, and in these moments your protector perceived your child as some sort of threat or as something to control. The protector doesn't have the where-withal to even know who that is—that that is your child and you are a grown-up. The protector acts and reacts. That's it's job. Most of our protector parts have been doing their jobs for a long time. It's automatic, self-protective (hello, fight-flight-or-freeze), and it sucks when we see we were hijacked. But this is what it's like being human.

It can be hard for us to own our errors. Most of us have strong inner protectors who like to defend—who strive to ward off shame at all costs. Maybe some parents believe it's giving in or it feels too vulnerable to show your child your imperfection. There might be fear that acknowledging your errors to your child will result in your son or daughter using them against you down the road. This belief might even come from experiences in your early life, and this is where one of your protectors got its data: in real life, in the past. Maybe you learned it's not safe to be that vulnerable.

In this case, I encourage you to get curious. Get to know the part that carries this belief and help it heal and release the past. Help it see that you are now grown. Give them an update on the current circumstances so they see who the players are. They're not the same, and the game has changed. Trust me—learning to repair and apologize to your child will be a miracle salve that will not only bring you more into your Self in difficult parenting moments, but it will model to your child how to do the same. I agree with Dr. Becky: Repairing is the single most important skill for parenting—or any relationship.

BE EMBODIED

One gateway to accessing Self is through the body. You might do this through breathing exercises, movement (e.g., yoga, tai chi, hiking), a mindfulness body scan meditation, or other ways that bring you into your body, like dancing, being in nature, walking on the grass with bare feet, or playing an instrument. Stephanie shared with me how she accesses Self when she most needs it:

> My go-to, in terms of accessing Self-energy, is to go outside because I often find that my system feels trapped by motherhood in some ways and this offers me some perspective. You know, because you're responsible entirely for this other human depending on you. So, especially if I'm alone with him and if we've been in the house all day. We literally put our bare feet in the grass. That's a practice that I'm teaching him, like, go walk in the grass. My wife taught him to pick dandelions, so he likes to blow those and then we play bubbles. Then we're both a little more regulated.

Practice being in your body. Heighten your awareness as you step up each stair or down the hallway (the many thousands of times you go up and down or back and forth each day). Maybe it's at the park when you're pushing your kiddo in the swing. Allow your breath to ground you in more presence and see if, for even a few moments, you can just be present and aware in your body. You might ask your parts inside to give you some space. *Just for three breaths, may I please just be here now in my body?* Notice what happens.

There are many reasons it can be challenging to stay present in your body. As a society, we prefer rationality (mind) over the body, and we've lost our way. Many of us live in our heads much of the time, and it might feel like retraining your attention to come back inside: *Come back down into my torso-buttocks-feet.*

If you've experienced any physical or sexual abuse, your body can feel like an especially unsafe place. Avoidance of being in the body can, for many trauma survivors, be an adapted way of survival. Coming back to being more fully present in the body can take time, patience, and healing.

I encourage you to experiment with this gateway to Self. Any of our senses can serve as a helpful bridge to being more present and embodied. Try aromatherapy or scented candles, drink a lovely cup of tea, or look out at a beautiful sunset (if you live near water, enjoy its view). Notice the comfort under a weighted blanket or enjoy the sounds of classical piano—whatever works for you.

Experiment to see what helps you be more fully present in your body as you invite your inner protectors to trust that it's safe and okay to be awake and aware there. Maybe try now: Take one slow, deep breath in through your nose, and one long exhale out your mouth. What do you notice? Who is doing the noticing?

CONNECTION AND COMMUNITY

When we are in Self, we feel connection; we don't feel the isolation and aloneness that many of our parts carry. Witnessing others' vulnerability can often activate our compassion—the stirring of the heart that naturally wishes for the well-being of others. In my experience, a gateway to feeling moved with compassion and feeling less alone is in a group or community—being in connection with others.

For some people, feeling compassion for others becomes an opening to more compassion toward themselves.

Now, not all groups or communities feel safe, so there's a caveat to recognizing the potential for accessing Self-energy with and through the company of others. In fact, I found that my experience in many groups was a triggering context for many of my parts. I couldn't feel open, calm, or compassionate because I found many of my inner protectors were at the ready—fearing others' judgment and rehearsing my own performance to ensure I would avoid harm, rejection, or judgment. I would feel exposed and insecure.

I was curious to make sense of my reactivity in different groups. Eventually, I realized that Self is available to us in very safe and supportive groups. There's no guarantee your protectors will step back, but I noticed that when I was in the company of women with energies and intentions of support, nonjudgment, and receptivity, then my parts relaxed and I could feel more Self.

Because finding your right tribe is so important, it's given the space it warrants in the next chapter.

LISTEN: TAKE IN FEEDBACK

One of the less pleasant places to notice an entryway to Self is in listening to others' feedback, especially your kids'. Your children will let you know—often in not-so-gentle terms nor in the ways you'd like—when you're speaking from a part and not Self.

For example, Noelle described how she realized she was not in Self-energy after hearing her kids' comments on how "grumpy" she was acting with them. She listened to their feedback, though difficult to hear, and worked hard to not become defensive. She recognized the truth in their experiences, and she realized she had been allowing the resentment and frustrations in her marriage to project out onto her moments with her children. Listening to them helped her shift out of protector mode—and from Self, she acknowledged her children's experiences, which further helped the trust and connection in their relationship. She then had the clarity and courage to take these feelings to her husband to address, reducing the risk that her kids would assume her burdens.

For me, it's been when my kid would just say—or even yell— "STOP!" during one of my rants. He eventually learned to use softer language, but at that age, this was his way of letting me know what he needed—he was overwhelmed and couldn't keep listening to me. I noticed quickly I was in a protector part because it was very difficult to respect his request. My manager "lecturer mommy" part didn't want to stop, even though I knew he'd had enough—and it's okay for him to feel that way. Realizing a part of me just didn't want to stop talking, I had to use HEAL to address this internal reaction.

Though I hate to admit it, for a period I was getting the same feedback from everyone in my family. With many family members, there was little room for my part that wanted to talk and talk and talk. I kept feeling silenced and stifled. This was pissing me off, so I had to go inside to figure out what was happening.

Working with this part, I was able to see this was most definitely a manager part who was trying to gain control in the house, and it was protecting a vulnerable exile who didn't feel heard in my childhood family. The youngest and quietest "good girl" in a family of loud and talkative people who constantly interrupted others, I had a part that felt ignored and that no one listened to, which this young part interpreted as rejection and believing she was unlovable (not important enough to pay attention to). Once I connected to this vulnerable part and was able to give her the care and attention she craved—like listening to her and valuing what she had to say—I felt much better. I had a lot of compassion toward this chatty part that really wanted to be seen and heard. She was trying to control things for my best intentions, but it was creating little ruptures with my family and leaving me away from the connection and belonging I craved.

I thanked this part for working so hard to be heard and understood—to not be invisible like the little girl felt. And I committed to her that when people in my family have had their limit, I will always listen to her. After telling her this, she instantly softened and no longer felt like she needed to rant and rave! She also no longer felt hurt, as from Self I could see clearly there was no ill will coming from my husband and kids. No one was trying to ignore me or dismiss me—as this part had sometimes felt and had created a narrative around (i.e., burden), given my childhood experiences.

This new understanding and dialogue I had from Self to this chatty part were transformational. Since connecting with her, I've been much more highly attuned to my children's and my husband's limits to my chatty part. Rather than this being a negative development, now my chatty part no longer needs to vent to them as she feels connected to me and is heard, understood, and welcomed into my heart.

When we feel disconnected from our children's reactions to us and are mainly concerned with managing, controlling, coaching them, and herding their behavior, as opposed to listening to them, hearing them, and being curious and open with them, this is a clue that we are parenting from a part. When you notice this, send that part some love. Try HEAL (Halt and go inside, Explore parts, Ask about its concerns, and Let Self lead).

SPIRITUALITY

I didn't grow up religious, but I always sensed myself as a spiritual being. As a child, I was drawn to existential questions and wondered about life, identity, and something greater that brings purpose to this human experience. I was drawn to meditation and mindfulness in a way that turning inward in stillness and silence felt like coming home.

My belief in being guided, held, and supported by unseen forces—ones I can feel, trust, and connect with through my energy and devotional practices—has carried me through matrescence, especially during times of challenge and crisis when I felt I had no remaining options. Faith and trust in something greater than me and my family—that connects us all—have provided a bedrock of support and guidance in the dark passageways of my forest walk of motherhood.

Whatever bridge to faith and trust you have or can find, I encourage you to nourish it. Maybe you have a tradition of religion or formalized faith and community. Perhaps you're like me and you've been drawn to your own resonance, connecting more with the term *mystic* or *seeker*. Or maybe you view yourself as agnostic or are new to the idea that there is a source beyond what we see that connects us all.

My meditation teacher, Jack Kornfield, described how heads of different faiths came together to discuss their traditions, seeking to find a unified language for the varied beliefs and contemplative practices of different peoples. The term on which they all could agree was the *Great Mystery*. Self-energy and the state of being connected and calm, with clarity of view, compassion, courage, confidence, creativity, and curiosity, are in line with this same energy—a source in which we all share and are connected.

Whatever words fit for you or are gateways to feel a deeper presence, awareness, and connectedness to something grander, I encourage you to recognize this source as a resource for you. It might be God or Christ, consciousness, Allah, or Buddha. Maybe, like me, you refer to your Spirit Guides. Perhaps it's nature. For many people, walking or sitting in nature has healing qualities that are hard to put into words. Maybe it's from spending time with your pet. Wherever you feel a deep presence and connection to a universal love, notice that.

Allow yourself permission to follow your own inclinations around this. Your Self—or what I've long called your *inner wise woman*—knows what she needs for healing. She will guide you to create this space in a way that has meaning for you. Do you have a spiritual or devotional practice that helps you connect with the Great Mystery?

HOLD IT LIGHTLY. IT'S A PRACTICE

It's not possible to always be in Self. We're designed with multiplicity for good reasons. Living a human life takes an inner village or committee. The real pathway to Self-led parenting involves an intention toward self-understanding, self-acceptance, and self-love. This comes about through turning inward and listening—getting curious about your inner reactions. Who's in there? What are their intentions? Is it possible to update them so they are more aligned with the here and now? Can we learn to collaborate and move forward in true service of our heart's desire—which is to lean in and savor our journey through motherhood?

It's a practice. It's a re-remembering and a coming back each time with curiosity, interest in your wounded or busy parts, and learning to love them all. What better modeling is that for our kiddos?

Now with a sense of different ways to accessing Self and working toward becoming a Self-led mom, let's dive deeper into why community matters. We can't do the work of healing alone. All the moms I've spoken to and worked with have at some point experienced the importance of connecting with other moms or other women. We can help one another grow and expand. Finding your village might be just the thing you need to help you get to that right next step toward your next level of expansion as a mother.

EXERCISE: LIST THE WAYS YOU ACCESS SELF-ENERGY

Explore for yourself where and how you best can access Self-energy. Take a few moments to pause, go inside, and reflect on the following questions (you may wish to write them in a journal):

- When do I most feel the 8 Cs (compassion, calm, curious, creative, confident, courageous, clarity, and connected)? Where am I? What am I doing when I most feel the 8 Cs?

- Try one of the practices listed in this chapter. Use it as an experiment. Maybe jot down in your journal how you felt before the exercise, what parts were there, and then how you felt after the practice. What did you notice?

- Keep a list of where you access Self and what helps you to do so. Refer to the list when you feel blended or taken over by parts.

CHAPTER 9
FINDING YOUR VILLAGE

Rarely, if ever, are any of us healed in isolation.
Healing is an act of communion.

—BELL HOOKS

THE SAYING "IT TAKES A VILLAGE" stems from truth. Raising children is not an easy job. No single person—even a mother—can or should be expected to meet all the needs of her child. We used to live in communities—not digital ones, real ones. In agricultural times, we'd have aunts, sisters, grandmothers, and friends share in childcare responsibilities. If a mama needed a minute, several people were available to help her.

I'm not sure where the myth that a good mother does it alone came from, but it reeks of patriarchal roots that pigeonhole mothers to feel isolated and judged when they inevitably need others at some point. Many times my mother-in-law saved me in a pinch, like the time my husband signed up our son for a hockey camp, only to have him suit up and fall on his face on the ice. He couldn't skate, and the camp was for hockey players. I got the call not twenty minutes after dropping off all my kids to camp while I headed to work, and my husband was out of town: "We recommend your son attend the learn-to-skate program. Can you please come and pick him up now?" Luckily, Nana was home and able to scoop him up so that at least that day I didn't have to declare yet another absence from work and cancel all my clients. Looking back now, I think I needed—and would have loved to have had—even more help. The problem is, because of the myth of the good mother, I felt guilty every time I asked.

Myths of the good mother are transmitted subtly and indirectly. Some mothers ensure that when their kids have babies (i.e., their grandchildren), they'll help out in ways that they didn't get. Other grandmas might take on the attitude, "Well, I didn't have any help, so why should you?" We continue to judge mothers for their fortitude to go it alone and praise them for their island-esque capacities. But the truth is that no mother can go it alone—not without detriment to her emotional, physical, and psychological well-being.

It's not just family members who judge mothers who reach for help. Sadly, even those in the healthcare field perpetuate dismissive attitudes and judgment when a mother can't do it alone. One mom I worked with, Juliana, shared that after months of trying to care for her toddler and newborn twins without the benefits of family or friends nearby, her mental health was so diminished that she was experiencing signs of paranoia, insomnia, and near total mental breakdown. Finally opening up to her OB/GYN, she was countered with harsh and uncompassionate words infused with the myth of the good mother: "Did you think it was going to be *easy* having a toddler and twin newborns?" As if somehow her struggling was her lack of being mentally prepared for the chaos that awaited her having twins.

The notion "You wanted this" is steeped in patriarchal criticism, implying that a good mother should never need help—that since she chose this path, she should be ready and equipped to handle it herself. It also gets male partners off the hook from stepping up and helping with child-rearing and parenting responsibilities—keeping them in the "I'll do what I want to, not all that is required" category.

This absurd idea forces mothers to blame themselves and feel ashamed when they inevitably realize it's impossible to meet all the expectations. The only way a mother can do it all alone is by completely depleting herself, causing unintended harm to her well-being and that of her children.

Some communities, often hospitals or early education groups, cater to this gap for moms. New mom groups can be super helpful spaces for mothers to experience support, belonging, and care at a time when often only the infants are getting TLC. Many moms I've spoken with have shared how profoundly helpful their early mom groups were. In Sarah Cassidy's book *Swaddled*, a compilation of mother's stories of matrescence, one mom described her moms' group this way:

> My new support group at the hospital ended up taking care of me. The ladies were like an outsourced and collective parenting partner, diminishing the loneliness in my marriage and in my early motherhood. I was hooked after the second meeting. I knew that I wouldn't be besties with every one of the women; that wasn't the goal. The instant and mutual respect we developed and held for each other was a great gift, and I'll always believe that that group saved me. It allowed me an awakening around what it meant and what it was like for me to be a mother. I was no longer alone.

A mom to two kids who were now in their twenties, Lisa was answering many of my questions in hindsight. When I asked what helped her the most during those years of motherhood, she said, "Groups of women":

> Throughout being a mom, what helped a lot was having
> support. I was in a mom's group for ten years, and before that
> I had a book club with women for ten years. So, I've always
> had a consistent group of moms. I have my friends, but there's
> something about the witnessing, I think, that happens in
> groups, even though it wasn't a parenting group per se. Check-
> ins and support from other moms really helped my part that
> wanted to be perfect. Like, in group witnessing I realized that
> no one's perfect, and so that part could probably relax a little
> over the years that I don't have to be perfect. I got perspective.
> I had all this empathy for the other moms, so, yeah, I was able
> to have more compassion for myself. That was really big.

When I hear from moms about how they had support, com- radery, and community in a mothers' group in those early years, honestly, I feel jealous. Maybe it's more like a loss, because although I tried, I didn't quite find my tribe when my kids were young. I had three maternity leaves in a city my husband grew up in, so I knew no one. I tried to connect with a couple of moms who were the wives of his childhood friends, but nothing clicked. I went to Mommy and Me groups in the community, but outside of the teacher facilitating songs and stories for our babies, I'd leave feeling more alone, having not made any new connections. Eventually I stopped going.

Maybe it's because I lean toward being an introvert. I can only take so much small talk, and the moms I would try to chat with would talk mostly about their babies, schedules, sleeping, gas, and colic. I felt like I got that information online. I wanted to have real conversations: I craved a conversation where we could talk about how we missed our work, how we felt resistance to scheduling our entire day around the nap schedule of an infant. I wanted to have a hearty laugh and know that I wasn't alone. I think most of the moms I met were all just in survival mode, or maybe just navigating alongside one another and unsure of how to drop the mask of perfection.

In later years I found solace, support, and—on some level—salvation when I joined a parent support group. During one of the hardest times of my life and parenting, this group of moms who got it helped me feel like I had a life raft. I could breathe and carry on, with more compassion in my heart, tools in my belt, and my knowledge that I can do this. My shame and self-blame melted upon hearing from other moms who were going through similar challenges with their kids. The weight came from navigating a situation with little support and understanding—it wasn't the kid, and it wasn't the mom. This was like a salve for a wound that was worsening with each self-critical thought I carried. I felt Self-energy come through sharing our experiences that were different from many parents. There was a communal feeling of understanding, care, and zero judgment. Feeling less alone and understood was like filling my gas tank, ready to keep going another week, until we would meet again.

Not every group needs to be deep. What each mom wants and needs from the group is unique to her. As an introvert grappling with changes in matrescence that I didn't understand, I longed for other, more extraverted moms to speak out and share how hard it is. I was tired of focusing on my babies and my whole world becoming all about schedules and feedings. But other moms thrived talking about all the details. As an example, recall Rachel. She shared this about connecting with other moms:

> I definitely have mom friends who I don't have a lot in
> common with besides our babies, but we still help each other
> out. And so, I would say, people could be open-minded. Even
> if someone's not your friend, having some people who are just
> mom friends, I think, is actually good. There can be different
> levels of friendship.

THE SISTER WOUND

Whether it's making new mom friends or joining a mom's group, some women feel cautious or hesitant to connect with other moms due to past experiences with other women. Some refer to it as the "sister wound." The sister wound is theorized as any distrust that's derived from emotional pain from relationships with other women, often from early life experiences of rejection, judgment, or humiliation from girls (including friends). It manifests in feelings of jealousy, insecurity, fear, and discomfort, and a desire to compare.

Sadly, many women have received the most judgment, shaming, and rejection from other moms, whether in person or online, mothers-in-law, sisters, colleagues, fellow church members, friends, and strangers—everywhere women are policing the "shoulds," the mother-blaming, the myths of the good mother.

You might wonder why women relate to one another this way. In-fighting among women can be traced back to the days of the witch hunts. The rise of the Catholic Church, which coincided with the male-dominated scientific revolution and medical movement in the fifteenth to the eighteenth centuries, led to the dismantling of the system wherein the community trusted and relied on the women in villages who were often the ones people went to for guidance and help—the healers, the medicine women, and the midwives. They were given the label "spinster," becoming socially and culturally reprimanded, with many killed under the guise of religious and patriarchal ideologies.

Women trusting other women and gathering in groups were and still are a threat to patriarchy. One sure way to diminish the power of those who are oppressed is to divide them. Better yet, inspire them to divide and compete against one another. We perceive other women as a threat to us and believe we have to compete with other women for attention, power, relationships, jobs, and social status.

Backstabbing, gossiping, and using sexist and derogatory language against one another, like *slut, whore, cunt,* and *bitch,* continue this alienation from one another and keep us women feeling small, staying safe to avoid being targeted ourselves, and becoming untrusting of one another. As Tina Fey's character says in her film *Mean Girls,* "You all have got to stop calling each other sluts and whores. It just makes it okay for guys to call you sluts and whores."

Being on the receiving end of mean girls hurts, and it leads to feeling like women aren't your sisters in the struggle but are a source of pain and oppression, leaving us further isolated and lost from feeling and experiencing a sisterhood of support. If we can't trust one another and have one another' backs, then we are divided and unable to access our full power and potential as women.

Using an IFS lens on the sister wound, we might see that women who judge and shame others are acting from a protector part. The harsh, judgmental, and shaming part that judges other moms is likely internalizing the same critical messaging inside herself. As you hopefully have come to understand from reading this far, our protectors have our best interests in mind, and most of them learned their strategies at a very young age. Being a bully or the judge and jury of others likely comes from a manager part that is trying to prevent that mom from experiencing pain and keep her safe in some way based on her past experiences. The narrative of competing against other women might also be a cultural legacy burden that, on some level, we've all absorbed, as seen in the ways we continue to pit women against one another and put up shields against trusting.

Consider the pop culture representations of this in news stories and social media sites that seem to obsess over "cat fights" between celebrity women. Or the witch hunt that can occur when groupthink decides that a celebrity should be canceled. There's been a rampant obsession online with judging and gossiping about Jennifer Lopez. There are tons of TikToks trashing JLo, talking about how much of a diva she is, how rude (not a nice girl), and how awful. Perhaps this woman has behaved rudely to people—but can you imagine any such groupthink hunt that would accuse a man of "being rude"? Powerful men across time have behaved in aggressive and "rude" ways and have never been criticized for "not being nice."

We have all absorbed the cultural and societal ideas passed on from generations that diffuse the power of women in groups. Calling girls in high school "sluts" was nothing more than diminishing a girl based on sexist ideologies that propagate the control of women, their bodies, and the extent of their power.

While IFS helps us understand ourselves and navigate matrescence with greater insight into our parts, it also helps us make sense of other people's reactions and behaviors. When a sister is behaving aggressively, harshly, or even in an attacking or bullying way, we know she is not acting in Self-energy but she is blended with a strong protector.

Given that our parts are often from childhood, it's not surprising that they can make us act like children, behaving in immature and sometimes unkind ways. When a dog's paw is caught in a trap, the dog barks and bites. It doesn't calmly allow you to help it get the paw unstuck. The same can be considered when we see our spouse, children, or other women behave in unkind ways. They are behaving as though some part inside feels caught in a trap—or is anticipating a trap. As the saying goes, "Hurt people hurt people." There is great wisdom in these four words.

Even with this more compassionate understanding of others' behaviors, thanks to understanding that all of us are made up of parts, that doesn't mean we need to accept their behaviors toward us. But it gives us a lens to make sense of our own parts when triggered by others' actions. For instance, if you had a negative or emotionally painful experience with girlfriends—say, being rejected by a friend or suddenly ousted from a group with no explanation (which seems to happen often for girls)—you will likely have an exiled part that carries the pain. If you couldn't process that in childhood or adolescence when it happened, your parts would have organized around this experience in a way to make you more vigilant, cautious, and protective in future interactions with women.

If you feel activated in groups of women, or if you avoid them entirely because of fear or a lack of trust, in IFS this situation would be considered a *trailhead*. Recall, a trailhead is a strong emotional reaction that introduces you to a part that was beyond your awareness. Trailheads can feel unsettling. We might wonder why we had such a big reaction to someone. But getting activated is a good thing because it offers an opportunity to get to know a part—to make the U-turn and investigate what part is reacting so strongly and why. It's a window into an opportunity for healing.

Some process groups and IFS groups are designed to help group members curate intentional and powerful healing with the understanding that they can speak for their parts and process the pain that's been suppressed. Learning to speak *for* your parts instead of *from* your parts (e.g., when blended) is a key IFS skill that is encouraged with couples and in relationships. When we are blended with our protectors, we lose our access to Self, which means we're less capable of using the skills that are often needed for productive, connecting communication.

It can be really hard to stay in Self when someone is coming at us from their protector part. But the sister wound is just that—a belief system over generations that pits women against one another. We each have the power to heal the sister wound and learn to support other women rather than tearing them down. Participating in a mothers' group may be the best context in which to heal ourselves and the sister wound.

Women's circles that are created with the safety of the space as a priority can give ample opportunities for women to tell and hear one another's stories of vulnerability. Understanding that the mom who may appear so confident and all together also struggles with perfectionism or feels fear and insecurity like you do has real potential to dismantle the veil that lives between us women.

Compassion is the antidote to shame, and curiosity is the antidote to judgment. When we get close to learning about and seeing the vulnerability in others, our hearts open and sometimes this is the key to being more compassionate and loving toward ourselves.

Shame wants us to hide, and in naming and being held with love and acceptance, we can be transformed. As the well-known shame researcher Brené Brown has said, "When we find the courage to share our experiences and the compassion to hear others tell their stories, we force shame out of hiding and end the silence." We each have the capacity to heal the sister wound or at least be part of its dismantling. We do this by showing up for one another, telling our stories, and practicing nonjudgment, curiosity, and compassion for other moms and ourselves.

SAFE SPACES

It might sound like I'm contradicting myself here, but I want to acknowledge that not all spaces will feel safe for telling your story. Yes, mothers' groups have the potential to be healing containers for all the members, but there are certain conditions—namely, that each of the group members shares the intention to dismantle the sister wound while learning to support and care for one another in matrescence.

Not everyone is self-aware or has the intention to work on themselves. Healing is probably the last thing on the minds of women in the New Mama group! That's understandable. It's also why I recommend facilitated groups. I may be biased as a circle facilitator, but I've had years of experience in groups as a participant and a leader. The groups that are successful are those in which members feel safe enough. There needs to be enough Self-energy for our parts to relax and open up. There also needs to be a leader or a facilitator who can help contain the space and ensure safety for everyone.

Rupture and pain can occur in a space where certain protector behaviors go unaddressed. It wouldn't be safe for our vulnerable parts to be acknowledged and healed in a space where there is judgment. I know the pain or discomfort of opening up with someone who doesn't respond with understanding. I bet you do too. They may mean well, they may think they have your best interests at heart, but a manager part who wants to give you advice because they think they've got it figured out is not the response a vulnerable mama wants. She wants to be listened to and held in presence, in Self. She wants to feel like you get it, or even if you haven't had the same experience, that you care. You are listening, not solving anything for her.

You have the right to be discerning in who you share your story with. It makes perfect sense to be cautious and reserved until more trust is built. It takes time to earn trust and evidence that someone is trustworthy. Your protector parts will need to see evidence that it's okay to share more and be more vulnerable as time passes. This healing process is likelier to take place when a group has skillful facilitation. This might also mean finding a group with other women who share in your identity representation, or your racial or ethnic background, or a specific group that connects everyone together in some way (e.g., infertility groups).

Jamie O'Neal, founder of the Mom Walk Collective (MWC), stated that she's come to understand that moms want validation, they want permission to be; they want fellow cheerleaders to encourage and support them in their journeys to trust their own instincts and choices as a mom. She said moms are not really looking for advice or to be told what to do. They want to feel that they're not being judged and that they're affirmed by other women in the choices they make, helping them feel empowered. She started the Mom Walk after she was three months postpartum and feeling lonely and isolated. She started with two other women joining her on her first walk, and the MWC has grown to offer walking groups for moms across 350-plus cities. If you're looking to connect with other moms, check it out. Maybe they have a walk near you!

CHOOSING YOUR MOM COMMUNITY

- What type of group do you want? Small talk and details or deep conversation?
- Facilitated or peer led? Topics provided or open conversation?
- Do you want a postpartum group for new moms or a group that's specific (moms of neurodivergent kids, parents of trans kids, or other specific issues)?
- Do you feel safer in a group with similar racial and ethnic backgrounds and identities?
- Open or closed? Open groups accept new members every session, whereas a closed group would be, for example, a six-week group, where no one can join midway.
- It must feel safe and nonjudgmental: All parts are welcome. This may need a facilitator to establish and help maintain.
- Don't give up! Keep trying until you find a fit. Maybe you have a village of one other mom whom you can be yourself with. Start there!
- It may be helpful to participate in a group, and then if you notice any trailheads, take that information and process it with an IFS therapist.
- Groups offer many opportunities for healing, growth, re-sourcing, and support!

YOUR INDIRECT VILLAGE

Circles and mom groups aren't the only format in which to feel the support of a village, especially if you can't seem to find an in-person group in your neighborhood—or perhaps you're not able to get childcare so that you can attend. Having other resources to access indirect support and wisdom can be a good for many moms.

I never would have learned about matrescence had I not put on Amy Taylor-Kabbaz's *Happy Mama Movement* podcast. This was an instrumental moment in my life. I was struggling on my own for months and couldn't understand why my knowledge and clinical skills were not working to make me feel better. I couldn't understand why I felt so unhappy, unsatisfied, and frustrated all the time. Hearing Amy describe matrescence was like a life raft. It gave me a thread to follow. I quickly bought her book *Mama Rising* and felt I had a village of other moms around the world who were with me. Here was a mom talking to other moms about all the ways their lives have changed upon becoming a mother, how they were transforming. I felt seen and like I had a tribe out there, even if I didn't know them personally.

Perhaps you're a book reader and you also have books that inspired you, answered questions you were carrying, or made you feel a bit less alone. Moms who can't manage to read more than a few pages might listen to podcasts or audiobooks while running errands or doing laundry, whatever works for you.

The world of social media offers myriad influencers talking about motherhood. I peruse TikTok and follow one mom in particular, Nicki Marie, who makes me laugh. *Bigtimeadulting* on Instagram is also a favorite of many moms. Their humor and folly at the realities of day-to-day #momlife is spot on, and often the laugh is what we need to help our nervous systems drop out of survival mode into remembering life is a ride—and we are not alone.

The Marco Polo app, if you're not yet familiar, is championing opportunities for meaningful connection. A video app that allows you to record yourself and send it to anyone in the world, Marco Polo has been instrumental in helping me reconnect with a friend who lives in Canada who has been a main support for me. Living in a new community, it has been slow and challenging to connect with other moms and find friends. Marco Polo vids with my friend up north has helped me fill my connection tank up in ways that work for busy moms (i.e., making short videos while I walk my dog and listening to hers on one of my many drives picking up a kid).

It's amazing, really, that carried in her purse or pocket, a mom can have instant access to a virtual village if and when she wants. It's incredible and not something to discount. Conversations, questions, and comments can help a mom feel understood. She's not crazy. What she's feeling and thinking are normal because lots of other moms are feeling the same way.

Social media can also be a trigger, with too many misrepresentations of the perfect mom. Be mindful when you sift through because scrolling sometimes can be overwhelming. The onslaught of opinions and influencers can seem very loud—at least sometimes for me. Be careful of falling down a rabbit hole of scrolling, which may be a firefighter behavior. Regardless of who professes to be an expert, guru, or know-it-all, you always know in your heart what's right for you. Never lose that connection. That's the one that matters most.

MANTRAS FOR MATRESCENCE

You may be familiar with the adage "When the student is ready, the teacher will come." This has been my experience. In tough moments I have prayed for guidance, answers, and support from the Universe. Often it has shown up in the written or expressed wise words of various people, whom I could call teachers, but they are all writers and wise women thinkers. When I reflect on my journey of motherhood—the last fifteen years thus far—these ideas, affirmations, or mantras I'm about to share were a lifeline that brought me validation, inner strength, and a pathway that carried me through to the next hard moment.

"YOU'VE DONE THIS A THOUSAND TIMES BEFORE"

One of the books I read that made a lasting impact on me was Tara Mohr's *Playing Big: Practical Wisdom for Women Who Want to Speak Up, Create, and Lead.*[1] An articulate writer, Tara gives voice to the many ways that women in our culture self-silence and keep themselves small. It's an empowering read, and I highly recommend the book.

Thankfully, because of following her, I received a short note in one of her newsletters that carried wisdom she had learned and was imparting to her community. She shared her fears about giving birth. She recounts in the blog how fearful she was and how a yoga teacher she admired expressed her surprise that her pregnancy was Tara's first, telling Tara she seemed as if she'd mothered "a thousand times before."

Mohr took on this phrase and it landed in my heart as a source of strength. She wrote,

> And then I had the thought, "You can act as if that's true."
> And suddenly, then and there, I decided I had done labor a
> thousand times before. And the minute I thought that, I found
> a part of myself who had done it a thousand times before. It
> was like she raised her hand and said, "Here I am." I can't tell
> you what part of me that was. Perhaps it was the part that is
> connected to every other woman on earth. Perhaps it's a part
> of me that is older than my thirty-some years, a part that has,
> in other times, given birth. I don't know what part of me it
> was, but I can tell you that part was right there to say, "Yes, you
> have done this before."

Maybe this can be your mantra too. I have found strength in it
many times when faced with an obstacle in motherhood that stumps
me, that triggers the part of me that doubts myself. I connect with
courage—one of the 8 Cs of Self—and it amplifies my sense of my capacity while helping me perceive a sturdy ground beneath me. *I have
done this a thousand times before.* I imagine a tribe of mothers to my
left and to my right . . . alive and with ancestors who've passed on.
Imagine your tribe of women, of mothers, and call on their strength.

"WHAT'S IN THE WAY IS THE WAY"

A wise mentor I learned from during my two years of training to
teach mindfulness is writer and meditation teacher Anne Cushman.
During one of our one-to-one sessions as she asked me about my
plans for bringing mindfulness to others and I played around with
options, I expressed my frustration that I felt like motherhood was in
the way of my career aspirations.

I shared with her how I felt confused and resentful that I had
to say, "No, not now," to the many amazing trainings and retreats

that I saw advertised. I felt envious of women who didn't have kids or whose children were already launched. What I perceived as their freedom of choice seemed to create a feeling in me of being trapped, as if I was in prison without a chance to follow my dreams. I felt like my career ambitions were thwarted, as though I simply couldn't expand as a professional while juggling raising my kids at the same time. I also confessed to her that I felt guilty for having these thoughts and feelings.

Anne shared something that day that gave me strength and helped me embrace acceptance, bringing grace to my growing pains of matrescence. Unsure of the original teacher who coined the phrase, Anne shared with me the following teaching: "What's in the way *is* the way." These seven words strung together helped me shift out of a mindset of seeing my children as a barrier to my ambitions.

Little did I know then how much this phrase would ring true for me and light the path of my true calling. It was many years before I would gain the clarity that mothers are actually the people I most want to help, but of course, I didn't realize it at the time. I thought everyone was and I had massive FOMO (Fear of Missing Out). My lack of trust back then created stress, worry, comparison, and jealousy. This phrase helped me turn to what was here. Present in my life at the moment was being a mother to these three souls. The suffering that came from feeling like I wasn't where I wanted or needed to be—the frustration from putting my interests and passions to the side for now—softened and eased my suffering. After all, suffering, by definition, is the resistance of the present moment.

This phrase helped remind me of my beliefs in something greater, and in my heart I couldn't discount that if I weren't meant to mother these souls, they wouldn't be in my life. The realization that motherhood was my calling—not my only calling, but certainly a very substantial and important one—helped me access an inner strength and trust that felt like assurance from beyond. I instantly felt like I was back on track.

This is the power of an affirmation that lands! Sometimes hearing certain quotations, phrases, or teaching is just the right next thread to carry us to the next difficult moment. It offers us a breath of air, like a gust of wind that can help us carry on further.

If you sometimes feel like motherhood is slowing you down, holding you back, or in your way of something else, I encourage you to sit with this phrase. Trust that your calling is always your calling. Unlike the motherhood mandate that believes motherhood is the only purpose and goal for women, you have many gifts and life experiences that await you—that are for you. In Buddhism, this is called your *dharma*. Your dharma will not disappear because you are raising children. You are not behind or on the wrong track. You are right where you need to be.

"WE CAN DO HARD THINGS"

I didn't follow Glennon Doyle's *Momastery* blog. I didn't know about her until Oprah picked *Love Warrior* as her book club winner. Reading it—followed by her more recent memoir *Untamed*—helped me feel like I had some sort of village even if I didn't DM her, post on any thread, or follow her on socials. Her memoirs helped me feel less alone.

An activist who founded Together Rising, a charity that's responsible for providing millions of dollars of aid to women and children around the world, Glennon Doyle is a leader and a truth-teller. Her books helped remind me of the feminist roots I had somehow forsaken. I felt strengthened by her voice that was calling out the societal bullshit that women were facing everywhere and every day.

She rallies women to live authentically and to debunk the societal myths that keep women small, silent, and disempowered. Her words felt like cheerleading chants to me, guiding me to what in my heart I long for also—to be part of the solution for women, not accommodate the problem.

Perhaps I needed to listen to a strong voice that aligned with a part of me that also wanted to live more authentically. I was caught in the day-to-day mode of autopilot, not realizing how much cultural and societal myths were affecting me. I was staying silent and ignoring the little tugs at signs of sexism that still very much pissed me off about this world.

Her memoirs helped me remember I was raising a daughter. I wanted her to have a role model who was fierce and strong. I wanted to prepare her for a world that would challenge her in ways that are clearly different than her brothers. I carried with me her phrase "We can do hard things," and I continue to share this with my daughter when she's doubting herself and feeling overwhelmed by life.

Perhaps it's not Glennon for you, but I share this example to show how we can find our village in many ways. Different voices will speak to each of us and call in our tribe of sisters. Connecting with the truths that an influencer writes or an author speaks can pull on your heartstrings in the right way.

Listen to it. Trust it and lean on it, maybe only until you have your own in-person tribe. The benefit of the digital age is we can listen to these leaders' voices for free on their podcasts. We can see our stories in other women who DM and post on their social platforms. We can, in an instant, see that we are not alone in our pain, confusion, or shame. Women out there are showing us the way. We can follow them, and we can also forge our own pathway with what rings true in our own hearts.

"I'M HERE"—LETTERS FROM LOVE

Meeting up with a friend and former colleague for lunch one day, I was given the next thread along my journey. This friend raved about and suggested for me Elizabeth Gilbert's Substack project called *Letters from Love*. She told me, "This is my Sunday prayer practice." My curiosity piqued, I checked it out and signed up for the five-dollar monthly fee that seemed doable. In this project, Liz interviews different people and invites them to write a letter from "the spirit of unconditional love" and share it. She shares her own each week, and members of this community are invited to write and share their own too. She describes this project as a way to help others know their own worthiness and preciousness.

She explains the intention in her writing:

> To condemn yourself as unlovable is to swallow a terrible lie.
> And to believe that you must earn love through perfectionism,
> or that you must seek love from others in order to become
> whole, turns all of us into hungry beggars. I believe there is an
> ocean of warm, affectionate, and outrageously unconditional
> love available to us all—and that it is conveniently accessible
> from within. I don't believe anyone is excluded from this
> ocean of love; it is only a question of learning how to hear it,
> how to feel it, how to trust it.

She teaches readers to trust love for themselves through offering different themes and inquiries each week. She also offers general guidance to write a letter to yourself with the prompt "Dear Love, what would you have me know today?"

Now, I'm a bit embarrassed to admit this to you, but while I have gratefully been reading and following Gilbert now for several months and finding my heart lit up and connected with amazing souls around the world through this community, I have not yet written a letter to myself from love. Maybe it's because I saved all my writing time for this book, but I have been impacted by reading these letters. I have been stirred by sentiments that draw me into Self-energy through their poetic words.

There are little golden nuggets each week, and some resonate in ways that seem to speak right to my pain and woes. I've also picked up affirmations or meaningful mantras as well as practices that keep me connected with my heart. One practice I borrowed from Liz is the quickest and easiest way to connect with what I know as Self, which busy and stressed-out moms sometimes need in hectic difficult moments.

"I'm here."

These two simple words seemed to help me connect almost instantly with the energy of Self. I believe that what Liz and her friends and colleagues are referring to in all their letters is Self-energy. You can call it Love, Soul, or whatever you want, but as far as I understand it, it's the same source. It's loving awareness. It's energy that prevails beyond all circumstances. It's not tarnished, changed, or altered with trauma. It is immune to damage because its very essence is love.

When I say, "I'm here," to myself, feeling the warmth from my hand on my heart, I quickly sense the Great Mystery and I know I'm not alone. Perhaps reading these letters or writing some for yourself will be a resource for you on your motherhood journey. Matrescence invites us on a journey of self-love, I believe. And your teachers guiding you to heal and know yourself as love are around you right now.

A loving note, dear mama—

If you have moments of feeling alone, please know you are among a tribe of mothers facing the same and different pains, worries, and woes of holding responsibility for another soul. You are not expected to be perfect, despite what some of your younger parts have come to believe. You are a soul on a journey alongside your beautiful children. Trust this path that you find yourself on and stay open to the teachers, guides, and answers that are there waiting for you to discover them. You are in a community with other mothers reading these same words right now. We get it. You are not alone. We are with you. We're here, beautiful mama.

EXERCISE: MEDITATION PRACTICE TO HEAL A SISTER WOUND

Bring yourself to sit or lie down in a comfortable position where your body is relaxed and alert.

Begin by taking a few slow, deep breaths, allowing the exhale to lengthen each time as you invite a settled presence into your mind and body.

Now, check by going inside and notice what's there. You might scan your body, observing any sensations, any tightness, any tingling, or any congestion—anything that's there in this moment.

Reflecting now on this topic of other women . . . notice inside what—if any—parts arise that have something to say or share around this idea of the sister wound (wait and listen with your whole body, without thinking or having an agenda).

Notice what arises. It might be memories from a time in your life, images of friends or girls or women who were not safe or friendly. Without judging, just invite in a sense of what burdens some of your parts might be carrying based on lived experiences.

After a few moments of listening with a kind attention to the parts that share with you, invite in now your understanding of parts. You might imagine the person or people who have come to mind and see if you can bring to mind a most generous interpretation. Without denying any of your own feelings or parts, expand now your awareness to include this other person to imagine their protector parts.

Check in to your heart center now. Take a few slow or deep breaths as you sense connection to Self—to your heart space. . . . If this feels too far out for you, that's totally fine. Keep offering a caring and kind attention to your parts.

You might invite in the Self-energy of this person into the scene in your mind if this doesn't naturally arise. See if you can sense or imagine this person's core energy behind their protective layers and their parts' efforts to keep them safe from harm.

Don't ask your protectors to leave you, but see if they are open to considering that the past is just that. Let them know that you now are an adult. Take a moment to update them to your current strengths, your self-trust, and your discernment about whom you will trust and to whom you will open your heart.

Notice inside if there's any readiness to release and let go of burdens carried from past experiences with girls or women. You might ask your protectors if they'd be willing to let go of the past even a bit. You might invite them to send those feelings or beliefs that came from any difficult experience with other females and send them out into the ether—into the air, fire, water, or earth.

Ask your parts if there's a new role they want to have in your system. Is there a way they can protect you while keeping connection to your heart?

Thank your parts who have shared with you and for any willingness to shift or change—to see a new way of being.

Now, to the extent that it feels natural or comfortable for you, imagine a tribe of women—of mothers—to your left. You turn and see them next to you, and you sense their support.

Next, notice a tribe of women to your right, standing strong and maybe arm-in-arm. These women are your people. You sense the shared strength of these women and mothers through time who have endured, who have faced challenges and adventures, who have known pain and sorrow—and yet they stand. They stand with you and support you now.

You can feel the energy from their support. You sense the awareness that you have done this a thousand times before.

Take a few slow and deep breaths and sense what this feels like in your body. When you're ready, open your eyes and move back out into the world.

CHAPTER 10

THE UNBURDENED MOTHER

*When we are open
and accepting of all our parts,
they relax and transform, and we
rediscover the wholeness and
wisdom of our Self.*
—DR. RICHARD SCHWARTZ

I HAVE HAD A PART, most likely a firefighter, that during times of being in therapy and working on healing just wanted to be done already! It would ask my therapist when she thought I'd be there—as if there were a ribbon I'd run through like a marathon to indicate, yep,

Angele is finally healed! I have seen and heard similar parts in clients over the years as well. Perhaps it's our culture where we often want a quick fix. But as Dick Schwartz has noted, "Very few people are constantly and fully Self-led."[1] But still, I think it's helpful to know what we're working toward. What would it look like and feel like, and what will your life be more like if you brave forward and help your parts heal and unburden? The mandala of an unburdened internal system is an image and vision of what is possible through following the IFS model of healing that was created and published by the lead trainer Mariel Pastor and supported by Dick Schwartz.[2]

The IFS motto "All parts are welcome" is aspirational as much as true. Despite some of the parts' behaviors that seem difficult for other parts to fully accept, the truth is that, at their core, each part has Self-energy within, and its purpose and unique gifts are ultimately served when it can be freed of the burdens it carries.

We can't rid ourselves of our parts—even the ones that we judge as unwanted—because they are parts of who we are. And hopefully, you've learned in reading this book that, at their core, all parts have some good intention or reason for doing what they do. They are us and, when able to trust the Self to lead, they have wonderful qualities and useful gifts that can help us in our lives when we can collaborate with and integrate them. It serves us well to learn how to embrace all of us.

Written words have their limitations, however, as a more accurate representation of us and our parts is as a system that flows in and out like shifting and moving energy. There is no end goal either, as we are always in process in our life, and despite what parts of us sometimes vie for, we never actually arrive. There is no one-size-fits-all. Each person will access Self and lead from it within their own culture and context.

Accordingly, I have adapted Mariel Pastor's mandala to illustrate the possibilities for mothers specifically. I wanted to show you the potential—what lies within you when you begin or continue your healing journey to release and unburden your fortuitous parts from their extreme roles and are open to living a more Self-led life.

I'm sharing this mandala with you because it has helped me understand the beautiful gifts within each of my parts, even the parts that have made choices I've regretted or parts I've struggled to accept in myself. It also points to the potential learning and growing that help us cultivate the qualities we aspire to in motherhood, as well as in our intimate relationships, our work and professional life, and our communities.

Please understand that while this image may serve as a sort of vision or North Star of possibility and potential, it is not a benchmark for self-judgment or self-critique. It is not your report card, nor your summit or destination. The only way I can write this chapter is to be fully honest and acknowledge that, for me, this experience—being a Self-led mother—is in progress. I am not an expert, nor am I killing it in parenting and motherhood. I am not an unburdened mother, and I am not proposing you try to be either. I am in it along with you, and I am passionately sharing what I have found helpful along my parenting journey.

THE UNBURDENED INTERNAL SYSTEM MANDALA FOR MOTHERS

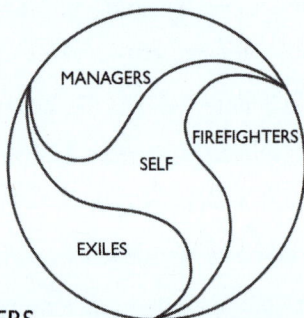

MANAGERS

Managers are the parts that aim to prevent pain from reoccurring. They do this by trying to control people, events, and other parts in the system.

Managers, when not in their extreme roles, can greatly support moms by balancing tasks and managing the mental load of motherhood. Unburdened managers help moms juggle responsibilities with ease and presence, embodying qualities like confidence, clarity, creativity, calm, and cooperation.

FIREFIGHTERS

These parts spring into action at the onset of pain or vulnerability. They are powerful automatic repressors that work to avoid burdened exiles from arising, to release stress and pressure and stop what feels painful or threatening in the system.

Unburdened firefighters support moms by signaling when stress is too high and encouraging healthy coping strategies to restore balance. Firefighters also play roles in voicing injustices and setting healthy boundaries with confidence and courage in the face of challenge. Firefighters bring energy and zest for moms, inspiring adventure, passion, humor, and healthy risk-taking. The adventurousness, courageousness, passion, creativity, and fun these parts embody can bring great joy to their relationships with their children.

SELF

The core essence within each of us. Self-energy acts as a healing agent. It is the wise, compassionate leader that tends to parts to help them unburden, heal, and transform the inner system.

When a mother leads with Self-energy, she stays present, aware of her own parts, and able to respond to her children with curiosity and less reactivity. A Self-led mother embodies the Eight Cs: Connection, Calm, Courage, Compassion, Clarity, Curiosity, Confidence, and Creativity.

EXILES

As tender and often young parts within us, exiles carry the deep wounds and memories of painful or traumatic experiences early in life. In their truest natural form, they bring curiosity, awe, delight, and wonder into a mother's system. They carry an innocence and joy that is contagious and pure.

Often intuitive and empathic, exiles value a connection to Self and others. For moms, these exiles can show up with presence with her children, connecting with them and being playful and joyous—rediscovering the world with them by embodying what's sometimes referred to as "beginner's mind." An unburdened exile is playful, spontaneous, sensitive, warm, open, trusting, and innocent.

Text by Angele Close, PhD, Internal Family Systems by Richard Schwartz, PhD
Adapted from *The Unburdened Internal System* by Mariel Pastor, LMFT
Original graphic by Janet R. Mullen, LCSW

SELF-ENERGY FOR MOTHERS

The symbol in the mandala is meant to indicate fluidity between Self and parts. When a mother has access to Self-energy, she can lead with Self and enlist the aid of her protectors as needed. This means she is less reactive to her children's behaviors and more able to address their needs calmly, with clarity and compassion. She is present with her children, attuned to their agency and their parts, while also aware of her own parts—able to speak for them and not be taken over by them. She can fluidly address her own inner world, respecting all parts with curiosity, interest, and care. She is connected to herself and her children, and she responds and engages with grace, trust, and ease. A Self-led mother exudes and embodies the 8 Cs: connection, calm, courageous, compassionate, clear, curious, confident, and creative.

UNBURDENED MANAGERS FOR MOTHERS

Managers can be a great help to moms when not in their extreme forms, such as when carrying burdens and protecting exiles. They help moms balance and function, accomplishing the many multiple tasks and bearing the mental load often required of mothers. An unburdened manager part can help a mom juggle tasks with more ease and presence, while working effectively in the role of caretaker and house manager, as well as nurturing parent. In their healthiest version, they can be described with qualities such as confidence, discernment, clarity, helpfulness, creative problem-solving, calm, and cooperativeness.

UNBURDENED FIREFIGHTERS FOR MOTHERS

Unburdened firefighters have an important role for mothers: They help signal the Self when stress levels are getting too high and overwhelming. An unburdened and healthy firefighter will engage in healthy coping strategies and use wholesome self-soothing and restorative practices to establish balance in the mother's system. This may require speaking for her parts to a spouse or partner and having what in IFS is called "courageous conversations." Firefighters also play roles in voicing injustices and setting healthy boundaries with confidence and courage in the face of challenges. This part might look like expressing concern when her children use inappropriate language or cross a family rule or value. Firefighters also bring energy and zest to moms, inspiring adventure, passion, humor, and healthy risk-taking. Qualities unburdened firefighters demonstrate are adventurousness, courageousness, passion, creativity, fun, and sensuality.

UNBURDENED EXILES FOR MOTHERS

Our exiles are often the most tender and young parts within us. It's not surprising, then, that in their truest natural form—when not needing to suppress or stifle themselves and when healed and unburdened from any traumatic experience—exiles bring curiosity, awe, delight, and wonder into your system. They carry an innocence and joy that are contagious and pure. They can be highly intuitive and empathic, and they value a connection to Self and others. These exiles can manifest for moms in showing up with presence with their children, connecting with them and being playful and joyous—rediscovering the world with them by embodying what's sometimes referred to as "beginner's mind" in some contemplative and spiritual traditions. Words that might describe an unburdened exile include playful, spontaneous, sensitive, warm, open, trusting, and innocent.

MY UNBURDENING

While I wouldn't describe myself as an unburdened mother, I have experienced the unburdening of many of my exiles and protectors. Unburdening these parts from their intense roles was incredibly helpful in how I felt internally in my thoughts and emotions, and it translated to a better relationship with my children and a more harmonious family. The more Self-energy I opened up through healing, the less I suffered from the challenges of parenting.

Before I learned about IFS, I felt angry multiple times each day while feeling more and more hopeless over time, seeing that my mindfulness practice was not helping me feel at peace, centered, or present with my kids. I had a strong critic who was subtly tearing me down at every juncture of parenthood. I resented my kids' needs, which felt like they were robbing me of time for things that filled me up. I was burnt out and felt like I was treading water until the next trigger pushed me down.

I was grumpy a lot and vacillated between drinking wine to chill out and find some fun and my task-oriented manager that lost my patience with my kids at times or sighed with exasperation when I heard, "Mommmmm!" for the seventeenth time. I had little tolerance for my son's emotional outbursts and found myself saying typical, old-school things parents would say that were the opposite of validation, and validation is what I know in my heart is the right way to respond to a child who is having a hard time. My default mode was trying to shut down my children's negative emotions, despite my years of training in Emotion-focused Therapy. Then, of course, I would feel guilty and ashamed of myself. I felt like I was failing as a mom and as a therapist: I was an imposter. The wear and tear of parenting left me feeling nearly depressed, as I was teary almost every day and my self-confidence.

Discovering IFS and learning that matrescence is a thing—and I was in it—was like finding a pathway through an Amazonian jungle. Getting to know my protectors instead of ignoring them, earning their trust, and, with their permission, going to my exiled parts to witness them and help them release their burdens have been the most mystical, powerful, and profoundly healing experiences of my life.

Learning about IFS through books and training, I now recognize what to expect if I follow its map to know my protectors and earn their trust to heal and unburden my wounded parts. But doing the experiential work myself, sometimes guided by a skilled IFS therapist, provided the real data to validate that this method is legit. Healing really is possible, because I feel it and I notice the positive ripple effects in my life.

With each exile I learned about, listened to, and helped release, I felt more energy freed up in my body. I noticed myself finding laughter in things much more than before. I felt a lightness as creative energy and inspiration came back into my being. I was more fun with my kids again, no longer engaging with them from my protector parts that struggled with boundary-setting and resented parenting. I can honestly say that I am closer than I've ever been to truly having compassion and love for myself, which in my opinion is what healing is truly about.

WHAT OTHER MOMS SAY ABOUT IFS

I cannot say enough that we are always in process. Like the weather, where storms move in and out, we have moments of clarity and connection with the Sun (Self), and we will be swept away at times by our parts. Where the clouds (parts) can sometimes block us from the Sun, we can see the weather for what it is, be curious about it and accepting of it, and the curious collaborative approach will help us soon feel the sunshine on our faces again.

Moms who've had some experience using IFS described to me that the process of slowing down, softening, and connecting with Self was incredibly helpful in parenting and matrescence. For example, Rachel, who didn't even question being an intensive mother, described having more compassion for herself with an IFS lens and easing up on one of her manager's drives to be the perfect mother:

> Every time I have a part that's like, "You are totally letting her get away with murder," or "This is reinforcing bad behavior," I worry. Sometimes I'm inconsistent because sometimes that part guides the intervention. And I, or maybe my part that wants to be perfectionist about it, want to just pick something and stick with it, and always parent that way. And . . . when I'm more compassionate to myself, I just land at, It's impossible to be 100 percent consistent—like, it's okay to be mostly grounded in one way of being. It's not possible to be perfect all the time.

Juliana, who was brand-new to IFS and didn't want to do parts mapping, described noticing the positive impacts of turning inward and seeing herself as having parts:

> I am noticing that the more I feel supported, and I dare to dig deep—the more I allow myself to rest and slow down—the better I am able to deal with emotional situations. Often when kids push me a lot, I can regulate myself better, and when I

> struggle with missing the freedom and wanting time without
> kids, I do talk to that other part of me [I call this part "Wild
> and Free"], acknowledging these feelings, and it helps me a lot.

Being able to turn inward and connect with your parts while accessing Self can help a mom be less reactive and more present in parenting. Emma, a survivor of childhood sexual abuse and mom of two kids, described it this way:

> Being able to find IFS and both start to work with and
> understand my legacy burdens and really to heal trauma
> wounds has made me far less reactive with my kids. Now,
> parts still get activated, and so I find the practice of just being
> able to slow down ... be here ... listen in, 'cause that's really
> what so much of IFS is, right? It's pausing. It's slowing things
> way down. It's being curious. It's doing that U-turn. What is
> happening inside? And parts are still activated, even though
> I've done some significant healing work, but it's much easier
> and I'm more in control from relating to my parts this way.

Tatiana, the mom who had a jealous part and a strong inner critic, recalled a situation when doing schoolwork with her daughter. She recognized that a strong manager part that drives her to be perfect was coming up and becoming frustrated with her daughter's imperfection. As she explained,

> I get angry or frustrated and concerned about what this
> means about me when my kid struggles. I have a part that
> tells me, "She has to do everything right. Otherwise I failed.
> It's my fault if it doesn't go right." I wasn't able to cope with her
> feelings when she made a mistake or was wrong about

> something. I call this part "The Frustrated One." It has a very low frustration tolerance. But I did act well and did not get fully taken over, I have to say. But it took a lot of overcoming, so I had to really control myself and notice it and be in Self. It was super hard, like one of the hardest things I've done.

Hopefully, from these mothers' voices and experiences, you get the sense that there's no drive for perfection and that turning inward and changing your relationship with your inner world is possible. It can help us in our tough parenting moments, and it's a practice.

WHERE TO START?

Something I have said often to clients when they're starting out in therapy is, "Way to go! Great noticing! We can't change what we're not aware of." Often the first place to start is just to notice. Coming out of autopilot is usually the first step for many people. The next few strategies provide some guidance if this is where you are. If you feel like you're a bit ahead in your self-healing journey and this isn't your first rodeo, then I offer you these practices as friendly reminders. In my experience, the journey of self-growth and awakening is a long game, made up of re-remembering and deepening.

PAUSE AND U-TURN (MINDFULNESS)

Mindfulness refers to being present and aware of one's experience with an open and nonjudgmental attitude to all that is arising. You may have a part that balks at this heading. I taught mindfulness meditation for years, and as a mother of three, I know how challenging it can be to slow down. Our Mama managers are often driven by a "Go-Go-Go!—We got shit to do!" energy. Yet we notice much less when we're moving too fast and on autopilot (i.e., living blended with a protector part).

After working with many moms, I've seen an uncanny theme that arises repeatedly: slowing down and turning inward is the essential key to living and parenting from Self. It's also a key to connecting with your parts and continuing to build a trusting relationship with them so they'll allow you—Self—to lead.

Dr. Becky Kennedy reminds us parents with "deeply feeling kids" that "presence is an intervention." Our manager parts tend to think they have to "do" to "fix" (which they often aim for through lecturing, coaching, or even criticizing, threatening, or controlling). You may have noticed in the mandala of an unburdened system that Self is in the present moment. It's often our protector parts that are aiming to keep us safe by anticipating the future or keeping the past in our minds to remember, "Never again."

Self is not preoccupied with worry but is present oriented and able to *be* rather than having an agenda to do. It lives in the space of right here and now. Spiritual teacher and author of the well-known book *The Power of Now,* Eckhart Tolle offers this: "As soon as you honor the present moment, all unhappiness and struggle dissolve, and life begins to flow with joy and ease. When you act out the present-moment awareness, whatever you do becomes imbued with a sense of quality, care, and love—even the most simple action."

Pastor's circular mandala represents the flow from Self (in the present moment) and our parts (that often take us out of present-moment awareness). The circular shape depicts flow and unity—it's a shape that denotes cycles and process. Self in the center seems to me like an anchor or the hub of a wheel, connecting to the parts like axles allowing the rotation and movement within the system. In essence, we have thousands of moments in our day when we can anchor back into presence while moving in and out of awareness.

As Mariel Pastor states, "Parts are not the problem." Our challenges are tied to carrying burdens that require attention, healing, and transformation, especially when they're out of our awareness. When our parts are unburdened, we can live our moments with greater presence. When unburdened, we can have access to our parts' Self-energy, which emboldens us to live with more vitality, creativity, joy, and aliveness. The more aware of our parts we are, the more able we can attend to them and help them unburden.

Western mindfulness meditation teacher and author Jon Kabat-Zinn emphasizes the importance of pausing to be more present. In his book *Wherever You Go, There You Are,* he wrote, "To allow ourselves to be truly in touch with where we already are, no matter where that is, we have got to pause in our experience long enough to let the present moment sink in; long enough to actually feel the present moment, to see it in its fullness, to hold it in awareness and thereby come to know and understand it better."

The importance of mindfulness came through in many of my interviews with moms for this book and in my own experiences parenting. For example, Emma described how her father was often Self-led. He embodied presence, and she tries to remember this as an anchor for herself in her aim to be a Self-led mom:

> What I do now is I stop, because [my dad] radiated so much Self-energy and I think just "be the model." I don't think I ever had a lecture from him ever. All parts were loved, and he always just led by example. And so, it's a good reminder for me when I have my parts that come in and want to get it right and do it perfect. And some days it's just, like, to be able to pause and to sort of show that part—"you just gotta be." That was more than enough.

Rachel honestly shared with me how she isn't sure she's able to access Self-energy often in her life. But on reflection, she said she most organically senses that she has access to Self in motherhood when things slow down, and somewhat by accident, she finds herself in this space of creativity, joy, presence, and the openhearted essence of Self:

> I think maybe this is like being with them in Self-energy when it's an unexpected day off, or they're home sick, but not too sick, but sick enough to stay home from school. I love days like this because we don't have an extracurricular activity. We don't have a plan. I've either shifted my schedule around, which is annoying to do, or I lose some money because I cancel a client or something, which is annoying. So I have parts that are like, "Oh, I lost money," or "Oh! Like this was hard," but then I just sit and play with them for a chunk of the day. So, what I try to do more is this idea of one thing at a time. For example, if I'm doing the dishes, I am doing the dishes. But if I'm playing with the kids, I'm playing with the kids. . . . It's an impossible thing because we're all so busy. And I certainly wouldn't take my own advice to cut down the extracurricular activities; it's good that we do some after-school sports and things. And I just always feel better when we don't. I always feel better when there's just a day that we just hang out and play.

She went on to name that perhaps she could be "more intentional" about finding these times rather than waiting for the Universe to allow them. This is not a bad idea at all. And it can feel counter to our culture where many kids are overscheduled. The daily responsibilities, duties, and activities can easily overwhelm the most organized mom while the busyness may bowl over opportunities to connect, to *be, to access presence and Self-energy.*

THE ONE-BREATH MEDITATION

During the lockdown of the COVID pandemic, when I was trying to homeschool my children in three different grades of curriculum—and losing my mind—my therapist at the time suggested the one-breath meditation. You might have a part that reacts to this idea with "Really? What the hell is that gonna do?" or "I'm so sick of people telling us moms to slow down and breathe!" Trust me, I get it. Sometimes I think that too.

Still, I must admit that when I practiced it, it helped. It didn't heal anything or take my 10/10 emotional gauge down to a calm and lovely 2 or 3, but I noticed it helped take me down to an 8 or 7, even if only for a few moments. As I walked up the stairs to attend to yet another demand from my child (feeling like I'm playing whack-a-mole with their needs for my attention), I would mindfully take one breath in and slowly exhale out of my mouth. Some meditation teachers suggest exhaling through a pursed lip—like you're slowly blowing out of a straw—but any practice of breathwork that lengthens the exhale is calming.

Taking that one mindful breath is a way to enter Self-energy—to anchor into the center of the mandala. Even if only for one breath, you open up a bit of space to notice. I also like asking myself, *Who's here?*—a helpful IFS-type question that helps me identify what parts are active. I can then intentionally unblend from the protectors and be more present and Self-led in such moments. One conscious breath with one question has amazingly shown me how I can access Self in any moment. It's doable anywhere, anytime. It is my daily practice. I invite you to try it out for yourself!

MINDFULNESS IN OUR DAILY ROUTINES

Sometimes, as busy moms, a one-breath meditation is all we can muster to add to our busy days. In his book *Self-Led*, Seth Kopald speaks to the reality that "routines are life." He points to the common challenge that it's often our parts that are dominating many of our interactions with our kids, which are the day-to-day tasks: teeth brushing, readying for bedtime, shuffling the kids out the door, or getting ready for this or that.

A loving note, dear mama—

Take a breath or two, and if you notice a self-critical part coming in reminding you of times you've lost your cool during daily routines, please ask it to step back. Remember, our parts have roles, and getting to work (or anywhere) on time is a good reason to be swift. Before I had kids, I was never late for anything. As a mom, this is one of my biggest triggers: At all ages, it can feel like I'm herding kittens to get us ready and out the door on time. Be kind and gentle with yourself, sweetheart. You are doing the very best you can, and that's all we can do!

I don't know about you, but I often felt bad once I'd arrived at work and realized I'd snapped too much or was too pushy or impatient with my kids. It never feels good to have these rushed and manager-led interactions with our children. Kopald points out the resultant impact on your relationship with your kids—their own protectors might put up walls and withdraw from you when you next reach out to have a connecting conversation—all because of the previous moments of rushing, snapping, or maybe shaming to get them out the door.

And when we can slow down and recognize the parts that are driving us to get us to do, we might invite them to step back and see if those parts would be willing to let us be present with our kids in the many moments that make up our daily routines. Kopald writes, "The additive effect of positive interactions during routines will do wonders for your relationship with your child."[3] He provides some helpful questions using an IFS lens that we can use to improve our experiences in routines with our kids, which I've included at the end of this chapter.

FINAL WORDS ON THE HEALING PROCESS

When traveling on a long plane ride from Brazil back home to Illinois, I watched an old movie about a family that survived the 2004 tsunami in Thailand. Through watery eyes, I was overcome, my heart wrenching with compassion for what this and other families went through, as images of each of my children kept appearing in my mind. Watching the tragedy of what the family endured, a mother torn apart from her two children, not knowing if they're alive or dead, I noticed all my protectors were acutely in my mind's waiting room. I felt nothing but raw, unwavering, fierce, and intense love as I thought of each of my kids. It was like I could see and feel beyond the daily squabbles and frustrations and sensed only soul-level love and connection to each of them.

I had been away from my kids by then for almost a week, and so I had rested, relaxed, and felt very much in Self-energy. My heart was completely open to the love I have for my children, along with gratitude for their health and well-being all at once, that nothing else tainted this profound and deep love and connection that had taken over all the energy in my mind, body, and heart. Or rather, through watching this traumatic story of near loss on the small screen, I had instant access to the love that's always there for my children but isn't always available during life's daily demands.

This overwhelming love I felt wasn't new to me, and I'm sure you know this feeling too—the profound heart opening that comes in moments, for instance, when looking at your infant sleeping or when they're hurt, and you comfort and soothe them without a thought. The bond of love is palpable as you feel better seeing that your comforting eases them.

If you've experienced any close, near, or heart-wrenching realities of the loss of a child, you know very well—probably more so than me—the deep love for your child that I'm trying to describe here with mere words. It's galactical. It's soul speak. And it's a taste and sense of love without burdens.

Always living in this level of awareness is not possible. As my meditation teacher Jack Kornfield explained to me years ago, "The heart opens and it closes" in order to live in this world. Understanding our parts and how we are made to survive and function in this human life, I now understand it as the full openness of the heart always being there—it is Self-energy. The more we work to connect with, witness, and heal our exiled parts, the more we can release our strong protectors from their posts relating to our past trauma and live life with more access to the heart that shines readily beneath our armored committee of inner parts. We can move through our life with less fear, less guardedness, and more openness to the love and beauty that are also a part of being human on this Earth.

In graduate school, my professor described the process of true healing and change to us young, keen counseling students as the shape of a spiral. Too young to truly know from lived experience, we were taught to share with our clients that growth and healing are not linear but rather are better represented in the shape of a spiral. You've heard the adage "Two steps forward, one step back." I prefer the spiral shape, which conveys a process of cycling through that is probably more accurate. We live in seasons, and while sometimes you may feel like you're slipping backward, really, you don't return to the beginning.

We don't unlearn or unawaken when we grow. We come to our life lessons again and again, each time with a different view or depth of understanding. We re-remember, in a sense, what some part of us knows, has learned, and seems to have forgotten or needs to learn in a new shade or hue. We may need to meet new parts or familiar parts who have fears or concerns with our growth and learning. Each trailhead is an opportunity to know one's Self more deeply and to aspire to the insight that's available for you to consciously curate the life you want to live.

Healing is messy, just like motherhood. It can feel like an emotional roller coaster when we begin to turn inward and listen to our inner world. Another common phrase in the psychotherapy field is, "It's worse before it gets better." My interpretation of this phrase, now that I understand multiplicity, is that when we are finally making the U-turn and start listening to, acknowledging, and appreciating our parts—the protectors for the ways they've been trying to help us and the exiles they protect—it can sometimes feel like a stampede inside, with many of our parts vying for our interest and attention.

Instead of a semblance of one personality or one dominant part who mostly controls the wheel, it's like every part fighting for the mic, which can feel unsettling. If you anticipate this in some way and understand these are like little children vying for your love and attention, you can ride the wave a little easier. As Dick Schwartz has advised us IFS trainees, you can ask them to go slow and to please take turns. Let them know they will each have a turn for your kind and caring attention.

Some days will feel more raw, your exiles acting like they're just beneath the surface and almost anything can trigger tears, exasperation, or deep pain. Other days you may feel more resourced, less fragile, and more grounded or centered—a bit steadier. All of this is fine. Neither is right or wrong. It's the joys and sorrows of human life. It's a process of expanding and contracting. It's the spiral process of our awakening and healing. It's the flowing in and around as in the mandala. You're doing great. You are right where you need to be. One breath at a time, sweetheart.

It's a trek that's worth taking—for what you will model to your children and what you won't pass onto them because you've healed many of your familial trauma patterns. And it's worth it because of you. You deserve to live more awakened, open, and aligned with your heart. You deserve to feel joy. Your creativity and your gifts are waiting to be freed, and the awe and beauty of this world are here for you to feel, see, and know. This is difficult when our protectors are more concerned with blocking us from feeling sorrow and despair. And it's possible, now that you are no longer a child who lacked an adult to lean on, that you can relearn how to feel all of the feelings. You can release and unburden the misunderstandings only children make because they don't know any better. Thank your protector for its service—for helping you survive. And now it's time for you to thrive.

As my trainer Mariel Pastor has written of the unburdened system, "A Self-led person brings an abiding sense of curiosity, acceptance, and openheartedness to their relationships, naturally inviting others' Self-energy to increase." When we can approach others—our children, our spouses—in relationship from Self we are much more likely to be heard, understood, and received. We are increasing the chances that their Self-energy will arise in resonance with ours.

This is the intention of Dick Schwartz as well as the many thousands in the IFS community—a number that is growing each day. The potential within IFS is that as each of us unburdens our past wounds and breaks the trauma cycles that we carry from our ancestors, we heal what's been passed down for generations. As each of us shows up more in Self in our lives, others will resonate with this energy.

We can see the wounds of our inner systems mirrored in the outer world in the deep polarizations, the hurt, and the pain that are rampantly projected onto and exacted upon others in sometimes heinous ways. And as each of us does our own healing, we unburden the collective legacy burdens. This Self-energy that facilitates our personal healing will transmit into our relationships with our children, our spouses and partners, our families and communities, and eventually offer hope for a new world.

EXERCISE: REFLECTION QUESTIONS ON HOW TO BE SELF-LED IN YOUR DAILY ROUTINES

(from *Self-led: Living a Connected Life with Yourself and with Others* by Seth Kopald, PhD):

1. How can we arrange our schedule differently to allow for more time for transitions?

2. What are things that trigger my parts during routines? Find those parts and get to know them (Practice HEAL or do the exercise from Chapter 3).

3. How often does my own stress overflow on my child as we are trying to get out the door? How do my parts feel when someone treats me that way?

4. What is my biggest fear if my routines don't go well? What messages do I hear inside? Allow those messages to be trailheads for your exploration of your parts and return to the exercise from Chapter 2.

A FINAL LOVING NOTE, DEAR MAMA—

FROM THE OUTSET OF CREATING AN OUTLINE for this book, I knew that I would end it with a "Love Letter to Mothers." It's not a conclusion or a summary but a parting word.

I tried to write this book as much as possible from Self and trusting that what wants to come to help other mothers will do so. It was from this intention that I received the idea to try Liz Gilbert's practice of writing a letter to yourself from the spirit of unconditional love (SOUL). And so, it's in my first attempt at this practice that the following letter from Love flowed.

As I finished the letter, I felt the stirring of tears flowing up and out. I closed my eyes and sensed the profound energy. The Great Mystery. I hope it lands like this for you too. And if it doesn't, or if you're curious, maybe try a letter from Love for yourself.

Love, what would you have me know about motherhood that I may share with the readers of Unburdening Motherhood?

You beautiful Goddess—you know not yet of your power. You are a beautiful imperfect angel of light. You have chosen this path in another dimension, and it is all as it should be.

But not easy.

No one said it would be easy. That was one of your errors of perception—which is so human.

If this weren't for you, it wouldn't be. So sometimes, darling, when it's hard and you're at the very edge, remember that. That I have faith and all-knowing in you that you are the perfect mother to these little souls, and I don't expect you to know all the answers. That would not be a human experience.

All growing has its pain and yes, you have many of these moments, it's true. And—my Dear—you have the bliss—you know also moments of love like no other that feel as though this is beyond. But trust me—it's real.

This love between you and your littles is cosmic—and it is only masked at times by the cloudiness of struggle, by the misunderstandings and foibles of humanness.

You see, my love, you are on the ground. You are on the front lines now, and so much weighs heavy on you. And the more you stray from your knowing of me—of how We support you and help you carry it all—then the steeper the steps will feel. And that's okay too.

These little ones are the mirrors of your wounds. Mothering them will give you a multitude of chances to see your beauty—your lovability—your perfect imperfection and goodness.

Mothering these lovelies is your journey to healing, my love.

Tell them, share this with all the mothers. They can heal. There are many of you looking, seeking, and ready for this Truth.

You have everything you need—inside—to heal. You are doing it, my beautiful—even now.

Ah . . . that breath. That re-remembering, it's a precious and mystical process and we love to see you shine and expand. There's no rush, sweetheart. Keep going—keep turning inside to see—to know—to love, and tell them, my love, tell them they are also perfectly loveable just as they are. Tell them they're not doing anything wrong—it feels hard because it is hard. Motherhood is a shero's journey.

Help them resist the blame and unfocused pain. Give them your hand and walk together, my sweet. A tribe of angels is growing. Hold their hands, sweetheart, let them know.

It's time.

NOTES

CHAPTER 1

1. Webb, J. (2012). *Running on empty: Overcome your childhood emotional neglect.* Morgan James Publishing.
2. Taylor-Kabbaz, A. (2020). *Mama rising: Discovering the new you through motherhood.* Hay House.
3. Yehuda, R., Daskalakis, N. P., & Desarnaud, F. (2015). "Transgenerational transmission of trauma and epigenetic mechanisms: A review of the literature." *Biological Psychiatry, 78*(5), 276–284. https://doi.org/10 .1016/j.biopsych.2015.02.009.

CHAPTER 2

1. Reich-Stiebert, N., Froehlich, L., & Voltmer, J. B. (2023). "Gendered mental labor: A systematic literature review on the cognitive dimension of unpaid work within the household and childcare." *Sex Roles, 88*(11–12), 475–494. https://doi.org/10.1007 /s11199-023-01362-0.
2. Calarco, J. M., Meanwell, E. V., Anderson, E., & Knopf, A. (2020, October 9). "'My husband thinks I'm crazy': COVID-19-related conflict in couples with young children." https://doi.org/10.31235/osf.io/cpkj6.
3. Warwick-Ching, L. (2020, July 29). "'Motherhood penalty' made worse by the effects of the pandemic." *Financial Times.* https://www.ft.com/content/19025754 -ad69-4cfa-9653-f8c8216539e9.
4. U.S. Department of Health and Human Services. (2024). "Parents under pressure: The U.S. Surgeon General's advisory on the mental health & well-being of parents." https:// www.hhs.gov/surgeongeneral/priorities/parents/index.html.
5. Trost, S. L., Beauregard, J. L., Smoots, A. N., Ko, J. Y., Haight, S. C., Moore-Simas, T. A., Byatt, N., Madni, S. A., & Goodman, D. (2022). "Pregnancy-related deaths: Data from maternal mortality review committees in 36 U.S. states, 2017–2019." Centers for Disease Control and Prevention, U.S. Department of Health and Human Services.
6. Rodin, J., Silberstein, L., & Striegel-Moore, R. (1984). "Women and weight: A normative discontent." *Nebraska Symposium on Motivation, 32,* 267–307.
7. Grajek, M., Tiggeman, M., Haines, J., & Tang, L. (2022). "Perception of body image in women after childbirth and its associations with postpartum eating behaviors."

International Journal of Environmental Research and Public Health, 19(16), article 10137. https://doi.org/10.3390/ijerph191610137.

8. Chen, M., & Chang, S. (2023). "The relationship between body dissatisfaction and postpartum depressive symptoms: A cross-sectional study." *Journal of Affective Disorders, 324,* 418–423.

9. Waltz, M. (2015). Mothers and autism: The evolution of a discourse of blame. *AMA Journal of Ethics, 17*(4), 353–358.

10. Serrellach, O., & Bulsara, M. (2021). "Emotional depletion in new mothers: A qualitative study of the experiences of Australian mothers." *International Journal of Women's Health, 13,* 1271–1280.

11. Howorth, C. (2017). "Motherhood is hard to get wrong. So why do so many moms feel so bad about themselves?" *Time.* https://time.com/4989068/motherhood-is-hard-to-get-wrong/.

CHAPTER 3

1. Schwartz, R. C. (2013). *Internal family systems therapy.* 2nd ed. Guilford Press.

2. Schwartz, R. C. (2021). *No bad parts: Healing trauma and restoring wholeness with the Internal Family Systems model.* Sounds True.

CHAPTER 4

1. Mulligan, C. J., Quinn, E. B., Hamadmad, D., Dutton, C. L., Nevell, L., Binder, A. M., Panter-Brick, C., & Dajani, R. (2025). "Epigenetic signatures of intergenerational exposure to violence in three generations of Syrian refugees." *Scientific Reports, 15*(1), 5945. doi: 10.1038/s41598 -025-89818-z.

2. McDaniel, K. (2021). *Mother hunger: How adult daughters can understand and heal from lost nurturance, protection, and guidance.* Hay House.

CHAPTER 5

1. Earley, J., & Weiss, B. (2010). *Freedom from your inner critic: A self-therapy approach.* Pattern System Books.

CHAPTER 9

1. Mohr, T. (2014). *Playing big: Practical wisdom for women who want to speak up, create, and lead.* Penguin Books.

CHAPTER 10

1. Schwartz, R. C. (2001). *Introduction to the Internal Family Systems model.* Trailhead Publications, 32.

2. Pastor, M., & Gauvin, J. (2021). *Internal Family Systems: Level one training manual.* Trailhead Publications.

3. Kopald, S. (2023). *Self-led: Living a connected life with yourself and with others, An application of internal family systems.* Exploration Services, LLC., 97.

ACKNOWLEDGMENTS

I NEVER WOULD HAVE GUESSED that my purpose would emerge through the growing pains of motherhood. The seamless early years gave no warning that eventually, my entire world—and the ways I thought I knew myself—would crumble and, ultimately, transform me. IFS becamse my life raft, and this book was born from a desire to offer that same lifeline to other mothers struggling through cycles of confusion, anger, self-blame, and shame. I am deeply honored to have been the steward of this work—and I know I did not do this alone.

I am grateful to my husband, Ryan, who helped my distracted parts re-focus and finally write the book! I'm also incredibly appreciative of the friends who cheered me on, reflecting back unwavering belief and encouragement. Thank you, Sarah Cassidy, for trusting your intuition—Amy Taylor-Kabbaz for helping us rise, and to Jillian Abby, for helping me shape early versions of the proposal and celebrating the joy of the writing process with me.

To my editor, Darcie Abbene—thank you for believing in me and in the power of helping mothers heal. And to Bob Land and the team at Health Communications Inc.—thank you for the clarity and opportunity to bring this book into the world.

With gratitude to Dick Schwartz, for giving language and shape to a process that has brought more healing and awakening than anything I've known. Thank you for taking the time to meet with me, for your generous listening, and for encouraging my passion to bring IFS to the experience of motherhood. I'm also grateful to Jeanne Cantanzaro, Susan Cahill, Mariel Pastor, Fran Booth, Seth Kopald, Tammy Sollenberger, Susan McConnell, Delta Larkey, and Toni Herbine-Blank—your teachings and presence have deeply influenced my understanding of myself, my clients, and the work I feel called to do in the world.

Finally, to the moms who so graciously offered your stories, your time, and your trust—thank you. Your voices made this book possible. The readers of *Unburdening Motherhood* will gain so much because of your courage and generosity.

ABOUT THE AUTHOR

DR. ANGELE CLOSE is a clinical psychologist, motherhood coach, and certified mindfulness teacher who helps mothers navigate the challenges of matrescence and parenting.

With nearly twenty years of experience working with adults and couples, she shifted her focus to maternal mental health after her own motherhood journey revealed the urgent need for more support, education, and healing resources for moms.

After experiencing profound personal healing through Internal Family Systems (IFS) therapy, Dr. Close pursued extensive IFS training and now integrates her personal experience and professional expertise to guide mothers in healing intergenerational wounds, breaking unhealthy patterns, and feeling more compassion, confidence, and joy in motherhood.

Dr. Close offers individual psychotherapy and coaching, as well as workshops, courses, and group sessions online. She lives in Illinois with her husband, three children, and their two dogs.